A Peculiar Imbalance

A PECULIAR IMBALANCE

*The Fall
and Rise
of
Racial
Equality
in Minnesota,
1837–1869*

WILLIAM D. GREEN

University of Minnesota Press
Minneapolis

THE FESLER–LAMPERT MINNESOTA HERITAGE BOOK SERIES
This series reprints significant books that enhance our understanding and appreciation of Minnesota and the Upper Midwest. It is supported by the generous assistance of the John K. and Elsie Lampert Fesler Fund and by the interest and contribution of Elizabeth P. Fesler and the late David R. Fesler.

Publication of the original edition of this book was supported, in part, with funds provided by Jola Publications, Minneapolis, and by the Elmer L. and Eleanor J. Andersen Publications Endowment Fund of the Minnesota Historical Society.

First published in 2007 by the Minnesota Historical Society Press

First University of Minnesota Press edition, 2015. Published by arrangement with the Minnesota Historical Society.

Published by the University of Minnesota Press
111 Third Avenue South, Suite 290
Minneapolis, MN 55401-2520
http://www.upress.umn.edu

Library of Congress Cataloging-in-Publication Data

Green, William D.
A peculiar imbalance: the fall and rise of racial equality in Minnesota, 1837-1869 / William D. Green.
Includes bibliographical references and index.
ISBN 978-0-8166-9730-4 (pb)
1. African Americans—Minnesota—Saint Paul Region—History—19th century. 2. African Americans—Minnesota—Saint Paul Region—Politics and government—19th century. 3. African Americans—Minnesota—Saint Paul Region—Social conditions—19th century. 4. African Americans—Legal status, laws, etc.—Minnesota—Saint Paul Region—History—19th century. 5. Saint Paul Region—Race relations—History—19th century. 6. Whites—Minnesota—Saint Paul Region—Attitudes—History—19th century. 7. Racism—Minnesota—Saint Paul Region—History—19th century. 8. Minnesota—Race relations—History—19th century. I. Title. F614.S4G745 2015
305.896'073077658109034—dc23   2014040587

Printed in the United States of America on acid-free paper

The University of Minnesota is an equal-opportunity educator and employer.

21 20 19 18 17 16 15   10 9 8 7 6 5 4 3 2 1

To my wife, Judi

A Peculiar Imbalance

Preface

THIS IS AN UNTOLD HISTORY OF MINNESOTA—untold because its people were so few in number that their presence is typically overlooked. It focuses on the political, social, and legal experiences of blacks living in the region between 1837 and 1869 and on the roles black Minnesotans filled as slaves and free men and women and as residents of Fort Snelling, of missions, of Indian communities, and of an early St. Paul evolving from a French-speaking settlement to an American city. It is about the impact of interracial relationships and the views of others on the formation of a black man's self-identity.

Our story begins at the ceremonial feast following the signing of the Chippewa Treaty of 1837, when Stephen Bonga, a free man of African and Ojibwe descent from an area near Duluth, ate a meal prepared by Harriet Robinson, a slave woman from Virginia who later married a fellow slave at Fort Snelling named Dred Scott. Did the whites in attendance view Bonga and Scott in the same way? Did the Ojibwe? Did Bonga and Scott?

And what about the people after them? The concepts of race and culture grew rigid as Minnesota was transformed from wilderness to civilization. The same light-skinned black man was labeled "mixed," then "colored," then "black" over just ten years. And though this is a history of blacks in early Minnesota, ultimately it is an examination of how Anglo-Americans equated the creation of civilization with the drawing of stark lines—plowing furrows in a field, clearing a path for a road, and categorizing people into distinct and unambiguous groups.

In 1840 a mulatto named Jim Thompson lived in the francophone community of Pig's Eye (old St. Paul), where, despite his race, his neighbors considered him equal to all other men. In 1849, however, when Minnesota became a territory, Thompson could not vote, run for office, or serve on a jury because of his race. In 1846 Thompson's children attended school with white American, French, Irish, Dakota, and racially mixed classmates. Ten years later his Afro-Dakota children were segregated from their classmates, including the children of Euro-Dakota descent, who were permitted to stay.

Society reveals its collective soul most clearly when it determines who may belong and what level of opportunity it will avail to each of its members. Thus, the combination of a person's political, social, and economic equality is a way of assessing the character of that society. That begs the fundamental question of whether, if any of the components is absent, one truly could be equal to the Protestant Anglo-Americans who made Minnesota's rules and set its policies. Can equality be qualitative?

During the 1850s blacks could acquire property and own thriving businesses that attracted loyal white customers, but they had no rights of citizenship, because of racial prejudice. At the same time the Irish Catholics of St. Paul, themselves a derided class by the Yankee elite, could vote but largely did not enjoy economic opportunity, because of ethnic and religious prejudice. This examination of the black experience in early Minnesota provides a window on this most basic of issues: how did Anglo-American Minnesotans weigh racial and cultural differences against the question of citizenship?

Anglo-Americans extended rights in a seemingly incongruous manner. During an era when anti-Catholic and xenophobic sentiment were widely felt across America, Irish Catholics and mixed-blood Indians were granted voting rights. Even full-blood Indians could vote merely through adopting the clothing style of white men. Protestant Anglo-Americans who governed Minnesota typically viewed the three groups as individual races separate from their own. The region's leaders were predominantly antislavery and relatively tolerant of black economic development, in contrast to the limited opportunity they allowed the Irish. Yet this same Yankee elite denied blacks the right to vote. It was a peculiar imbalance.

The black experience in early Minnesota is unlike that of the same period in the surrounding states of Iowa, Wisconsin, North Dakota, and South Dakota—and as unique as the evolution of Minnesota itself. Wisconsin's development over a much longer span of time did not provide the crucible of events offered by the Minnesota experience: no panorama of major changes occurring in relatively quick succession and no known man of African descent whose life singularly reflected a panoply of social roles that black men could fill. Iowa lacked Minnesota's diversity, for fewer Indian and mixed-blood cultures existed there.

The northwestern part of Minnesota Territory, which in time became North and South Dakota, lacked a different kind of diversity. The region had Indian and mixed-blood cultures but virtually no black presence. Without the established navigable waters of the Mississippi to provide an avenue on which free blacks and fugitives could come north, the Dakotas were largely inaccessible. Within the upper midwestern region encompassing the head of the Mississippi River, no other state shared the dynamic and racial composition of Minnesota.

Although this is a Minnesota story, St. Paul is the primary setting. That city was Minnesota's political and commercial center, and as such it attracted the largest concentration of dreamers and adventurers. At the head of the navigable waters of the Mississippi, it became an easy destination for new arrivals, including the majority of blacks entering the region. With the exception of events outlined in chapters 5 and 6 (the birth of the Minnesota Republican Party, black suffrage, and the Eliza Winston case, all of which occurred in St. Anthony and Minneapolis) and chapter 7, addressing the Hazelwood Republic and the campaign for Indian citizenship, the focus is on activities in St. Paul.

I make no attempt to include everything there is to know about civil rights, nor do I provide an encyclopedia of every notable black Minnesotan of the mid-nineteenth century. The record for many of them is sadly incomplete and often contradictory, but enough information exists for analysis of how law and social convention impacted their lives.

In terms of style this book takes the form of an extended essay. The subject is complicated and multilayered, reflecting the sensi-

bilities of the people who lived in Minnesota. I refrain from ana-
lyzing legal doctrine, striving instead to keep an eye on the central
theme—what it meant to be a black member of early Minnesota
society.

In regard to the use of terms, "Minnesota country" appears several times in chapters 1 and 2 to describe the general region surrounding the Upper Mississippi River valley before the formal establishment of boundaries to the territory and, later, the state. I
refer to African Americans as "blacks" and Native Americans as
"Indians" except in reference to specific tribes. Furthermore, in
discussing the rights of various racial and ethnic groups, I discuss
the rights of men only, for this, alas, was a period in which "liberalism" did not extend to gender equality.

Acknowledgments

I WISH TO THANK Sally Rubinstein for helping me to develop my vision for this story and Ellen Green for sharpening and defending that vision. Thanks also go to Alan Woolworth, who was always available to give me insight into various events, as well as offer that one article that best captured an elusive aspect of race relations in early Minnesota. Ruth Bauer, Deborah Miller, Deborah Swanson, and Hampton Smith gave invaluable assistance by helping me to consider the questions I needed to ask, and Thelma Boeder of the Methodist Archives provided me with important material on the life of Jim Thompson. I also wish to thank the late Sumner Bright, whose kind words first inspired me, years ago, to explore this area of Minnesota history. I am indebted to the Minnesota Historical Society and the Minnesota Humanities Commission for grants that allowed me to perform my research and to Dennis Schapiro for his friendship and belief in this project. I want to acknowledge my son Nick's interest in my research even though he chose not to take one course in history during the four years he attended college. Finally, I am grateful to Judi, my dear wife and partner, who saw me through the difficult times while I was writing this manuscript and still had enough energy to read every word of it.

1
So Many Borders Not Observed

THE JULY 1837 SETTLEMENT between the Ojibwe and the United States of a treaty making "white man's country of the large delta between the St. Croix and the Mississippi" was occasion for a feast. Held at Fort Snelling, the celebration was attended by a contingent of federal officials led by Henry Dodge, territorial governor of Wisconsin, whose jurisdiction stretched west to the Missouri River, and the nearly 1,400 Ojibwe warriors who had gathered during the talks.[1]

The feast promised to tax the resources of the fort. Given the magnitude of the social aspect of the treaty signing he planned, Indian agent Lawrence Taliaferro likely called on the services of all his slaves as well as those of other owners for the dinner held near his quarters. His own Harriet probably helped to prepare the food. Physician John Emerson's Dred Scott and others likely served up and replenished the platters of beef and bowls of beans.[2]

One of the men served was the interpreter for the Ojibwe, a black man named Stephen Bonga. The Indians called him "brother," the term used earlier to refer to his father. As Bonga and the slaves serving him were the only black people present at the fort on that summer day, they no doubt took note of each other.[3]

How Bonga and the slaves viewed each other is unknown. Despite his African descent, Bonga probably thought of himself as separate, as unlike the slaves. The Ojibwe likely had selected Bonga, certainly not the only man fluent in both Ojibwe and English, because they trusted him. His father, Jean, was a black man and a slave brought by a British officer late in the eighteenth century from Haiti to the head of Lake Superior in the service of the North West Fur Company. Impressed by his quick grasp of their

3

language and customs, the Ojibwe pronounced Jean a free man in their country.[4]

Jean married an Ojibwe woman, as his son and his son's son would do, therein becoming a member of the tribe. Jean's son, Stephen, inherited his father's character. Taliaferro later wrote that even the Dakota, longtime rivals of the Ojibwe, "thought much of the negroes—called them black men, or black Frenchmen, Wah-she-che-sappo." They probably had the Bongas in mind. Indeed, the Dakota seemed to perceive Bonga and the slaves as separate, for they viewed blacks as unable to plan and good only for assisting the white man with his labor, "making him dependent . . . the white man's servant."[5]

No record describes Bonga's appearance during the negotiations. Still, the slaves likely saw him as a curious amalgam—a man who vaguely looked like them though he dressed in a quasi-Indian manner. He spoke with the accent of a man for whom English was not his mother's tongue, a man whose bearing perhaps was anything but servile, who enjoyed the privilege of sitting at the table with men of power. The slaves served him as if he were not, in fact, one of them.

They and he shared African blood but little else. The world of slaves existed in the context of black and white, master and slave, civilized and uncivilized. Their home was where their master took them—at this moment within the walls of Fort Snelling. Most slaves at the fort were known by only their first names. They were without a recorded past, without the gravitas that family histories might have provided to white men.

Bonga knew whence his father came. The son's world, his home, his family legacy, existed in the freedom of the north woods, where one's identity was cast not in terms of black or white but of red and mixed blood. Without the reinforcement of a black community—slave or free—his identity probably lay with the Ojibwe culture. The only other "black" people living in the region were his relatives, descendents of Jean and his Ojibwe wife. Being of the people who nurtured him in the land where he was born, Stephen Bonga, joining the feast at the long table, probably viewed his blackness as incidental. He was not like the slaves. He was a free man, free to leave the fort when he completed his work—unlike the slaves, who must stay there.

During the 1830s slaveholding was not unknown in Minnesota country. French fur traders owned slaves. Army officers owned slaves. Even Governor Dodge, then residing near Prairie du Chien, the nearest American outpost to Fort Snelling, owned slaves. Thus Taliaferro was not an exception but one of many engaging in a practice directly contravening federal law prohibiting the expansion of slavery on the northern frontier.[6]

In 1787 drafters of the Northwest Ordinance, mindful that the thorny nature of slavery could imperil the unity of the nation, sidestepped the issue. Congress incorporated language governing the territories northwest of the Ohio River and extending to the eastern bank of the Mississippi. The relevant provision was in article 6: "There shall be neither slavery nor involuntary servitude in the said territory."[7]

Despite this seeming clarity, the meaning of the article was ambiguous—slavery already existed in the region. Moreover, the text of the ordinance referred to "free" people and the "free" population, implying recognition of slave and free. Furthermore, French inhabitants of the Illinois country, who held slaves under the French and English colonial governments and retained them after 1776, argued that the intent was not to ban slavery outright or "to affect the rights of ancient inhabitants" but to prohibit its expansion into the territory. Several members of Congress agreed. For decades slavery continued in the territories that became Indiana, Illinois (as late as the 1840s), and Wisconsin. Over time Northern slavery diminished as growing numbers of antislavery settlers replaced the "ancient" inhabitants.[8]

With the acquisition of Louisiana Territory from France, America doubled in size, opening prospects for new settlement and lending urgency to the determination of boundaries demarcating free and slave. In 1820 a divided Congress worked out a compromise that split Louisiana Territory along the 36' 30" parallel extending west from the southern border of Missouri, which was admitted to the union as a slave state. More than ten thousand slaves of a population of sixty-six thousand lived in the state. Slavery had been entrenched there since the settlement of St. Louis, and most of the territory's leading citizens were slaveholders. By 1819 Southern slaveholders streamed into the region. Their defiant ownership of slaves showed how weak federal law was on the edge of the frontier. The distinction between "ancient" inhabitants and newly arrived slaveholders was irrelevant. By the 1830s St. Louis was a major slave market.[9]

In St. Louis a University of Pennsylvania medical school graduate, John Emerson, purchased "the Blows' boy Sam." Emerson acquired a commission as an army medical officer in 1833 and took his new manservant with him when he reported for duty at Fort Armstrong at Rock Island, Illinois. By 1834, blaming ill health, he requested reassignment to a warmer climate and waited impatiently for the response. In the meantime he heard from others of promising entrepreneurial prospects in real estate just across the river in Iowa, land recently ceded by the Sauk and Fox bands. Though the United States had closed the land to settlement, squatters had already built log cabins and cleared the underbrush, hoping to establish claims qualifying them, in due time, to buy prime riverfront at the minimum government price. Emerson, still assigned to Fort Armstrong, purchased 640 acres there. "Years later," wrote historian Robert Dykstra, "old-timers professed to remember that the good doctor's slave, a diminutive black man, occupied the claim on his master's behalf." By spring, however, the slave known as Sam—who later insisted his name was Dred Scott—had accompanied his master north to Fort Snelling, never to return to the Iowa homestead.[10]

Dred Scott was not the only slave to reside on the free soil of Iowa during the 1830s. Isaac Campbell, a prosperous Indian trader and merchant in Keokuk, at the mouth of the Des Moines River, permitted his slave, John, to work for wages and keep them. In 1834 army officer Stephen Watts Kearney brought to Iowa Country his household, which included a slave woman. The first recorded death at Bentonsport, a town on the lower Des Moines, was a slave woman named Aunt Mornin. Two female slaves cooked meals for construction crews putting up government buildings at the new

Sauk and Fox Agency. Two others, purchased in Missouri, belonged to a white trader who already owned several slaves. Even when the new Iowa territorial constitution expressly prohibited slavery, Southerners continued bringing their slaves with them when making a residence in the territory. This included those recently appointed to high governmental positions. Eyewitnesses have written that territorial governor and former congressman John Chambers of Kentucky, along with territorial secretary O. H. W. Stull of Maryland, both appointed by President William Henry Harrison, arrived in their new homes accompanied "by a small troop" of slaves. Their quarters contained "seven or eight colored people" who were flogged, otherwise mistreated, "and kept in profound ignorance of the fact that when they touched the soil of Iowa they were *free*." Not until the 1840s did antislavery sentiment grow to such a pitch that slavery was no longer tolerated. Clearly, it was not a case of Iowans following the requirements of federal law but rather a reflection of Northern antislavery settlers outnumbering proslavery residents.[11]

On the frontier federal proscriptions against slavery meant little without the support of state and territorial leaders, the outrage of a critical mass of antislavery residents, or the willingness of the U.S. government to exert its otherwise limited power to enforce federal law. In Minnesota country federal power resided at Fort Snelling. But its purpose, in keeping with the strategic plan laid out by Secretary of War John C. Calhoun, was to protect trade and preserve the peace, not to abolish slavery—an institution with which the officers, many from Virginia families, were familiar. Given the context of the 1830s, a decade after the enactment of the Missouri Compromise, this fort, like others in areas north of the 36' 30" parallel, incorporated a small slave community, its members rented or purchased by officers and traders.[12]

Through the antebellum period Southerners dominated the federal government. Since the nation had been founded, the South had provided 11 of 15 presidents, 17 of 28 Supreme Court justices, 14 of 19 attorneys general, 21 of 34 speakers of the house, 80 of 134 ambassadors, and enough officers to dominate the army and the navy. Most of these men were slaveholders. Practically all supported a man's or woman's right to own slaves. Their voices, embodied by the Democratic Party, spoke without significant challenge from its political rival, the Whigs. And in the 1830s when patronage became a fixture in the politics of Jacksonian America, personal contacts often secured political appointments and desirable assignments.[13]

John C. Calhoun of South Carolina, who in the late 1840s foresaw Northern antislavery sentiment dominating federal policy, enunciated the Southern position, arguing that slave states reserved the right to veto federal legislation contravening their interest. Calhoun maintained that if the government exceeded its power and abused its trust in working against the interests of any state, it could be dissolved. This same man was secretary of war under President James Monroe, vice president under John Quincy Adams and Andrew Jackson, secretary of state under John Tyler, and subsequently a senator from his home state.[14]

Federal officials like these supported measures that strengthened dependency on slavery and endorsed the servant allowance system in the military. Congressmen who had passed the Missouri Compromise evidently were not inclined to design antislavery policies for the men who protected the nation's borders. Accordingly, as the military presence and culture appeared on the frontier, so did slavery. The army paid any officer an allowance for "keeping" one servant—officers were expected to uphold a certain status even on the frontier. While some officers simply pocketed the allowance, often equivalent to a private's wage, others frequently used it to purchase or rent a slave. Furthermore, an officer with his wife and family at the post was more likely to serve with higher morale if his wife was free from the drudgery of housekeeping, as befitted her station.[15]

Such practices were especially prevalent at Fort Crawford, Fort Winnebago (Portage, Wisconsin), and Fort Snelling. John Emerson, who came from a family that did not own slaves, purchased Dred Scott just before he reported to Fort Armstrong, as did John Bliss before he proceeded to Fort Snelling. Col. Josiah Snelling, the builder and first commander, for whom the fort was named, had a slave to wait on his family, as did Nathan Jarvis, who preceded

Emerson as fort surgeon. Col. Zachary Taylor, commander of the post in about 1830, later a major general in the army and eventually president of the United States, likewise brought slaves to the outpost.[16]

The growth of steamboat traffic on the Mississippi made it easy for agents from Fort Snelling to access the St. Louis slave market, which facilitated their importation to the fort. When Lt. Thomas Stockton married, he asked James Langham, the Indian subagent and a Taliaferro subordinate, to acquire a slave for him at Jefferson Barracks in St. Louis. Langham, himself a slaveholder and frequent visitor to St. Louis, had become useful in bringing slaves to the fort. Of all the men—both civilian and military—who bought, held, or sold slaves at Fort Snelling, Major Taliaferro owned the most, over his tenure from 1821 to 1839 estimated to total twenty-one slaves. He brought some from Virginia; others were perhaps inherited from his wife's father in Pennsylvania; all were used at the agency or hired out at the fort.[17]

Maj. Lawrence Taliaferro—the rank was ceremonial, for he was a civilian—was a Virginian born into a patrician family of Italian descent that had settled in the King George County area in 1637. (In this same region of Virginia, Booker T. Washington was born, the *T* coincidently standing for Taliaferro, his master's family name.) President James Monroe, a fellow Virginian and family friend, appointed Taliaferro to the post of Indian agent. Taliaferro was "courtly and dignified, a gentleman of integrity whose nearly twenty years of Indian service were marked by an understanding attitude" toward the Dakota and the Ojibwe.[18]

Taliaferro had an aristocrat's appreciation for the Indians' use of ceremony and an honesty that made him, as William W. Folwell wrote, "cordially hated by all who could neither bribe nor frighten him to connive at lawbreaking to the harm of Indians." Taliaferro was "the most important and influential civil official on the upper Mississippi."[19]

His mission in life was to civilize the Dakota by transforming them into farmers, creating a place he called his "Lake Harriet Experiment," a precursor to the Hazelwood Republic, launched more than twenty years later by Indian agent Joseph R. Brown. To Taliaferro and the army, being civilized meant being educated, married, a Christian, and mindful of one's station, which often meant being a master of slaves.

Taliaferro was as unusual an Indian agent as he was a slaveholder, taking personal interest in upholding the moral character of his post, especially when the "ladies" of the garrison complained about the number of illegitimate couplings, typical in frontier settings. They apparently were unaware that Taliaferro, whose wife remained in Pennsylvania through most of his tenure, had fathered a daughter with a Dakota woman. To raise the moral standard, Taliaferro performed marriage ceremonies for blacks, whites, and Indians. That a slave of Dr. Emerson wanted to marry his slave made no difference to Taliaferro, who saw holy matrimony as fitting for their mortal souls as for those of any white couple, an attitude uncharacteristic of Southern slaveholders.[20]

Days after the treaty signing with the Ojibwe in 1837, Taliaferro officiated at the wedding of his slave Harriet Robinson and Dr. Emerson's slave Dred Scott, apparently relinquishing his ownership of Harriet. Perhaps, Taliaferro was free to be magnanimous since, after his frequent furloughs to Virginia and Pennsylvania by way of St. Louis, he often returned with slaves. Officers and traders were always interested in renting them for periods of time.[21]

Such entrepreneurial interests notwithstanding, Taliaferro long planned to free all his slaves. When Maj. Joseph Plympton proposed purchasing Taliaferro's slave Eliza, Taliaferro declined, writing in his journal: "I informed him that it was my intention to give her freedom after a limited time but that Mrs. P. could keep her for two and perhaps three years." In 1840, when he retired, Taliaferro freed his slaves, proud that he did so without coercion or compensation but in a "solemn act not influenced by any earthly powers."[22]

Within this world of servitude, the masters of slaves at the fort apparently treated them with relative benevolence. Like Taliaferro, they preferred the nicety of calling them "servants." Most officers apparently did not view the slaves as disposable; many slaves learned skills useful in making their masters' households comfortable in otherwise brutal surroundings. So assigning them to other officers was a common practice. In the Taliaferro era officers at the fort sold three slaves but only to civilians—an unnamed slave woman to Alexis Bailly; Horace to trader Hypolite Dupuis, who later sold him back; and James Thompson.[23]

To sell a slave downriver was unusual. Of the fifteen to twenty slaves working at the fort and Indian agency, only three experienced such a fate—Bliss's "nice-looking yellow girl," who had become the source of great distraction for the soldiers; a slave woman known simply as Rachel; and Langham's slave woman Mariah, after she allegedly confessed to murdering his daughter and was accused of torching his house. Except in Mariah's case— "the *vile* negro" forced to wear "an iron collar, ball and chain, and handcuffs"—punishment was either slight or unrecorded.[24]

Taliaferro hired out his slave boy, William, to Colonel Snelling, "the latter agreeing to clothe him." While in service to the colonel, William, attempting to shoot a hawk, instead shot a small boy named Henry McCullum, nearly killing him. In another instance William collaborated with another slave in distributing whiskey to young Dakota men. After writing that the man renting William had the Indians hit his slave with their pipestems, Taliaferro concluded: "But it was not known if they had inflicted any blows on William." In neither instance was severe reprisal carried out against the boy.[25]

There is no evidence of mistreatment by any master of slaves at the fort. Given the character of Taliaferro, who seems to have documented any abusive behavior occurring there during his tenure, he would have recorded any ill treatment of slaves. In keeping with his duty as Indian agent to maintain civil relations with the tribes, Taliaferro noted numerous incidents of soldiers assaulting or having sexual relations with Indian women and of cases of venereal disease among the Indian women at the fort. He was not concerned only with the abuse of Indians, for in August 1830 he recorded that a Dakota man had struck a slave girl.[26]

Taliaferro did not report any officer abuse of slaves. A code of silence may have shrouded the bad behavior of officers and compelled Taliaferro to omit such entries, but Reverend Alfred Brunson, who lived near the fort in the late 1830s, probably would not have felt so constrained. Even within the confines of the military, of living in a fort on the edge of wilderness, and of the convention

of slave ownership, less-structured officer-slave relationships sometimes occurred. The relationship between Capt. George Day and
his slave, Jim Thompson, examined in chapter 2, illustrates this
point.

Slaves seem not to have performed any labor forcing them to
work closely with the enlisted soldiers. Under the presumed protection of their officer-masters, slaves were not typically subjected
to the prejudices of "virtual animals" whose "finer sentiments of
civilization," as Taliaferro wrote, disappeared after being stationed
ten years at the fort. A significant portion of the enlisted men were
Irish, a group by this time notorious for its antiblack sentiments,
from which prudent officers may have distanced their slaves.[27]

In at least one incident, such protection was more than presumed. During winter months it was policy to provide heating
stoves only to officers and to enlisted men with wives. One day in
the winter of 1838, when Q.M. Lt. Daniel McPhail was allotting
stoves to the officers, Dr. Emerson requested one on behalf of his
slaves, Dred and Harriet Scott. The quartermaster refused, declaring that there were too few to go around, whereupon Emerson
called him a liar. They exchanged words, and the quartermaster
punched the doctor in the face. Emerson left momentarily, returning to the store with pistols that he trained on his assailant. Major
Plympton had the doctor arrested, but as there was no other doctor
closer to the fort than Prairie du Chien, he dropped the charges.[28]

In fact, as the stove incident shows, within the confines of the
fort, the Scotts lived as a married couple in their own separate
sleeping quarters. The 1836 Wisconsin territorial census listed
Dred Scott as a head of household. Without the designation "servant," "slave," or "dependent," the listing was that of a free man in
free territory.[29]

Fort Snelling was a small community. During the entire 1830s
just thirty officers served there, six or seven at a time. With most
of them owning no more than one slave—Taliaferro had more than
three at a time throughout his appointment—the slave population
was small and therefore not a threat to stability. Adult "servants"
spent practically all of their time working for the master's family;
there is no evidence of a sense of commonality among them.[30]

On this outpost of long and frigid winters surrounded by white men with weapons, isolated from the rest of the world by the iced Mississippi, slaves were not likely to cause trouble. Moreover, since food within the fort was limited during the winter, the tie with a master drawing military rations was a sure way for slaves to receive food and shelter. There was little chance for escape, due to the likelihood of freezing to death or starvation. Also, the Dakota might capture any fugitives and return them for payment and food, just as they returned some deserting soldiers. And perhaps many of the slaves, particularly those belonging to Taliaferro, did not feel the need to run because their masters, and the other officers using their services, had told them they planned to free them. Emancipation meant being cast from the fort—it had room only for army personnel and their attachés. Many of the slaves could understand their military masters more easily than they could the French-speaking Red River refugees squatting in the area as early as 1833.[31]

The welfare of the Fort Snelling slave was relatively secure so long as he or she could avoid being sent to the St. Louis slave markets. Paradoxically, in that city slaves might succeed in suing for their freedom, whereas the fort had no administrative infrastructure authorized to issue "free papers." In St. Louis, before the supreme court of Missouri, Rachel, a slave, sued for her freedom, basing her claim on having lived on the "free soil" of Fort Snelling. She won.[32]

In the fall of 1830, subagent Langham acquired Rachel from a St. Louis slave market and delivered her to Lt. J. B. W. Stockton, who, accompanied by his bride, was on his way to report to Fort Snelling. After a year at the fort, Stockton brought Rachel to Fort Crawford at Prairie du Chien, whence he was transferred. Finally in 1834, coincident to Rachel's pregnancy, Stockton took her to St. Louis to sell her.[33]

Eventually purchased by slave dealer William Walker, who planned to sell mother and child separately in New Orleans, Rachel filed suit to restrain Walker "from carrying her or said child out of the jurisdiction . . . till the termination of said suit." The Missouri

court had to decide whether it was the arbiter of the social convention of absolute slave ownership or of the spirit of federal law.[34]
At the trial Rachel asserted that the Northwest Ordinance of
1787 and the Missouri Compromise of 1820 established the territory on which Fort Snelling stood as free soil. In bringing her to the
fort with the intent of setting up his household, her master had effectively expanded slavery into free territory, thereby violating federal law. Accordingly, she argued, such action extinguished her
slave status.[35]

Walker, in turn, argued that while federal law clearly prohibited
slavery on free soil, the Missouri court had found exceptions to the
rule, noting one precedent holding that the slaveholder, not intending to take up permanent residence on free soil but detained
through no fault of his own, would not be required to forfeit his
property. Walker argued that as an army officer Stockton essentially was detained on free soil through his orders to report to Fort
Snelling. According to Missouri legal precedence, he had no intent
to take up permanent residence—Stockton could be reassigned at
any time, and was—so Rachel remained a slave.[36]

The lower court agreed—Rachel was a slave, and Walker, her
new owner, was free to take her to New Orleans. Rachel's only recourse was to appeal to the state supreme court. There her court-
appointed counsel, J. Spalding, claimed that no law or public authority required or compelled Stockton to take Rachel to Fort
Snelling as a slave. Rachel's servitude was based solely on her master's desire for convenience, which the law does not protect. The
court agreed with that position. By introducing Rachel to free soil,
wrote Justice Mathias McGirk, Stockton "and those claiming under him [Walker] must be holden to abide the consequence of introducing slavery [to free soil], contrary to law."[37]

In the June term of 1836, Rachel became a free woman. Three
months later, Roger B. Taney, who one day voiced the majority
opinion in *Dred Scott v Sanford,* was sworn in as chief justice of the
U.S. Supreme Court.[38]

Rachel's case may seem paradoxical, but from the mid-1820s
the Missouri courts had created a strong precedence for granting
freedom to slaves on the basis of their residence in free territory.

Rachel v Walker affirmed exceptions under which a master might keep his slave if the master was otherwise detained on free soil—exceptions that Stockton did not satisfy.[39] Ultimately, however, the paradox of legal precedence rested with the court. Though the sentiment of "free soil, free labor" had been established in the reasonably clear language of federal law and thus jurisdiction in federal courts, Rachel and other Missouri slaves (including Dred Scott, who, in 1850, initially won his freedom in the same forum) used the state courts to litigate their cases. In fact, as a proslavery writer lamented in a St. Louis newspaper, a growing number of lawyers specialized in advising slaves planning to sue for freedom. The case had special significance, for its decision proscribed the paradoxical convention of slaveholding officers living on federal military reservations on free soil.[40]

News of Rachel's success probably reached Fort Snelling. Its residents likely met any communication from St. Louis, the nearest connection to the outside world, with interest. Surely news about people associated with the fort was of special import. Taliaferro received letters from Lieutenant Stockton and Q.M. Josiah Brant, who had helped arrange Rachel's purchase.[41]

Yet, characteristic perhaps of a time when the affairs of distant states had little impact on frontier forts, Taliaferro's journals mention nothing of Rachel's success. Instead, Indian affairs, tensions between the Dakota and Ojibwe, and Alexis Bailly's irksome trafficking in whiskey overshadow the matter. By 1837 the fort was preparing for negotiations with the Ojibwe, and the concerns of Fort Snelling slaveholders, if there were any, apparently had disappeared. The affairs of Missouri mattered only to Missouri.

In October 1837, after several requests for assignment to a post in a temperate climate, Dr. Emerson received orders to report to Jefferson Barracks in St. Louis. Leaving Dred and Harriet Scott at Fort Snelling with the intent of sending for them in two months, Emerson journeyed to Jefferson Barracks, where he was surprised with new orders sending him to Fort Jessup in western Louisiana. Feeling settled there, he married Irene Sanford of St. Louis, and she joined him there.[42]

Before long, however, Emerson came to despise the dampness of Louisiana and once again petitioned for reassignment—back to Fort Snelling, the "best post." Before gaining reassignment, Emerson sent for the Scotts; they arrived at Jefferson Barracks in the spring of 1838. By September Emerson had begun his journey back to Fort Snelling, accompanied by his wife and the Scotts. After visiting friends and his wife's family in St. Louis on September 21, the Emerson party climbed aboard the *Gypsy,* a small sternwheeler of light draft moving slowly up the Mississippi in low water, expected to arrive at Fort Snelling on October 21. "Thus," as Don Fehrenbacher has written, "Dred [and Harriet] was taken not just once but twice into territory supposedly closed to slavery by the Missouri Compromise."[43]

Brunson, returning to his mission near Fort Snelling from a conference in Upper Alton, Illinois, with a layover for supplies at St. Louis, was also on the boat. He recognized Dr. Emerson and his entourage from the year they had all been at the fort. He later described a momentous event—on the otherwise uneventful four-week journey—somewhere north of the Iowa-Missouri border. Harriet Scott gave birth to a daughter. The proud parents named her Eliza, possibly for their mistress, Eliza Irene Sanford Emerson. Thus this child born in free territory, to slave parents about to resume their residency in free territory, was destined to live out her youth in slavery.[44]

Brunson, harboring abolitionist sensibilities and reminiscing years later on the birth of Eliza Scott, did not comment on the child's fate or, for that matter, on Emerson's ownership of the Scotts. Indeed, he said nothing of the slave ownership of officers and traders around the fort. For him the souls of Indians took precedence over the issue of slavery at the fort. Regarding the general ministration of the fort, which presumably included the treatment of slaves, he wrote, "If all military governments were of the same mild, just, and paternal character, there would never be just cause for revolutions in any country." Though he did not judge slaveholders, he was clear as to how he would comport himself on the issue of slave ownership: he would not countenance it.[45]

2

The Story of Jim Thompson

JIM THOMPSON was one of the most unlikely persons Reverend Alfred Brunson would encounter. Jim's life, once Brunson freed him from slavery, provides the best means for examining the legal, social, economic, and even religious standing of a black man living on the Minnesota frontier in the decade before it was a territory. His story begins with Brunson's effort to establish a mission at the Dakota village of Kaposia.

In the weeks before the U.S.-Ojibwe negotiations in May 1837, Brunson concentrated on establishing missions among the Ojibwe and Dakota. He already had authority to do so under the signature of Secretary of War Lewis Cass, who at the time headed the Office of Indian Affairs, in the U.S. War Department. Major Taliaferro supported Brunson's project as he did all missionary work among the Indians. Three missions of the American Board of Commissioners for Foreign Missions and two Swiss missions fell under his jurisdiction.[1]

Little Crow, son of Big Thunder and father of Little Crow the younger (who would lead the Dakota in the U.S.-Dakota Conflict of 1862), had left orders to invite Brunson to his village of Kaposia. As a grand gesture of welcoming, he "had a bark house prepared for them."[2]

That a non-Christian chief would invite missionaries to convert his people may seem odd, yet tribal leaders did precisely this. While Little Crow may have believed his people could benefit from the beneficence of a Christian god, his reasons for doing so may have been merely pragmatic. As a quid pro quo to receiving the government annuities promised in the treaty of 1837, he may have agreed to send the children of his tribe to learn the white man's ways at the mission school. He may also have felt that the Methodists could

17

stem the spread of liquor consumption among his people. Whiskey was everywhere—among the traders, the soldiers at the fort, and the Red River refugees settling around Fort Snelling. The mission under these Methodists, who preached moderation in all endeavors, might at least serve as an island of sobriety.[3]

In any event, Little Crow lent his support for Brunson's plan, and his offer "with great pomp and dignity" of the bark house solidified his intentions. The bark house, however, as Brunson later noted, "had been inhabited too long by Indians for any white man to be able to stand the vermin." The missionary began to build a log cabin. Then, due to his "ignorance of the Indian tongue," he turned to finding an interpreter.[4]

To help him communicate with the Ojibwe, Brunson planned to enlist the services of Stephen Bonga, whom Brunson characterized as "pious," "religious, and inclined to the missions."[5]

The missionary also needed someone to translate "the truths of God to the ignorant and unlearned" for the Dakota. Men who speak Dakota and English were available, but they were not to Brunson's liking. He described them as knowing "nothing of religion nor could they interpret spiritual things, because they did not understand the meaning of the terms we use to convey such ideas, and, further, the Indians had no words in their language corresponding with ours on that subject." Beyond a lack of facility to translate the word of God into Dakota terms, Brunson criticized their character, for the men "demanded high wages," and "being Catholic in their religious notions, and having learned the traders' tricks and morals," they would surely "take every advantage of the poor Indian and all others with whom they dealt."[6]

Brunson was looking for a special kind of man: "To convey to the Indian mind the truths of God's Word, from the want of words in their language, the teacher or interpreter had to use imagery, figures and comparisons. To do this to good purpose he must understand and feel the idea himself; hence the necessity of a converted man for that service." Bronson found such a man at the fort—a mulatto who was the slave of an officer from Kentucky. His name was Jim Thompson.[7]

George Monroe, nephew of President James Monroe, had

brought his young slave Thompson west from Virginia. Upon reaching Kentucky, Monroe gave him to sutler John Culbertson in payment for his debts. In 1827 Culbertson brought Thompson to Fort Snelling, where he sold him to Capt. George Day, in whose service Thompson remained until 1837.[8]

Thompson enhanced his value to his master and the fort community by learning the surrounding countryside and becoming fluent in the Dakota language. All this suggests the considerable intellect and charm of Jim Thompson, as well as the liberal nature of the master-servant relationship. Brunson wrote, "He was a slave, and the price demanded for his redemption was twelve hundred dollars, and for any other purpose two thousand dollars."[9]

Finding that Thompson had "been converted, had something of the missionary spirit, and was above the average of his race in education and mental ability," the missionary offered to Captain Day the purchase of freedom for Thompson, provided he could raise the amount from friends in the East.[10]

Supplying a context of the times, fellow missionary Stephen Riggs later wrote, "This was the time when the antislavery feeling ran highest in Ohio, and multitudes of people were only too glad to contribute to the fund that was started in Cincinnati, for the purpose of obtaining for James Thompson his liberty, that he might serve in the Methodist church in giving the gospel to the Sioux [Dakota] nation." Accordingly, he was set free, and in turn, noted Brunson's daughter years later, Thompson served as "a capable and faithful interpreter."[11]

To what extent Thompson's services as interpreter were needed is unclear. David King, a lay minister who had established the mission with Brunson and served as the mission's teacher, had begun studying Dakota, though he did not use it. Presbyterian and Congregational missionaries had been translating the Bible for the Dakota. Brunson believed that the Indians, both children and adults, should be taught in English. "The knowledge of this language," William Watts Folwell has explained, "would enable them to do business with the whites and would open the whole range of its literature including the Bible."[12]

Thompson's skills, then, would have had minimal educational

use. Perhaps his ability was better used to help Brunson converse with Little Crow and other Dakota leaders who did not speak English. This would have permitted King to focus on his time-consuming teaching regimen. More plausible, however, is that Thompson's value was not as an interpreter but as a diplomatic and symbolic gesture that bound the mission and the Dakota together. Thompson was married to one of the daughters of Cloud Man, the Dakota leader of the Lake Calhoun band who had transformed his encampment into an agricultural experiment Taliaferro called "Eatonville."[13]

Marriage to a daughter of a village leader must have been significant. Cloud Man's daughter Lucy (Stands Sacred) had a daughter by Capt. Seth Eastman, who was stationed at Fort Snelling, and Cloud Man's daughter Hannah (The Day Sets) had a daughter Mary by Major Taliaferro. Thompson, then, through the alliances made by his wife's sisters, was connected with some of the region's most influential men. He was an important addition to Brunson's fledgling mission community.[14]

The Indian village of Kaposia, where Brunson established his mission, sat on the west bank of the Mississippi, about ten miles below Fort Snelling, four miles below present-day St. Paul, in what now is South St. Paul. With the erection of several log buildings that Thompson helped to construct—a mission house, schoolhouse, and store—the community was ready to begin its work. The future of the mission seemed bright; its efforts were "being prosecuted with commendable vigor."[15]

Brunson later reported that Kaposia, a sign of progress and of the extent to which the Indians were being converted to civilization, had one hundred acres planted and that the school was in operation. Thompson, as interpreter, could indeed assume some of the credit, and he proved himself useful in yet another way. In June 1838 Brunson, with a party of three white men and Thompson, undertook a journey up the Mississippi when the Dakota and Ojibwe were on the verge of war. Thompson, knowing the river well, served as the party's pilot, and his hunting kept the party fed. But it was his wholehearted connection with the religious group that cemented the bond. Brunson "preached to my four companions, and we had a prayer-meeting, in which all participated."[16] Such harmony belied troubles at the mission. In the fall of 1839, two years after he had established it, Brunson left his post. His account suggests complicated circumstances. As early as the fall of 1838, the school was floundering due to "the irregularity of attendance" of Dakota students. Taliaferro "informed Brunson that the chief [Little Crow] had decided not to send the children to school until he had received his annuities under the treaty of the previous year."[17]

Without a significant number of Dakota students, critics in the Illinois Conference, which sponsored the mission, complained that Kaposia was too expensive. Brunson was so ill that he had to spend the winter of 1838–39 away from Kaposia, and he fell under the attack of those same critics, who accused him of profiteering in land acquisition in Prairie du Chien, where his family still lived. When he responded forcefully to the charges, the matter was allowed to rest, but the stress proved too much. That fall Brunson resigned from the mission and active ministerial work.[18]

By then, however, the Kaposia missionaries were dispirited, and the demise of their work was inevitable. Thompson left the mission about this same time.[19]

When Brunson's successor, Reverend B. T. Kavanaugh, arrived, he found the mission "depleted by resignations, the Indians unfriendly and even insolent." Along with Brunson and Thompson, teacher David King left the mission, soon to be replaced by farmer and teacher Thomas Pope. He also noted the Indians' "dissatisfaction" with Brunson's manner of doing business.[20]

Little Crow had begun calling for the close of the school for another reason—he disagreed with Methodist teachings against violence and war, and he did not want the boys of his band to be "spoiled as soldiers." Such teaching, he felt, ran contrary to a basic concept of Dakota culture—that boys were not considered fullgrown men until they had personally taken part in combat with the enemy. Absent the warrior's training, his young men might become like the soldiers at the fort, their indolence leading them to boredom, mischief, and drunkenness. Perhaps some of his young men were getting liquor at the mission.[21]

Thompson was later vilified for selling whiskey to the Dakota, which explains Folwell's characterization of his departure as "early dismissal." "The happy freeman's piety," Folwell noted, "did not long survive his emancipation [from Captain Day;] his morals were or became depraved." Reverend Stephen Riggs, a Presbyterian missionary to the Dakota and a contemporary of Brunson, wrote, "Thompson was a very indifferent interpreter and not a reliable man." Prof. Earl Spangler wrote, "Thompson became intemperate in the use of liquor, and corrupted instead of converted the Indians."[22]

Intemperately, Return Holcombe wrote, "Really Thompson was a sort of fraud. His pretensions as a Christian were hypocritical. He was very immoral and liked whiskey and Indian women, without regard to the quality or character of either. He spoke poor Dakota and worse English and was unintelligent and ineffective."[23]

If that was true, Thompson's act may well have been not only one of betrayal of the Kaposia mission and movement and a supreme act of ingratitude but also one of harm to the Indians. On the drinking habits of Indians, missionary Gideon Pond wrote, "They bade fair soon to die, all together, in one drunken jumble."[24]

Holcombe wrote more colorfully:

> The red man soon acquired the drinking habit and were slaves to it. . . . They could hardly live if they were not drunk. At some of the villages they were drunk for months together. They would give guns, blankets, flour, corn, coffee, horses, furs, traps—anything for whisky. They mutilated and murdered one another; they fell into the fire and water and were burned to death or drowned; they froze to death, they died of delirium tremens, they committed suicide even, and these tragedies happened so frequently that for some time the death of an Indian in one of the ways mentioned attracted but little comment or notice.[25]

But neither Brunson nor the Kaposia Methodists who lived and worked with Thompson ever said a word about him providing liquor to Dakota students. Not one insinuation, not one accusation appears in the records. The reasons for the absence of recrimination may be many. Thompson, while at the mission, may, in fact, have been innocent. Or the Methodists were generous, perhaps not wanting to tarnish the integrity of their having freed a slave. Or they avoided speaking ill of one of their brethren, especially someone they liked.[26]

Just as likely, Thompson did indeed give whiskey to the Dakota, but in a manner that his brethren may have deemed to be in moderation. The Methodists of this era, preaching moderation in all things, were certainly not in favor of liquor, but they also were not entirely antiliquor to the extent the Presbyterians were. The *Book of Discipline* told preachers to "use only that kind, and that degree of drink, which is best both for your body and soul."[27]

For laymen one of the conditions required of those who desired admission into the Methodist society was to avoid "drunkenness: or drinking spirituous liquors, *unless in cases of necessity*." Indeed, Methodists opposed drunkenness, but they may have varied in approach to the use of intoxicating beverages in the early to mid-nineteenth century. The strong push for prohibition did not start until after the Civil War, more specifically until after the mid-1870s. In this context, lay Methodists on the frontier in the late 1830s and 1840s likely took liberties.[28]

Regardless of Thompson's exploiting the situation, liquor clearly remained the major problem for the survival of the mission. In a letter to Brunson, Kavanaugh blamed the troubles on the groggeries in St. Paul, "for all order, peace and safety were destroyed by drunk Indians." On October 25, 1842, King wrote to Samuel Pond, a missionary who with his brother Gideon worked with Cloud Man: "Our missions and school have been all abandoned. The property is all for sale."[29]

Traders commonly sold intoxicating liquors to their Indian customers. Even though the American Fur Company officially obeyed the act of 1834, which prohibited the importation of whiskey into Indian country, "individual traders in its employ . . . did not resist the temptation to attract business by surreptitiously offering spirits to the Indians."[30]

Alexis Bailly, Henry Sibley's predecessor as director of the company, took part in this trade. Traders at the northern posts felt it necessary to use liquor to secure a deal with Indians, knowing that if they did not, their customers would simply go farther north, where Canadian traders would gladly supply them. Reports of these activities found their way back to Congress, acknowledging the fact that no military presence, no Indian agent (even a man of Taliaferro's stature), not the American Fur Company itself could embargo the importation of whiskey to Minnesota country.[31]

For traders there was no law "human or divine that could check their greed," for so long as they did not actually bring liquor onto Indian land, they were not violating any law. When subsequently the territorial legislature enacted legislation providing for prosecution of anyone selling liquor to Indians, especially in the border regions, the law was virtually unenforceable. According to Folwell, "Composed chiefly of traders and their satellites, no grand juries could be assembled which would indict, no unbiased trial juries could be impaneled, and no witnesses could be discovered who would reveal the illicit transactions."[32]

Boredom and tedium led soldiers to drink. By 1839 whiskey shops cropped up on the east side of the Mississippi and quickly became a source of trouble for the commandant at the fort. On June 3 soldiers went to a shop owned by Joseph R. Brown. Once there they consumed so much liquor that forty-seven of them were thrown into the guardhouse that night. In another instance, drunken soldiers threatened to kill officers.[33]

Despite this problem even the army recognized the occasional usefulness of liquor. During the summer of 1838, Lt. Peter V. Hagner brought a detachment of 145 recruits on a harrowing journey from New York to Fort Snelling. While in transit, he purchased whiskey that "enabled [the soldiers] to bear up physically & morally under the disheartening & tiresome duty" and then applied for reimbursement from the government. The surgeon general recommended reimbursement for the purchase and use of whiskey but that it should come from the funds of the Commissary General of Subsistence rather than the quartermaster's department. In the spring of 1839, Hagner was reimbursed.[34]

Business was good, and no doubt for this reason Thompson, after leaving the mission in 1839, moved to the east bank across from the fort to set up his own grog shop. Holcombe wrote: "After his dismissal Thompson took his Indian wife and children up to the east bank of the Mississippi, opposite Fort Snelling, where he opened a shop, for the covert and illegal sale of whisky to the soldiers, the Indians, or whoever would buy."[35]

If, to the army, liquor was an evil, for a time it was a necessary evil, much to the consternation of some. Even though the army apparently raided Thompson's shop several times, the reprisal was not severe enough for at least one noted chronicler. Holcombe wrote:

> The situation was bad enough, but it seems that it might have easily been improved. The commandant at the Fort had but to send a file of soldiers to the shack of the liquor seller, destroy his stock and his establishment, arrest him and send him out of the country, threatening him with death if he returned, and then the offending evil would have been removed, and his superiors would never have called him to account for such a procedure. But Major Plympton did not take this course. He arrested and imprisoned the settlers because their cows trespassed upon the drill ground, but in only two instances did he attempt to punish the liquor sellers.[36]

Holcombe listed men simply known as Menk, Pierre Parrant, Donald McDonald, and Jim Thompson "the negro" as the east-bank liquor dealers. But he did not include Joseph Brown, soon to be justice of the peace of St. Croix County, Wisconsin Territory, which then included the east bank of the Mississippi as well as the entire delta region between the St. Croix and the Mississippi.[37]

Brown was one of the largest dealers in the area. In a letter to the surgeon general of the army, the fort surgeon wrote, "At this moment there is a citizen named Brown, once a soldier in the 5th infantry . . . [who is] actually building on the land . . . a very extensive whisky shop."[38]

By summer 1839 Major Plympton saw clearly that liquor threatened the security of the fort. For the remainder of the year, he lobbied the War Department for authorization to extend the borders around the Fort Snelling reservation so that he could not only clear "settlers on the ground that several persons had established whisky shops . . . [but also] to afford further protection to the garrison."[39]

By May 6, 1840, following an order from the secretary of war, the U.S. marshal of Wisconsin Territory, supported by a detachment from the garrison, removed the settlers and their goods from the Fort Snelling Reservation and destroyed their log cabins.[40]

Once again the disgruntled settlers moved, this time to a point downriver. There they settled in "scattered shanties" in a "nameless settlement on a site selected almost by accident," on land that was good for cornfields and potato patches, near a shanty occupied by a whiskey seller named Pierre Parrant. Noted for his one eye that had "a singularly distorted and unnatural caste, so that it resembled that of a pig," Parrant was nicknamed "Pig's Eye," and "the locality of his shack bore the same designation." Jim Thompson was the community's first resident of African descent. His neighbors included such well-known men as Abraham Perry, Benjamin and Pierre Gervais, Joseph Rondo, and Pierre Bottineau.[41]

By this time Thompson apparently had long since stopped selling whiskey. One year earlier, on May 21, 1839, the first steamboat to dock at St. Paul Landing was the *Glaucus,* commanded by Capt. John Atchison. Six barrels of whiskey were unloaded for Donald McDonald, resulting in a transaction that ultimately put Thompson out of business. He appears, therefore, to have been out of the whiskey-selling business even before he and the Red River squatters were removed from the Fort Snelling Reservation. Still, to some chroniclers of the times, he was a difficult man to forgive. To critics of Thompson, in 1846, Auguste Larpenteur, "the first aristocrat of St. Paul," reportedly noted that five stores in town were peddling liquor. There was neither law nor custom against it, "so why pick on Jim?"[42]

Indeed, the Methodists, who had delivered Thompson from slavery and perhaps had the strongest reason to see him as undermining their mission, instead embraced him as one of their brethren. His name appears in the record books of church membership, and by 1840 his wife, Mary, and her sister; Hannah Taliaferro, the major's "Indian wife," and her daughter; and the Swede Jacob Falstrom and his wife, Marguerite Bonga Falstrom, sister of Stephen Bonga, had likewise been formally received into the Methodist fellowship. So committed was the Thompson family to the Methodist church that, when Kavanaugh closed the mission and moved downriver to Red Rock, where Newport is today, the Thompsons apparently made trips to prayer meetings there, faithfully keeping their membership active.[43]

The best example illustrating how rigid antiblack law was made flexible in preterritorial Minnesota is found in Thompson's role in the Deniger trial. On the evening of January 25, 1841, Jean Baptiste Deniger, in the company of the ten-year-old mixed-blood girl Ursula Labissoniere, stopped at the Thompson cabin, presumably to warm herself against the winter's chill. Noticing that Deniger was drunk, knowing what he was capable of doing in that state, and fearing for the girl's safety, Jim engaged their visitor long enough for Mary to sneak Ursula away, intending to take her to the Methodist mission. After a time realizing that Ursula was missing, Deniger hurried to his sleigh parked outside and whipped the horse into a gallop, heading down to the frozen river where he could overtake Mary before she reached the mission. He succeeded in cutting Mary off the track-lined snowy path and stopping her sleigh. Though Mary fought him, he pushed her off, pulled the girl into his sleigh, and raced away.[44]

Shortly after Deniger left the Thompson cabin, Jim labored through snowdrifts to his neighbor's to borrow a horse and sleigh and give chase. On the path he met Deniger, but he did not see that the girl was with him. Deniger kept her hidden, threatening to cut her with his knife. Jim proceeded toward the mission for a short distance. Apparently, he looked back over the path on the frozen river to see that Deniger's horse and sleigh were standing on the edge of the ice. At some point Jim looked back again and noticed that the horse and sleigh had not left the spot. Thinking Deniger might have had an accident and knowing that he was intoxicated, Jim returned to the spot. What he found was Deniger with his pantaloons unbuttoned, lying on Ursula, the girl's "lower parts" uncovered and drenched with blood. Deniger held a knife in his hand.[45]

Thompson pulled Deniger off the hysterical girl, saying he should be ashamed of himself. Deniger replied that all girls liked such things and that Ursula was his wife, at which point Ursula cried out, "No! No!" Deniger then threw a buffalo skin over Ursula's head, yanked her to her feet, and pulled her into his sleigh. Thompson reached for her, insisting that he take the girl back. Deniger pushed him, and Thompson lost his grip on the girl in the scuffle. Deniger jumped on the sleigh and whipped his horse into a gallop to escape. Thompson gave chase, overtook Deniger, rescued Ursula, and took her back to his cabin.[46]

Another neighbor of Thompson's, Jacques Lefevre, having heard Deniger say at the cabin of Joseph Monjeau that he planned to rape Ursula, apparently had not believed Deniger would do such a thing. He was shocked when he later heard from Thompson that she had been "ravaged" by Deniger. Lefevre felt compelled to go to Thompson's cabin to see for himself. He checked Ursula's clothes and heard from her mouth that Deniger had "ravished" her.[47]

On February 13 Henry Hastings Sibley, newly appointed justice of the peace to Clayton County, Iowa Territory, issued a warrant for Deniger's arrest, basing probable cause on the affidavits of James Thompson and Jacques Lefevre. By then Deniger was a fugitive from justice. Constable Edward Brissette was dispatched to track him down and succeeded in capturing him below Lake Pepin. He brought him back in irons.[48]

At the hearing Francois Chevalier, another neighbor of Thompson's, testified that he had heard Deniger say he intended to "do something." As pretext for giving her a ride, he said he would take Ursula to the home of Joseph Brown, where Ursula had once lived. His testimony, along with those of Thompson, Lefevre, and Monjeau, all but assured a conviction. Nevertheless, Sibley reported, "Friends of the culprit begged hard that he should not be severely punished, and after keeping him in durance vile for several days, I agreed to release him if he would leave the country, threatening him with dire vengeance if he should ever return. He left in great haste and I never saw him afterwards."[49]

From this case many questions arise. What was Thompson's status in the community? Why did Thompson attempt to spirit Ursula to the Methodist mission at Red Rock instead of to legal authorities such as the justice of the peace or the Indian agent at Fort

Snelling? The rape occurred somewhere along the east shore of the river, which places the crime in what then was St. Croix County, Wisconsin Territory. Why, then, was the case tried in Clayton County, Iowa Territory? Indeed, what was the nature of American law on the Minnesota frontier? And as a black man did Thompson's race hinder his ability to testify against a white man? Indeed, what did being black mean to Thompson? What did being an American mean?

Jim and Mary Thompson seem to have been very much a part of the community in which they lived, free from the stigma that white Americans assigned to blacks. In this rugged place, in these harsh times, racism was a foolish indulgence, for survival relied on kinship. The settlement—which by the end of the year became known as St. Paul, named by newly arrived priest Lucien Galtier after "the apostle of nations"—was predominantly French and Catholic. French was the only language spoken by most of the residents of the community. Thompson, to conduct his daily activities, must have learned to speak in that tongue. He certainly seemed to understand the people around him.[50]

One logically might have considered returning the girl to her father, yet there was no indication Thompson did so. The record shows only that the Thompsons intended to get Ursula to the mission, which suggests Thompson knew that her father, Joseph Labissoniere, was probably absent, hunting or trapping, or that, like many mixed-blood fathers, he had "given" his daughter to the mission where she could learn the "white man's ways" and thus be suitable for a white husband. In 1853 Ursula, in fact, married a young white man named James Victory. In any case, the decision to move her was immediate.[51]

Why then did they take the girl to the mission, instead of the nearer Fort Snelling, or to the justice of the peace? Without testimony one can only surmise the reason. If Joseph Labissoniere wanted Ursula to be raised at the mission, the Thompsons may have returned the girl to her "home." Another theory rests in the Thompsons' devotion to the mission. By January 1841 they were devout Methodists. They attended prayer meetings no matter the season; perhaps they viewed the mission as sanctuary. To supplicants so willing to undertake the trek to be in community with the Red Rock Methodists, the missionaries embodied a moral authority casting Red Rock as a refuge.

Fort Snelling may have seemed unwelcoming since Thompson, along with most of the Pig's Eye settlers, had been forcibly removed from the reservation eight months earlier. Also Deniger said he intended to take the girl to the house of Joseph R. Brown, "where Ursula once resided." Brown *was* the justice of the peace, and Deniger had been a witness for Brown for a sale of land six months before the rape. Brown may have even been one of the "friends of the culprit who begged hard [to Sibley] that [Deniger] should not be severely punished." In any event, Brown did not hear the case after Deniger was returned for trial, a tip of the hat to the integrity of American jurisprudence.[52]

By 1841 the part of Minnesota between the St. Croix and Mississippi Rivers—including St. Paul—was called St. Croix County, the westernmost section of Wisconsin Territory. That's where the crime was committed, and thus it fell within Brown's jurisdiction. The western shore of the Mississippi, including Fort Snelling and Mendota, were part of Clayton County, Iowa Territory, an area extending along a line about twenty miles south of Prairie du Chien north to Pembina, then west to the Missouri River, "an empire of itself"—Sibley's jurisdiction. He was the only magistrate in the region, and as Prairie du Chien, the county seat, was "some three hundred miles distant," he "had matters pretty much under my own control." "In fact," he wrote, "some of the simple-minded people around me firmly believed that I had the power of life and death."[53]

In fact, it's not at all certain American law had any practical meaning to the residents of Minnesota country. Legal authorities in both counties provided little sense of refuge, as indicated in the Thompsons' intent to take Ursula to the mission. Whether residents knew or cared which territory they lived in, especially during the 1830s and 1840s when jurisdictions were shifting, is unclear. Many years later, Sibley mused, "It may seem paradoxical, but it is nevertheless true, that I was successively a citizen of Michigan, Wisconsin, Iowa and Minnesota Territories, without changing my residence at Mendota."[54]

Confounded by a population largely speaking non-English languages, the administration of justice must have been bewildering. The same circumstances existed at the end of the decade, when Sibley told of the vexations of another justice at Mendota, "a very worthy, upright Frenchman, but indifferently versed in the English language." Sibley wrote:

> I was sitting in my office next door to the court room, when the justice entered hastily, and said to me in French: "That infernal [English-speaking] lawyer has been talking to me until I am tired, and I have not understood one word in ten that he has said," and he then asked me what he should do. . . . When I told the counsel afterwards that he had thrown much eloquence and erudition to the winds, he was astounded, "for," said he, "the justice never took his eye from me while I was speaking, and I flattered myself upon having produced a profound impression."[55]

By 1841 America had its flag firmly planted on Minnesota's soil and a garrison to defend it, the first semblance of a jurisprudential infrastructure, the audacity to believe it could work, and a population willing to use, though not always comprehending, the legal mechanisms. But none of this necessarily made the residents *feel* American. Neither did other Americans deem them such. Even Sibley's colleague, a justice in this legal system, was considered a "Frenchman."[56]

If Labissoniere, Lefevre, Chevalier, Monjeau, and Deniger were labeled "French" or "Canadian," what was Thompson, a freed black slave born on the plantation of America's fifth president and now a resident of the nascent St. Paul? At the fort he was a "mulatto slave," and at the mission, a "negro." Official documents, census data, records, and chronicles kept by Americans—except the first court record following Thompson's freedom—referred to him by his race. Sibley's warrant for Deniger's arrest does not refer to Thompson's race at all. He was simply a "deponent," one who gives a deposition. This simple designation illustrates the ambivalent racial nature of American law on the frontier.

Elsewhere in Iowa Territory, south of Prairie du Chien, a black man was legally prohibited from giving testimony in a trial in which a white man was a party. Robert Lucas, a Virginian by birth, whose "erect military bearing, collar-length hair, and severe features [that lent] him an uncanny resemblance to Andrew Jackson, his political hero," was territorial governor of Iowa. He had appointed Sibley to his post.[57]

In 1839 Southerners and Northerners sympathetic to slavery and antiblack sentiment dominated the Iowa territorial legislature, as reflected in its handiwork. Governor Lucas, whose Jacksonian penchant for the executive veto had brought him into fierce conflict with the legislature, signed into law a bill limiting public education to "every class of white citizen." He also signed a bill on elections barring anyone "not a free white male citizen" from voting, a militia bill requiring enrollment only of "free white male persons," and a bill mandating that "a negro, mulatto, or Indian, shall not be a witness in any court or in any case against a white person."[58]

To Iowans south of Prairie du Chien, the reason for the prohibition was simple: they wanted to give blacks no legal benefits that might attract black migration to the region; the legislature also banned interracial marriages in 1840. Historian Eugene Berwanger wrote, "Iowa's proximity to [slaveholding] Missouri and the fact that many Iowans considered 'free blacks' the most wretched and miserable element of the population, guided the actions of the Hawkeye legislators."[59]

Many Iowa delegates to the first state constitutional convention in 1844, not content with denying the ballot and membership in the state legislature and militia to blacks, also demanded, unsuccessfully, the incorporation of a black-exclusion provision in the constitution of Iowa. One delegate, a former New Yorker, said he would "never consent to open the doors of our beautiful state [to Negroes]." "If free Negroes were not prevented from settling in Iowa, the neighboring states would drive 'the whole black population of the Union' into it."[60]

But Mendota and Pig's Eye were far from that maddened crowd. Thompson, the mulatto, had indeed testified against Deniger, the white man. Without a doubt, Minnesota country was still wilderness, despite the civilized trappings of county designations. The American flag fluttered over the confluence of the Mississippi and Minnesota Rivers before the national identity and social custom of prejudice were established. Territorial and county boundaries were drawn before such demarcations were relevant to the people living there.

Sibley's self-assessment—"I had matters pretty much under my control, there being little chance of an appeal from my decisions"—reflected the conceit of the newest world order. In the final analysis the safety of Ursula Labissoniere lay not with the magistrate of St. Peter's–Mendota or the garrison at Fort Snelling but at the mission of Red Rock and, ultimately, in Thompson's own cabin.

"Civilization," legal historian Lawrence Friedman has written, "advanced in undulating waves, generally along river valleys. . . . The land was not empty before the Americans came." Nor was it so after they arrived. For a time, in practical terms, Americans reluctantly coexisted with other social systems. The Dakota still controlled much of their territory. And "in the Mississippi Valley, a cluster of Frenchmen lived by a half-remembered form of the law of France."[61]

The inhabitants of Pig's Eye were clearly not concerned about being overrun by free blacks and fugitive slaves, let alone by Americans. Jim Thompson was the only African American living among them, and he, in effect, had become one of them.

What then did Thompson's race mean to him? One can only speculate as to how Thompson viewed himself during the time between his residencies at Kaposia and Pig's Eye. Judging from his early years in Minnesota as a slave, he did not fit neatly into any category. He seemed even to disregard the limits of being a slave. His personality, charm, and intellect all reflected one who, in seeing the wilderness outside the gates of Fort Snelling, also saw the opportunity to be more than a slave.

As Thompson became more a part of that world, his "blackness" became less relevant. He probably was not thinking about it as he melded into the largely French-speaking community of Pig's Eye. Or when he was confronting Deniger—the drunk white man brandishing a knife—on that wintry night. Or even when he was giving the deposition to Sibley. (He probably knew nothing about the racial bills that Governor Lucas had signed into law in Iowa. In the remote possibility he did know, Thompson seems not to have cared if Sibley did not.)

By 1841 Thompson, a man half black, half white, had a Dakota wife and, within two years, a three-year-old daughter, Sarah, and a newborn son, George, the name of his father's first master. In 1856 Thompson succeeded in listing Sarah and George, both one-half Mdewankanton Dakota, as official members of the Lake Pepin Mixed Blood Reservation.[62]

Thompson followed his son, who had embraced his Dakota kin to live on the Santee Reservation in Nebraska, shortly before his death in 1884 and long after the day when other blacks began to reside in St. Paul. Yet he convalesced in the West St. Paul home of his daughter, the second wife of Thomas S. Odell, a former New Yorker employed in the platting of St. Paul in 1847.[63]

Thompson's remaining years reflected the fluidity with which he could, throughout his life in Minnesota, move from one culture to another. In that sense his people were the people of his children. If anything, to Thompson race consciousness was fluid, dependent only on the receptive nature of the people around him. To the Yankees who transformed Pig's Eye from an outpost into an American city, however, Thompson, a man for whom many claimed great admiration, was simply a "colored" man and "the African." Their portrayal trivialized a life that they did not understand. As an American living among Americans, he became again a man whose "blackness" relegated him to a life limited by his race.[64]

In late 1841 Pig's Eye underwent a transformation. Lucien Galtier, the Catholic priest who presided over a small congregation at Mendota, extended his stewardship to the growing settlement at the foot of the bluffs, not far downriver. Some had been his parishioners at Fort Snelling, become wayward when the army removed them from the reservation. Now, in October, Father Galtier intended to establish a place of worship at Pig's Eye. Two farmers in the new congregation donated land on which he built "a rude log chapel, which on the first day of November he blessed and dedicated to Saint Paul, the apostle of nations," for living nearby were people of different "nations" and faiths, principally Dakota and a few Protestants. With no other features from which a name might arise (Pig's Eye was an increasingly unsuitable name for people settling there), the village was soon called "Saint Paul's Landing," then "Saint Paul's," then simply "Saint Paul." By 1842 nearly thirty families lived in the settlement, and with the exception of three or four households, all spoke French.[65]

Although St. Paul rested officially on U.S. soil, it was decidedly not American. Jim Thompson did not seem bothered that his home, Pig's Eye, was now St. Paul, a French-speaking, Catholic community whose affiliation with America was at most incidental and at least irrelevant. His "minority status" as a Methodist did not stigmatize him. The competitiveness inherent in the governance of American states and territories was nonexistent. He had no difficulty in choosing the wilderness of St. Paul over the civilization of St. Louis slave blocks, the Monroe plantation in Virginia where he was born, or even Fort Snelling. He could stand up without fear of reprisal by any man.

When the notorious Irishman Edward Phelen stole a pig belonging to Thompson, he went to Phelen's cabin and retrieved his pig. When Phelen learned of what Thompson had done, he challenged Thompson to a fight, and Thompson agreed to the terms: "If you lick me the pig is yours, and if I lick you the pig is mine." Thompson won the fight, and Phelen conceded, inviting the spectators as well as Thompson to his shanty for a drink: "Ever after that Thompson and Phelen were good friends." St. Paul was Thompson's home, and the new opportunities it opened to him anchored his commitment to the place.[66]

In time "law followed the axe." By 1845 the number of residents in the settlement was growing, and the names of the residents were increasingly American. Battles between the Dakota and the Ojibwe occurred less frequently near the settlement as more whites cleared the woods to build cabins and cultivate fields. Thompson was in the thick of this activity, helping construct many of the cabins. As the 1840s progressed, Thompson's name was mentioned as one who could make a superior roof, secure the sturdiest cabin, and provide the surest hands. He was credited with helping to erect the first St. Paul house, owned by Phelen and his partner, John Hayes.[67]

Thompson ran the first ferryboat across the Mississippi and acquired more property as well. And in 1849, in his most memorable contribution to the city and his religious community, he helped construct the First Methodist Church on Market Street, furnishing 2,000 feet of lumber and 1,500 shingles for the roof. He donated the proceeds of the sale of property he owned to help pay for the church.[68]

By the time Minnesota was ready to become a territory, St. Paul indeed had undergone a major transformation. It was no longer a foreign settlement on a "broken hillside" but a town quickly becoming an American city. As St. Paul proper was platted and survey lines were drawn, civilization arrived. By then Jim Thompson had left his legacy. He saw the coming of the new Minnesota from the comfort of his home, warmed by memories and surrounded by friends, including his next-door neighbor, a lawyer and surveyor—Benjamin Brunson, the son of his old friend from the Kaposia days.[69]

3

The Liberal Civilization

WHEN BENJAMIN WETHERALL BRUNSON left his home on the morning of September 27, 1849, he may well have felt, as his friend and neighbor Jim Thompson did, that St. Paul was very much his town. Sure, Jim had contributed to the developing townscape, financing and constructing cabins and now houses and stores going up around St. Paul. But Ben held a claim of equal if not more significance. He had brought "lines" to St. Paul.

For a burgeoning community lines were everything. Lines made the wilderness knowable. Lines, in the guise of metes and bounds, elevated man to master of his plot of land. Lines, through furrows in the soil, molded the landscape into a source of bounty and nourishment. Lines marked streets and city blocks. Lines, in short, transformed wilderness into civilization.

By 1847 people settling in St. Paul were demanding greater ownership of real estate, thereby enhancing the value of property to a degree that must have astonished the earliest settlers. It became necessary to have portions of the town laid out in lots, the work to be done by competent and ambitious young men.

Benjamin Brunson, his brother Ira, of Prairie du Chien, where they had grown up, and Thomas Odell, who had left the army and was now working as their chainman, began their surveying in August. This resulted in the tract recorded in the Registry of Deeds as "Saint Paul Proper." The tract contained approximately ninety acres, encompassing the main business district and the settled residential neighborhoods. The owners of those lots were some of the leaders of early Minnesota—Robert, Lambert, Jackson, Brunson, Cavalier, Sibley, Bass, Larpenteur, Forbes, Simpson, Rhodes, LaRoche, Coty, and Guerin. Thompson lived among these men.[1]

Benjamin Brunson, in other words, surveyed St. Paul's first

"straight" streets. In this fast-growing town, cabins that Jim Thompson may have helped to build were overshadowed by houses and buildings and eventually dismantled with great frequency.

One might imagine young Brunson, age twenty-six, glancing at the Thompson house as he walked past it to work on that day in September 1849. Perhaps Jim was at the door, and the two waved warm greetings as the younger man passed by. Perhaps there was an attachment there. This man Thompson, who had worked with Brunson's father in the old days, perhaps understood something otherwise inaccessible about a father who rarely was home during his youth. Perhaps the wave to the fifty-year-old Thompson was an act of gratitude to the contribution of the Old Settler, a recognition of the embodiment of a time about to pass forever.

But on that September morning, Brunson probably focused on the work to take place at Central House. There in the territorial legislature he would propose a law creating a different line, one that separated men who could vote from men who could not. Today, his work was that of a founding father and the creation of the U.S. Territory of Minnesota.

The groundwork for this day had been laid nearly three years before, when on December 23, 1846, Morgan L. Martin, the congressional delegate from Wisconsin, introduced a bill to organize Minnesota Territory. The bill died in the Senate in 1847 because the population was insufficient to warrant such designation. Senator Stephen Douglas's effort to create Minnesota Territory in 1848 likewise failed. Joseph Brown, by then a representative of St. Croix County in the Wisconsin territorial legislature and a chief proponent of both initiatives, knew that Wisconsin in that same year was about to become a state. Seeing in that a propitious moment for Minnesota, he worked to get the region organized.[2]

The western boundary of the new state was fixed along a line drawn from the St. Louis River southward to where the St. Croix River met the Mississippi River, then along the river to the states of Iowa and Illinois. The question then was what would happen to that region between the west bank of the St. Croix and the east bank of the Mississippi—the part cut off from Wisconsin and not a part of Iowa.[3]

On August 26, 1848, a convention was held in Stillwater to plan a course of action. Delegates drafted resolutions and memorials to be sent to Congress and President James Polk, calling for legislation to establish territorial status for Minnesota, "bewail[ing] the unhappy plight of citizens 'virtually disfranchised,' lacking officers, and depending for security only on 'mutual good understanding.'" The delegates sent Henry Hastings Sibley to Washington as an unofficial delegate to act on their behalf. In October his status became official in an election in which he defeated another fur trader and future rival, Henry M. Rice.[4]

Soon after Congress gave Sibley a seat, Senator Douglas introduced in the Democratic-controlled Senate another Minnesota bill, this one naming St. Paul its capital. This passed with little challenge. But the bill met resistance in the Whig-controlled House, reflecting the tense nature of partisan politics. The Whigs, raising the ire of Senate Democrats, withheld approval until after the presidential inauguration of Zachary Taylor, a Whig who had a Minnesota connection as former commandant of Fort Snelling. On March 3, 1849, the measure passed, received presidential approval, and became law.[5]

Then an incoming Whig, General Taylor, instead of the outgoing Democrat, President James Polk, appointed the first territorial governor along with all other territorial officers upon the advice and consent of the Senate. The most important appointment was that of governor, and it went to a thirty-four-year-old Whig from Pennsylvania—Alexander Ramsey.[6]

Hindsight reveals the relative speed with which Minnesota moved to stand at the threshold of territorial status. Credit belongs to a few men who by forceful, focused, and indefatigable leadership made it clear to Congress that their interest was America's interest, that their mutual concern was urgency. The requirement established in the Northwest Ordinance that five thousand free inhabitants trigger the process was ignored since it frustrated progress. The philosophy amounted to "Build the territory, and they will come." This was a place of vast opportunity attracting a steady stream of settlers. Still, the virtue of freedom carried with it an inalienable right to shape one's future by staking and protecting one's rightful claim with the full backing of law now that civilization was coming to the frontier. This indeed was the essence of the spirit of America and the mandate of the Northwest Ordinance, "the Magna Carta of the west."[7] Adopted in 1787, the Northwest Ordinance was the first charter of local government passed by federal authority for newly established western settlements. According to William Anderson, "First in time, it was destined to be the first also in importance." The ordinance established federal jurisdiction over the region north of the Ohio River and east of the Mississippi River, including the eastern portion of Minnesota, even though no known American citizen had made the area home. By moving to the district from any section of the country, settlers gained full suffrage rights regardless of race.[8]

As soon as a district attained a population of "five thousand free male inhabitants," it was to create a legislative assembly, of which one house should be popularly elected. The ordinance encouraged settlers to build schools, admonished inhabitants to be just to the Indians, required common highways to remain free to all citizens of the United States forever, and mandated that new states be forever a part of the Union, its inhabitants to bear their portion of the federal burden. Slavery was prohibited. As the district became a territory and later a state, the new society was dedicated to "the fundamental principles of civil and religious liberty."[9]

Under the Northwest Ordinance there was no concern about race or even whether a man was a citizen of the United States. He only had to inhabit the region. Under that rule Jim Thompson, an inhabitant, was equal to any other.

On March 3, 1849, the Organic Act creating Minnesota Territory was finally passed, signed, and put into effect. But when the new governor arrived in St. Paul on May 27, he found that the non-Indian population of the entire territory—counting blacks, mulattoes, French Canadians, and mixed bloods and including 317 soldiers at Fort Snelling—was still less than five thousand. To meet this required number, it was necessary to include the large settlement of mixed-blood traders at Pembina, the northwestern-most region, which later became part of the state of North Dakota. Ironically, all of the male inhabitants of color necessary to make Minnesota "eligible" for territorial status later were denied their civil rights by the law they helped make possible. Such was the urgency by which civilization was brought to the Minnesota frontier.[10]

Although the Organic Act mandated that only free *white* male inhabitants above the age of twenty-one years could vote at the first election and hold elective office, a provision in section 5 empowered the territorial government to reassign suffrage rights to inhabitants of color. Those rights were extinguished when the Organic Act replaced the Northwest Ordinance as the basic charter of government for Minnesota Territory. What rights the Organic Act took from Thompson, the territorial legislature could return. This option, of course, was not the likely choice. Each week brought steamboats laden with new settlers from Northern states that had enacted black laws, and many of these people were the same ones who had endorsed such legislation.[11]

Nonetheless, the debate was really more than whether inhabitants of color should be able to vote. It was a clear indication of Minnesota's evolving notion of race, the black community's value to society, and an expression of territorial self-interest and self-image.

Just how much Thompson himself—or, indeed, any other inhabitants of color—yearned for suffrage can be overstated, for this was a time when the early settlers of the territory were just as concerned about staking a claim as shaping a new society. Carrying out one's civic duty took second place to the drive to survive and prosper. J. Fletcher Williams, a chronicler of the time, observed, "Indeed, some of our old settlers declare that . . . they used to have to *force* office on men—that such a thing as 'office-seeking' was unknown in those poor but honest times."[12]

In those early days the "white-only" language of the Organic Act had to seem peculiar, an absurd notion that scarcely reflected the reality of race and color in early Minnesota. Observing the residents of St. Paul in 1845, Williams wrote, "At this time, by far the largest proportion of the inhabitants were Canadian French, and Red River refugees, and their descendants. There were only three or four purely American (white) families in the settlement. . . . English was probably not spoken in more than three or four families."[13]

Life on the frontier tolerated racial intermingling. There was a sense that the community had a duty to educate children regardless of their race. In a letter written in 1846, Reverend Thomas S. Williamson, a physician and missionary seeking a teacher for a school he had established, declared, "[The teacher] should be entirely free from prejudice on account of color, for among her scholars she might find not only English, French and Swiss, but Sioux and Chippewas, with some claiming kindred with the African stock." Williamson must have been referring to Thompson's children, who were eight and three.[14]

On the frontier there was no need for a governmental infrastructure. Exercising one's voting franchise was not as urgent as making peace with surrounding tribes, trapping, farming, and surviving the winter cold. The social convention of racism did not exist and so did not stifle a free man's power to define himself. Whiteness for its own sake in a world that was predominantly one of color had little clout, even less currency on this frontier, and was hardly a distinction warranting the power to exclude.

But the world was rapidly changing.

On May 17, 1849, when traveling journalist Ephraim S. Seymour landed at the wharf of St. Paul, he found a town bursting at the seams:

> Its new frame buildings, glistening with the reflection of the rising sun, imparted to it an air of neatness and prosperity. . . . Everything here appeared to be on the *high pressure* principle. A dwelling house for a family could not be rented. The only hotel was small, and full to overflowing. Several boarding houses were very much thronged. Many families were living in shanties, made of rough boards, fastened to posts driven in the ground, such as two men could construct in one day. It was said that about 80 men lodged in a barn belonging to [Henry] Rice's new hotel, which was not yet completed. Two families occupied tents while I was there.[15]

The throng he saw was diverse and absorbed in the heady business of a new age:

> We are now near the dividing line of civilized and savage life. We can look across the river and see Indians on their own soil. Their ca-

noes are seen gliding across the Mississippi, to and fro between savage and civilized territory. They are met hourly in the streets. . . . Here comes a female in civilized costume; her complexion is tinged with a light shade of bronze, and her features bear a strong resemblance of those of the Indian. She is a descendant of French and Indian parents—a half-breed from Red River.[16]

If Ephraim Seymour had met Jim Thompson, he might not have realized that he was standing before the only Old Settler who was African American. Seymour proffered the conventional view of French-speaking residents: "There goes a French Canadian, who can converse only in the language of his mother tongue. He is an old settler; see his prattling children sporting about yonder shanty, which was constructed of rough boards, with about one day's labor. There he lives—obliging fellow! exposed to the sun and rain, and rents his adjoining log cabin at $12 per month."[17]

Seymour then described the men who probably determined the political fate of the region: "Let us pass on to that group that converse daily in front of yonder hotel. They appear to be principally professional men, politicians, office-seekers, speculators and travelers, discussing the various topics growing out of the organization of the new Territory—such as the distribution of the loaves and fishes, the price of lots, the rise of real estate, the opportunity now afforded for the acquisition of wealth or political fame."[18]

Within a month's time civilization had come so quickly that newly arrived settlers found no shelter anywhere in St. Paul. Boardinghouses and hotels simply could not be built fast enough. Seymour wrote, "On the 13th of June, I counted all the buildings in the place, the number of which, including shanties and those in every state of progress, from the foundation wall to completion, was *one hundred and forty two*. Of the above, all, except about a dozen, were probably less than six months old."[19]

The rush of immigration and trade in the territory seemed unremitting. The *Pioneer,* whose editorial policy was to promote development, reported, "On Wednesday of last week, three steamboats arrived at our landing. They were all heavily laden with merchandise for this point." Even observers in Illinois took note:

"We learn that whole colonies are on the move to Minnesota, from the Middle and Eastern States, and from Canada."[20]

And still one was as likely to hear French spoken on the street as English. The town in 1849 was an outpost, with French fur traders and mixed-blood "attachés." The newly formed Court of the Third District, which included St. Paul, convened at the end of August. Judge David Cooper presided, and Henry Sibley was foreman of the grand jury. When Judge Cooper read the first charge to the jury, Sibley observed, "Only three out of the twenty-odd members understood, the rest being French." Maj. William Forbes, also a member of the first Territorial Council, had to translate.[21]

This was a place in clear need of an "American stamp." The *St. Paul Pioneer* excitedly reported on the arrival of the *Highland Mary,* carrying five hundred passengers, a common load for those days: "On Friday morning . . . the smoke of a steamboat was visible at St. Paul, and the very heart of the town leaped for joy. . . . As she came up in front of Randall's warehouse, the multitude on shore raised a deafening shout of welcome. . . . Such has been the anxiety here for the arrival of steamboats, that nothing else was talked of. St. Paul seemed likely to go to seed." The newspaper also printed an editorial urging, "Let us do everything in our power to welcome, encourage, and build up those who have come to unite their fortunes with ours." The editor noted that the hotels would quickly fill up and suggested that residents should extend the hospitality of their homes until the new arrivals could build "tenements."[22]

In June 1849, 840 people lived in St. Paul. A year later the population had grown to 1,294. Jim Thompson ceased to be the only black man in town. Both the 1849 and the 1850 censuses listed 40 blacks or mulattoes living in the capital city.[23]

At the intersection of Minnesota and Bench Streets stood the hotel noted by Seymour where professional men and office seekers discussed the business of the new territory. Robert Kennedy's Central House was a log building that he had enlarged and repaired during the summer to accommodate travelers and boarders. It now served as the temporary capitol, where the House and the Council met. At ten o'clock on Monday morning, September 3, 1849, Representative B. W. Brunson of St. Paul had arrived and, with fifteen other representatives in the front west room on the ground floor of Central House "sitting on rough board benches and chairs," began "to work out as they may this old problem of self-government through the appalling labyrinth of parliamentary rules and tactics that perplex their souls," processing the bills stacked before them.[24]

There was a bill to incorporate the Minnesota Mutual Fire Insurance, a bill to appoint commissioners to prepare a code of laws for territorial Minnesota, a bill to incorporate the Minnesota Historical Society, a memorial to Congress related to the purchase of Dakota lands west of the Mississippi River, and a series of bills for relief of various ferrymen as well as for divorce grants. During the afternoon session Brunson introduced Bill No. 11 prescribing the qualifications of voters and elected officeholders and describing the right to vote as limited to free white men. Seated across from him was Reverend Gideon Pond of Oak Park.[25]

Pond, thirty-six years old and a native of Connecticut, had come to Minnesota in 1834 with his brother, Samuel, fully intent on spreading the Christian faith among the Dakota from the mission they established near Lake Calhoun with the band of Cloud Man. Like Taliaferro, Seth Eastman, and Jim Thompson, the Ponds had secured allegiance with the chief through the marriage of one of Samuel's nephews to one of the chief's granddaughters. For eighteen years Gideon Pond and his brother worked "to give the Dakota a written language and literature of their own." To do so, they created an alphabet, assembled a dictionary, wrote grammar texts, and compiled readers, all for use in converting the Dakota to Christianity.[26]

Now, standing at more than six feet, the robust and pious "Grizzly Bear" (as the Dakota called Gideon Pond) was an imposing figure when he rose to debate the restrictive language of Bill No. 11. He moved to have the word "white" stricken from the first line. The motion failed. Pond then moved to amend the bill by inserting the phrase "and all free male colored persons over 21 years of age." This, too, failed. The suffrage rights that could have been extended to blacks were lost for another twenty years. Pond—

given his work with the Dakota—probably was acting on behalf of native friends rather than blacks. A series of amendments following appeared to reflect greater sympathy for the rights of mixed-blood residents of the state.[27]

William R. Marshall of St. Paul, a native of Missouri, who as governor of Minnesota in 1869 was instrumental in securing black suffrage, proposed the following amendment: "All persons of mixed blood, of Indian descent, of civilized habits, shall enjoy all rights and privileges granted in the first section of this act to whites." The motion failed. Then Virginia-born Henry Jackson of St. Paul offered "that nothing in the foregoing act shall be so construed as to prevent the voting of half-breeds, unless they are mixed with the African race, which shall be prohibited." The motion failed. At this point Morton Wilkinson, destined to be a U.S. senator, moved that "all civilized persons of Indian-descent, who have adopted the habits and customs of white people, shall be entitled to the right of suffrage." The motion failed. All motions to expand suffrage to Minnesota's people of color—black, Indian, or mixed—failed. The question was called, "Shall the bill pass?" The last version of the bill was narrowly adopted, nine to seven.[28]

In contrast, the Council's deliberations were less contentious. But its members wanted the franchise to include "persons of a mixture of white and Indian blood" who "adopted the habits and customs of civilized men." No provision to include inhabitants like Jim Thompson was mentioned. On October 27 the "half-blood" provision was accepted. But for the provision to become law, the House of Representatives had to adopt the language, and it had already voted against a similar amendment. On October 31 the Council learned that "the House of Representatives have refused to recede from their amendment [to Bill No. 11]." Conceding to the lower house, the Council adopted the Brunson language on the afternoon of November 1. With that, Brunson's restrictive bill became law.[29]

The effect of the law was both immediate and expansive. By denying Jim Thompson and all other nonwhite men the franchise to participate in congressional, territorial, county, or precinct elections, the law also barred them from serving on county juries because such service required that persons be selected from voting lists. In time this law further barred them from serving as referees in civil cases and from holding offices in villages because such candidates had to be "qualified as a juror."

In 1851 the law expanded to bar blacks from running in village elections through its provision that any person elected to office had to be "entitled to vote at the election at which he shall be elected." A similar law in 1853 prohibited black participation in town meetings. While these subsequent laws were not necessarily intentional expressions of antiblack sentiment but rather logical increments of citizenship, the cumulative effect was one of increasing restriction on the rights of Minnesota's free black inhabitants. Bill No. 11 was a simple reflection of the sentiments of the original voting population of Minnesota.[30]

Brunson's newspaper, a self-styled journal that occupied "high moral and conservative grounds," nonetheless characterized the voting provision of the territorial constitution as "very liberal."[31]

In stark contrast to the socially progressive and racially inclusive liberalism in American politics of the mid-twentieth century, the liberalism of Minnesota in 1849 was Jacksonian in context. It was a brand of politics extending opportunity to virtually all of the nation's white male citizens, a liberalism suspicious of economic and political elites. Brunson's words celebrated a new age when privilege was eliminated. Men, no matter how common, now had opportunities never before available—provided they had the talent and energy to exploit them. Being white was the foundation of their opportunity, an ideal that the majority of the legislators could support. And yet, except for Henry Jackson, these legislators did not express antiblack sentiment. Rather, their desire was to minimize controversy, especially since the black population was so small. The urgency to create a territorial constitution was more important than the principle of universal male suffrage, especially since the men in "civilized" Minnesota (St. Paul, St. Anthony, Minneapolis, Stillwater, and various smaller settlements) were already increasingly Anglo and increasingly Anglo-white. On this issue it was a matter of choosing their battles.

As Brunson surveyed property lines and city blocks to bring St. Paul out of the wilderness, he drew lines that delineated free black male residents as second-class persons, without the rancor or hostility so characteristic in other midwestern states. With lines, civilization had come to Minnesota. Such was the birth of the liberal civilization.

4

A Peculiar Imbalance

DURING THE EARLY 1850s Minnesotans created a society in which Irish Catholics, the least acculturated and most derided of whites by the Yankee elite, were granted political rights but afforded limited opportunities to economic development and relegated to fill the city's laboring class. "Civilized" Indians and mixed bloods, the most "foreign" of people in a land that originally had been theirs, personified a lifestyle that would give way to the culture of the plow and get the right to vote—provided they offered strategic and economic benefit to the American fur trade or merely dressed as white men. At the same time, blacks—Protestant and acculturated to a society governed by an elite that was primarily Protestant, Northern, and antislavery—could acquire property yet be denied political equality. In terms of citizenship, Minnesota was a society that altogether reflected a most peculiar imbalance.

Two of the blacks who had recently come upriver from Galena, Illinois, were William Taylor and his wife, Adeline. Taylor soon opened a barbershop next to the St. Paul post office on Third Street, near Minnesota, and lived in a house across the street, facing his business. He personified a new kind of black presence. Like Jim Thompson, he was a married man and a property owner. But there the similarity ended.[1]

While Thompson had lived in Minnesota for twenty-three years, Taylor was a newcomer. Thompson embodied Minnesota's past—he was a former slave, married to the daughter of a Dakota leader, and trilingual in speaking English, Dakota, and French. Taylor came to Minnesota a free man, married to a black woman. Neither of them had experienced the transformation of a frontier settlement to a civilized American town.

While Thompson for a time resided in St. Paul, he was equally

at home in the wilderness. Taylor was a townsman. His trade provided a service for the burgeoning group of white professional
men, politicians, office seekers, and speculators staking their fortunes on the future of Minnesota, men who preferred the elegance
of expertly trimmed hair and beard, men who hired others to provide the brawn. Thompson, however, did not serve the vanity of
professional white men. While he knew many of the men who later
became Minnesota's power brokers and had confronted the likes of
Deniger and Phelan, he was not one to trim their hair.

Thompson and Taylor were indeed different men. If they had
met, they would have been cordial, but their differences would
have been as obvious as the clothes they wore and the manner in
which they spoke—the English of the fifty-year-old Thompson
was probably accented by years in the Minnesota bush, in fran-
cophonic Pig's Eye, and on Dakota land, where English was rarely
spoken. Taylor represented change coming to St. Paul from downriver, where race relations had long been starkly defined along
lines of black and white. In Minnesota the greatest differences had
been between the Ojibwe and the Dakota.

At midcentury black people had begun to trickle into Minnesota country, though their immigration was hardly noticeable.
By the time of the 1850 census, black people constituted .64 percent of the overall known, non-Indian population of 6,077 in the
territory, just 40 people. Of this number, 30 lived in St. Paul. An
employed male headed all but one family.[2]

In contrast, the growing number of white men arriving weekly
were single and destined to be laborers. As James M. Goodhue, the
first territorial newspaper publisher, wrote on August 16, 1849,
"There are a great many smart bachelors, who will have to continue
odd, if their other halves don't come along." With wry humor an editor of the *Minnesota Pioneer* suggested they "take up with some of
the Wenonas of the Sioux nation, who could have been bought any
day then for a few dollars each." Edward Neill, who would serve as
chaplain in the territorial legislature, wrote, "Vice has travelled here
[to St. Paul] with telegraphic speed" and complained of "the numerous conveniences for becoming a drunkard" and the desecration
of the Sabbath by "billiard rooms and ball alleys."[3]

The *Register* noted: "The number of retail liquor establish-
ments in Saint Paul and other towns of the Territory, is a leetle too
great for a sound and healthy state of public morals. This is the
subject of remark by strangers, and gives us a bad name at home
and abroad, to say nothing of its evil effects upon society."[4]
In this setting black residents were careful to be discreet.

Five black men were barbers, and they were the only barbers in
Minnesota. The blacks listed eleven different states as their places
of birth—many of them were born in Virginia or Kentucky. Most
of the black adults were literate, a far higher percentage than adults
in the white community. The blacks in St. Paul lived in every ward
of the town.[5]

In short, this was a respectable and well-integrated population.
Even the *Pioneer,* a conservative newspaper, characterized the
black community as "attentive to their business, and . . . no idlers
as they are represented to be, in the slave states. They are a useful
class and here on the confines of Barbarism do as much to put a
civilized aspect upon the face of society as any other class."[6]

Indeed, there was no outward display of bigotry by the white
neighbors. Still, the absence of a segregated neighborhood; the
practice of interracial marriage among blacks, Indians, and whites;
and the ever-increasing white population all contributed to making
a discernible black community microscopic and politically insignificant. Nevertheless, during the legislative session of 1851, suffrage
rights were extended only to "all persons of mixed white and Indian
blood who have adopted the customs and habits of civilization."[7]

On the surface the act to enfranchise mixed bloods while barring blacks was puzzling. The blacks of St. Paul fully embraced the
customs and habits of Yankee civilization. While all blacks spoke
English, most mixed bloods did not. Furthermore, the blacks lived
among whites and internalized many of their values. But the culture of the majority of mixed bloods was vastly distinct from that
of the Yankee community. The Northwest Ordinance and the Organic Act excluded both Indians and mixed bloods, regardless of
whether they were "civilized." And yet, by 1851, one group of people of color enjoyed more legislative support than the other.

One explanation for this was that antiblack sentiment was long embedded in the national psyche. The white settlers from eastern and lower midwestern states feared that universal suffrage might attract a flood of blacks to the area. In essence, the black people they knew were the black hordes they imagined, rather than the individual barber, cook, or interpreter who lived next door.[8]

Indeed, the pioneer legislators, all self-made men, had established their positions largely through contacts with Indians and mixed bloods. With few exceptions individual legislators had spent years in trade, commerce, and farming without contact with black people.[9]

Even missionary Gideon Pond, the only legislator who argued to remove "white" from the suffrage bill, which would have permitted blacks to vote, had spent most of his adult life working with the Dakota. He was not likely thinking about black residents; rather, his use of the word "colored" may have been as an imprecise term meant to include the people he had converted to Christianity. Only Henry Jackson's restrictive amendment expressly denied the vote to a person with a drop of black blood: "That nothing in the foregoing act shall be construed as to prevent the voting of all half-breeds, unless they are mixed with African blood."[10]

A second reason for enfranchising "civilized" Indians and mixed bloods rested in the sense that, as a colorful people, the mixed bloods were often viewed in idealized and whimsical terms. Mixed bloods had "free, half-wild manners . . . untrammeled by the restraints of more refined society . . . [who lived a] generous improvidence and half-nomad life, part hunter, part farmer." As J. Fletcher Williams wrote, they "were . . . a study. Nearly all of them were swarthy, half or quarter-breeds, or *Bois Brules,* as they were termed, and dressed in a costume, a curious commingling of civilized garments and barbaric adornments. They were usually clad in coarse, blue cloth, with a profusion of brass buttons, and a red sash girt around their waists. Add to this a bead-work cap, and an Indian's moccasins, and you have a fair picture of the Red River half-breed."[11]

In other words, their race did not lend itself to codification in the simple terms of black and white. They clearly were their own category.

A third reason lay in the value of their trade in furs, their inter-
cessions with various Indian tribes, and their knowledge in chart-
ing the region for settlement and economic development in territorial Minnesota. From the 1820s to the 1870s, mixed bloods helped
establish Minnesota's first overland roads. They traded furs for
goods and supplies between St. Paul and posts in the rich Red
River Valley and various Canadian settlements to establish a main-
stay for Minnesota's economy in the late 1840s and 1850s. According to Williams: "All of the money received for the sale of furs
would be generally spent in merchandize in our city, and large
sums in addition . . . [on] [s]taple groceries, liquors, dry goods,
blankets, & c., hardware and tools, household utensils, ammunition
and guns, clothing, boots and shoes, glass, sash, farm implements,
even threshers and mowers." The arrival of the caravan of mixed-
blood traders was always an important event for the merchants of
St. Paul.[12]

Their value to the territory was strategic as well as economic.
While the black population was essentially urban and politically
insignificant due to its small number of residents, the mixed-blood
population was numerous and scattered throughout the territory.
The single-largest concentration of mixed bloods was in the Red
River Valley and the Pembina region in the northwest section of
the territory. Here their political worth was most evident. The region had considerable economic potential, one that the British
Hudson's Bay Company had long exploited. In mid-1849 the residents there petitioned Governor Ramsey to seek federal presence
in the region, thereby protecting the mixed bloods' as well as the
territory's interests against the British.[13]

This set the stage for the fourth reason. In support of the petition, Ramsey, in a message to both houses of the legislature, argued that the mixed bloods' racial, cultural, and language differences should not distract the legislators from seeing their economic
and strategic value to the region.

Ramsey wrote, "I herewith communicate to your honorable
bodies the translation of a memorial, numerously signed by half-
breeds, residents of Pembina, on the Red River of the North. . . .
[A]s they are, in common with ourselves, Minnesotians, and as

such deserving of our warmest sympathies, in their remote and comparatively unprotected and uncared-for home, I have thought it proper to invite the aid of your influence." The Pembina mixed bloods would not drain territorial resources, for they were self-sufficient, residing "upon a fertile soil, that produces or is capable of producing in abundance, wheat, rye, corn, potatoes, and all the vegetable and animal productions necessary to human subsistence and comfort." Their contribution to the territorial community would be beneficial, for the buffalo that ran in abundance offered "meat, hides and tallow" that could be converted "into articles of profitable merchandise."[14]

But it was also a wealth coveted by a foreign power, Ramsey continued:

> The interference of the settlers within the British lines with them, in this their main pursuit, demands that the National Government should abate the evil, and jealously maintain the integrity of our Territory by repressing the intrusion of subjects of a foreign power, that churlishly refuses all reciprocity; and so preserve to our people advantages which nature has bestowed almost exclusively upon our Territory, wherein not only the larger animals of the chase, but those also valuable entirely for their furs, prefer to range, because their subsistence is easy from the abundance of their natural food spontaneously produced by a fertile and congenial soil.[15]

These Minnesotans, argued Ramsey, living under constant threat of foreign invasion, deserved territorial protection and, in time, territorial security:

> If, by establishing a military post at Pembina, and extending over the settlement our civil law, through organized counties and courts of justice, we can confine the British hunters . . . exclusively to their inferior hunting ranges, the advantages of immigrating to Minnesota rather than remain in British Territory, would so greatly preponderate . . . the first step towards any efficient relief is . . . the extension of our land system, or a modification of it thereto; and the organization of counties and courts therein, so that our fellow-citizens of mixed blood on the frontiers may enjoy in common with ourselves the precious privileges of free, just and liberal institutions.[16]

Economic and strategic factors counterbalanced the foreign or different quality of the predominantly Catholic, Franco-Ojibwe mixed bloods inhabiting faraway Pembina, thus elevating their importance to the territory. This apparent bonhomie did not easily transfer to the French Catholics and Catholic mixed bloods living in St. Paul, among whom the Protestant missionaries proselytized, illustrating the double standard the territory's power elite was willing to employ.

Political equality, especially when extended to people with no intention of living among the Anglo-Protestants, was not the same as social equality. At the same time that Ramsey appealed on behalf of the mixed bloods of Pembina, Edward Neill, chaplain of the territorial legislature, reported with alarm that the "Papists" were still the most numerous class in St. Paul. He believed they were planning a cathedral.[17]

Father Augustin Ravoux complained, however, that French families in his parish were receiving pamphlets critical of the Catholic Church. He called the Protestant propaganda "assaults of the Old Serpent, and his satellites" and "containing devilish lies." He demanded that Presbyterian missionary T. S. Williamson, who had campaigned to build a multiracial school, desist his anti-Catholic activities. Both denunciations were the outgrowth of deep-seated tension, which intensified as the town of St. Paul struggled with its American identity.[18]

This was the essence of the peculiar imbalance. The Anglo-Protestant elite spoke more benevolently of the "foreign" Catholic people of Pembina than of the Catholics who lived among them in St. Paul. Against these white neighbors, not blacks, they directed xenophobic, even racial, terms of derision. Despite this contempt for Catholics, Yankee suspicions of their disloyalty, and a determination to deny them economic opportunity, the political elite granted Catholics the vote.

Yankee Protestants viewed America's frontier not only as the embodiment of the nation's future but as its very soul. To the extent the frontier was populated by the so-called foreign element, as Catholics were viewed to be, the soul and future of America was threatened by a distinctly un-American presence—people who bowed to a foreign leader. Nevertheless, the Jacksonian Democrats, still largely in control of the federal, state, and territorial governments, made it easier for Catholic immigrants to attain the franchise, thereby making them the bane of Yankee Protestant Americanism.

In a sermon first preached in Philadelphia in 1846, Reverend Albert Barnes outlined the task of the benevolent mission, emphasizing "Americanization," political and moral stabilization, and religious evangelism. Focusing his attention on the task of Americanizing and Christianizing the immigrant multitudes in the West, Barnes first described the two main tendencies there—the "Puritan mind" and the "foreign mind."[19]

According to Barnes, the Puritan tradition, which had been "modified by the institutions of New England," was "strongly imbued with the love of civil and religious liberty; with hatred of oppression and wrong; with the value of the simplest and purest forms of the Protestant religion; and with a desire to promote the cause of sound learning." In sharp contrast, Barnes found the "foreign mind" to be "mostly bred up under monarchical forms of government; little acquainted with our republican institutions."[20]

Barnes's views reflected those of the American Home Missionary Society, perhaps the most influential among home missions. This mission played consciously on a "popular fear of Catholicism" to raise funds for its societies. Anti-Catholic propaganda flowing from the American press between the 1820s and the 1850s exploited the fear of Catholic plots to control the West. But mission preachers "cordially welcomed" European immigration even as they raged at the presence of Catholicism.[21]

This philosophic framework explains a note appearing in the *Minnesota Chronicle* after the 1849 election of the first territorial representatives, in which the French of St. Paul, who dominated the town, elected men neither French nor Catholic. "They have behaved well," wrote the editor. "They voted independently and without dictation from any quarter. They gained greatly in the opinion of their American fellow citizens. True, they were deceived somewhat by a defected candidate; but deception is what all are liable to;

still they acted as freemen, they were not led up in a body, or in detail, and forced to vote for certain candidates. . . . They had redeemed themselves from reproach—they have proved that in a land of freedom they spurn the slavery from which they escaped." The governance of the territory was to be largely an Anglo-Protestant affair.[22]

Heartened by the election and intent on saving the souls of Catholic children, Neill pushed for legislative support to build Protestant-based schools. On October 9, 1849, allies wrote in the *Report of the Committee on Schools* that the curriculum should include "three great departments of education," which were "physical, intellectual and moral . . . morality and religion should be regarded as the most essential elements of education," and "Christianity should be impressively urged, and clearly explained, as present in the Bible." Perhaps wary of stoking the flames of anti-Catholicism, especially with expediency dictating respect for the Catholic constituents, legislators cautioned the authors to exclude "bigotry, fanaticism and narrow-minded sectarian prejudice." Still, they passed a law to create a public school whose curriculum loosely embodied the Protestant ethic.[23]

But mission leaders pushed for more. On December 4 the Provisional Committee on Schools met to plan public schools for the town. Neill recommended that the committee erect on school land a structure for use as a schoolhouse six days of the week and as "a sanctuary on the seventh." In the minds of these Protestants, the call reflected the close ties of their religious belief with a republican government. "Any incongruence between the principle of separation of Church and State and the proposed religious uses of this school apparently did not occur to Protestants like Neill, at least not until their catholic neighbors reminded them."[24]

On June 19, 1850, the papal office in Rome announced the establishment of the Diocese of St. Paul, and by July 2, 1851, Bishop Joseph Cretin had arrived to preside over the new see. Using funds donated by the Society for the Propagation of the Faith, a Catholic mission agency based in Lyons, France, Cretin constructed schools and clerical residences to buttress "the lonely sentinel of Rome on the upper Mississippi."[25]

But in the combustible atmosphere of Protestant-Catholic relations, such activities only increased mutual suspicions. Diatribes
from both sides intensified. The intolerant attitudes of Protestant
educator Harriet Bishop toward "the motley throng" of "deluded,
ignorant" Catholics was matched by Ravoux's denunciations of
"bigoted ministers" who "vomited now and then their pestiferous
poison." To secure the American imprint on Minnesota, Neill and
other mission leaders just worked harder to expand Protestantism
in Catholic St. Paul.[26]

By the end of 1851, the Protestants had established five churches
and several benevolent societies in St. Paul. If this number is any indication, St. Paul seemed well on its way to the moral order that
both Neill and Governor Ramsey envisioned in 1849. Ramsey,
wanting also to establish a Whig presence in the territory, had as-
sisted in the development of the "high moral tone" noted in his first
speech to the legislature. Though he tried to show impartiality—
contributing money to the Presbyterian, Methodist, and Catholic
churches—his admiration for Neill drew him to becoming active in
Neill's church. By June 8, 1851, Ramsey had accepted election as
the president of the Minnesota Bible Society. Even here he sought
to strike a balance, openly admiring Neill's zeal and vision while re-
fraining from outright attacks on Catholicism. He dreamed of a secure cultural and religious hegemony—a Minnesota with St. Paul
its Winthropian "City upon a Hill," while embracing the Catholic
mixed bloods of faraway Pembina.[27] It was expedient to avoid alienating the significant Catholic vote.

As increasing numbers of foreign-born immigrants arrived to
stake their claim in St. Paul's boomtown prosperity only to find diminishing opportunity, the balance was sorely tested. Lost in this
ambition was any reconsideration of the civil rights of the tiny black
population, predominantly Protestant and, but for African descent,
in industry and sobriety much like the Yankee Protestant citizenry,
endeavoring to press the American imprint on Minnesota.[28]

In 1850 throughout the territory, foreign-born outnumbered
native-born residents by a substantial margin. But by 1860 the
native-born population predominated. In contrast, St. Paul's population shifted over the decade from being mostly native born to

largely foreign born, as Irish and German immigrants transformed the town into a European enclave. The Irish alone outnumbered native-born residents. Meanwhile, the French Canadian community rapidly diminished in relative size during the
1850s, more quickly than in Minnesota as a whole. Furthermore,
in the town where the Yankee business elite dominated the economy, most foreign-born workmen found employment only in the
lowest occupational levels, thus adding another class dimension to
the culture of early St. Paul.[29]

In view of the town's position as the capital of a newly organized territory near the head of navigation on the Mississippi, it is
perhaps not surprising that in the 1850 census 29 percent of St.
Paul's employed males stated that they worked in nonmanual occupations. Lawyers, merchants, doctors, clerks, hotelkeepers, and
editors converged on St. Paul in large numbers. The *Pioneer* noted
that by 1852 about forty lawyers lived in the small town, all of
whom "burrowed into a nest of considerable affluence" a short
while after their arrival. By purchasing or facilitating the purchase
of valuable property, these men launched and controlled many of
the business corporations chartered by the territory. Of about
thirty business and professional leaders in St. Paul, most were
from New York, Pennsylvania, and New England, and most were
listed as incorporators of such enterprises as the St. Paul and St.
Anthony Plank Road Company, the Minnesota Mutual Fire Insurance Company, and the Louisiana and Minnesota Railroad Company. Of thirty entrepreneurs only three were foreign born.[30]

By 1852 cultural and social cohesiveness became more apparent.
As one indication of this trend, Alexander Ramsey noted in his di-
ary the "remarkable improvement in the dress and appearance" of
the congregation at Edward Neill's Presbyterian church. Its members appeared as "well-dressed" and "fashionable" as one might
see in an eastern city. In fact, Neill's church was by this time attracting a number of prominent men, including *Pioneer* editor and
territorial printer James Goodhue, fur trader Charles Oakes, and
investor-lawyer Henry Masterson.[31]

If the elite could not control matters politically, they could do
so through socioeconomic connections and the bonds of Anglo-

American nativity and Protestantism. Indeed, privilege transferred to the native-born population, thus creating a wider social
and economic cleavage between that group and the large French
Canadian and Irish-born Catholic community.

Privilege was evident even within St. Paul's working class.
Foreign-born laborers were less likely to achieve higher occupational status in St. Paul than were native-born workers. New
England–born workers held a clear edge over other native-born
workers. In contrast, the largely French Catholic workers born in
Canada and the newly arrived Irish immigrants fleeing famine-
ridden Ireland together occupied the bottom of the economic
structure, all a likely consequence of anti-Catholic sentiments.
The wretched condition of the community of Catholic laborers
could be seen in the state of the children.[32]

A Catholic seminarian, Daniel J. Fisher, arriving in town in
1852, described his pupils as "dirty little ragged Canadian and
Irish boys." The Catholics of St. Paul were "very poor" and consisted mostly of "half-breeds, Canadians, and Irish." He continued:
"Every day, morning and afternoon, I practice patience with these
little fellows—try to teach them who God is, and then to instruct
them in the mysteries of A, B, C. I left New York to go among the
Indians, and I was hoping for strength to undergo the hardships of
a savage life, or to meet a martyr's death . . . but . . . to take the
charge of the impudent and insulting children of unthankful parents was the greatest mortification I ever underwent."[33]

Even Goodhue observed the "condition of the lower landing"
where ragged, unschooled children ran about the streets and
vices ranged from "lying and profane swearing" to the "higher
calendar of crimes." Catholicism for these people was more cultural than religious, for they were characterized as "very irreli-
gious and indifferent."[34]

Despite the growing number of Catholics, their political influence was limited at best. Ward boundaries intentionally dispersed
the foreign born among the wards of the town, effectively prevent-
ing their formation of a political power base. Thus their voices
were not heard, and St. Paul's first modern underclass took form.

But as the number of Catholics increased and the political tide gradually changed, their impact became more reactionary and less geared toward empowerment.

The newly formed *Minnesota Democrat* gave voice to the politics of grievance fostering frustration among the working class, the Catholic poor in particular.[35] The target of their anger was not the Whigs, a party with little influence, but the Furs (sometimes called "Moccasins"), whose source of wealth and power was shifting from the fur trade to urban commerce.

In 1851 *Minnesota Democrat* editor Daniel Olmstead took aim at the Yankee elite in the wake of the recent legislative election: "Why is the fur company so violently opposed to the Democratic Party? Because [it] is in favor of the Equal Rights of the People and therefore opposed to prostituting the legislative power of the territory to the service of the Fur Company or any other pecuniary interest. . . . Why is the Fur Company so zealous in advocating the election of the monopoly Whig ticket? Because the candidates on the ticket will, if elected, become as servile and obedient to the command of the company, as the most submissive voyageur that ever entered service."[36]

The *Democrat,* reprinting an excerpt from the New York Catholic newspaper *The Celt,* reminded St. Paul Catholics of their vulnerability to Protestant fanaticism. Going to the heart of Catholic concern about schooling, Olmstead attacked the educational policies of Reverend Edward Neill, by then the territory's superintendent of public schools. First he quoted Neill's sermon: "May not the real cause of opposition to our system of public instruction be that it trains the pupil to exercise the right of private judgment, and even think and do as Rome does not on many subjects?" Then he followed up: "If Mr. Neill and those who act with him want to convert Catholics, why not grown up Catholics, and teach them to exercise 'private judgment.' Why pounce on the weak, the credulous, the uninformed? Why prowl about the cradle, and count your prey by the daily list of births? Why cut into our posterity under the pretence of making them heirs to a higher and better hereafter?"[37]

In February 1854 the paper reported on a riot in Cincinnati that culminated in numerous injuries and the burning in effigy of Gaetano Bedini, the pope's nuncio. For its part the Whigs' *Weekly Minnesotian* insinuated that the anti-Bedini demonstration was justified.[38]

Such protestations by the *Democrat* spearheaded its replacement of the *Pioneer,* the party's official newspaper, as the newspaper of note for the poor and working classes of St. Paul. In 1854 Daniel Olmstead, who had also staunchly defended the Catholics against the anti-immigrant sentiments of the Know-Nothing movement, outpolled William Marshall for the mayorship. Democratic candidates also won seats in the legislature. Increasingly suspicious of Catholics and stymied by the ascendancy of this branch of Democrats in the territorial government, St. Paul's Yankee Protestants grew bitter. Their relations with St. Paul's Catholic immigrant population grew in rancor. When news reached St. Paul that Catholics had forcibly removed a claim jumper from church property in Dakota County, the *Weekly Minnesotian* and the *Democrat* exchanged insults.[39]

Despite the burgeoning political influence of the St. Paul Catholic community in the Democratic Party, the Catholics generally remained at low economic status. Catholic spokesmen echoed their resentment. Louis Robert, one of a small number of French Canadian Catholic entrepreneurs, viewed the temperance movement sweeping St. Paul as an unjust imposition on the town's poor. August Larpenteur, another wealthy businessman, criticized the treatment of Catholic citizens. In an 1851 letter, Daniel Fisher wrote, "The Yankees have all the influence, the wealth and power, although they are not near as numerous as the others. . . . [T]here is no money—as all the wealth is controlled by a Fur Company who owns nearly all the shops and employ a great number of workmen and never circulate any money—they loan it at 60 percent!! They pay their men in provisions." The Catholics of St. Paul were, in short, frozen in poverty, captive to their own anger.[40]

Fisher's comment indicated the extent to which political tension existed not only between the Democrats and the Whigs but also within the Democratic Party, which included the urban, Catholic laborers and the Furs who were their employers.

The Furs were the patricians of Minnesota's Democratic Party; their economic interests did not always coincide with those of their labor-class brethren. Paid low wages, the laborers felt it was at their expense that their Fur employers had created a new class of privilege. Business and power trumped party loyalty. Political equality created by the right to vote did not change the quality of life. The politics of St. Paul's Catholic labor class were the politics of resentment.

By the end of the season in 1854 when the frozen Mississippi was closed to navigation, a record 256 steamboats had docked at the newly incorporated "city" of St. Paul, exploding with unprecedented prosperity. The Catholic laborer could walk down Third Street after dark and see all the new shops where, three years before, there had been wilderness—"the lights gleam from the dwellings, in multitudinous twinklings, like fire-flies in a meadow." Yet not one shop was owned by anyone like him. By fall the currency in circulation—freebank notes issued by local banks when there was no unified banking system or single national currency—depreciated to bury him further in poverty. The debts he had accrued could land him in "the miserable little log jail, about fit for a pig-pen" where "a Frenchman named Boulange, died . . . a prisoner of debt." Temporary relief of a grisly sort came on December 29 when a crowd, largely St. Paul residents from the labor community, assembled on St. Anthony hill to witness the hanging of Yu-ha-zee, a Dakota convicted of murdering a German squatter who had settled on land belonging to the doomed man's tribe. According to a witness, "The large crowd looked on it more as a joke than as a solemn act of justice." A newspaper reported that "Total Depravity" was out early in the morning on execution day.[41]

William Taylor owned one of the shops on Third Street, personifying those blacks who fared relatively well, being "attentive to their business," quietly nurturing their own claims. A few of the small shops on Third Street indeed belonged to black people, illustrating that they had achieved "a reasonable degree of assimilation into the economy of the area, as well as responsible and energetic conduct. . . . Minnesota had opened the doors of opportunity to those who sought and were willing to work toward a better life." None of this—the prospect of material success in a community that treated blacks with relative respect—went unnoticed by the young black man James Hilyard, who worked on steamboats delivering the new settlers to Lowertown. In time he too made St. Paul his home.[42]

Not only free blacks like Hilyard but fugitive slaves helped by Taylor on their way up the Mississippi viewed St. Paul as the promised land. Taylor, his nephew Joseph Farr, David Edwards, and James Heighwarden, "the principal agents in the business," brought the Underground Railroad up from Galena, Illinois, to St. Paul before sending slaves to their final destination in Canada.[43]

Although at first there was no organized society coordinating their efforts, Farr said that they did "whatever we could." A fifth black man, Eugene Berry, worked on the *Dr. Franklin* that steamed from Galena with hidden fugitives on board. A sixth man in Galena, known simply as Johnson, delivered the slaves to the steamboat. Once the boat arrived in St. Paul, someone waiting at the wharf spirited the fugitive to Taylor's house on Third Street until it was safe to leave for Canada.[44]

Curiously, while it appears that white neighbors suspected such activities, they did nothing to discourage the efforts of Taylor and his colleagues. Even slaveholders acted with restraint when dealing with him. "I can't tell you," Farr later said, "how many slaves we got away, but we were so industrious that the slave owners gave up bringing their slaves with them when they came up here, long before the war."[45]

Even more curious was the absence of reprisal from the poor whites who viewed the fugitives as a threat to their livelihood. There was always the sense—as borne out in the black code debate of 1854—that fugitives might choose to stay and compete for work. Perhaps the tacit respect of the city's power elite provided protection as well. Just as likely, many St. Paul residents, along with other Northerners, felt disinclined to return slaves to their owners.

With the passage of the Fugitive Slave Act of 1850 came the federal mandate of Northerners to become, within their own communities, veritable agents of the slaveholder. Designed to appease Southern interests, the law sought to ensure a speedy return of runaways. Any claimant who could establish proof of ownership by affidavit before a special federal commissioner could take possession of a black person. The captive had no recourse to the common legal safeguards of a jury trial or judicial hearing. The law awarded ten dollars to the commissioner if he decided for the claimant and five dollars when he ordered the release of the captive. "Critics," wrote historian Leon Litwack, "called it an open bribe." But it was the last provision that most concerned Northerners: the act empowered federal officers to call upon all citizens to help enforce its provisions and specified fines, imprisonment, and civil damages for concealing or rescuing a fugitive. According to Litwack, "It posed an obvious threat to free Northern-born negroes: any of them might be 'mistakenly' identified as fugitives and carried to the South. In other words, men like Taylor were theoretically at risk."[46]

Free Northern-born blacks usually did not become ensnared in the net of the Fugitive Slave Act, but it did happen. Litwack expanded: "Whites might differ on extending political and social rights to Negroes, but many of them shared a common revulsion at the sight of slave-hunters rooting out respectable Negroes from their jobs and families . . . [which] seemed to defy any code of common decency." The slave master who, as Joseph Farr remembered, came to Taylor and respectfully sought help in recovering his slave might well have tailored his behavior to the sensibilities of the St. Paul middle-class community.[47]

In contrast, unskilled blacks labored under different circumstances. If they were able to get work, it was likely to be in direct contact with unskilled white laborers. For the black laborer, getting through the day was a challenge, unless he maintained an obsequious demeanor—difficult for new arrivals who felt they had left their servile status behind.

A black porter named Bush, working at the St. Paul Winslow House, joined Zena Brought, a white carpenter, at lunch in the kitchen of the hotel. Brought told him "it was no place for him" and that the other black laborers typically ate outside. Bush said he did not care to go outside and that he had a right to eat where he wished. At that, Brought threatened to forcibly remove Bush. According to the *St. Paul Times,* "Bush threw off his coat remarking that he was in a country where he could act in a measure for himself—that he was no slave, and that if Brott [*sic*] wished to strike him . . . he would defend himself."[48]

Brought was not finished with Bush. A few evenings later a young man came to the hotel to ask Bush to help him bring in his bags. Later that evening, as Bush and the young man were walking up St. Anthony Street, the young man produced a weapon and forced Bush to a place where other young white men waited to beat him. During the scuffle the men pummeled Bush's eye with a brick and twice threw a rope around his neck. Bush freed himself both times and finally was able to escape. He sought shelter in the Auction Store of Moses and Cleland, where "under the counter he hid, asking protection of the proprietors of the store, who . . . did everything they could to keep off the desperadoes."[49]

Nonetheless, as Bush cowered under the counter, he was "severely beaten by one of the party, with a wire whip, and traces of blood can be seen where he lay." The storekeepers drew their guns and, holding off the men, told Bush to make his escape, but Bush wanted to speak to them. When he came around the counter, the men struck him on the head with a club, seized him, and forced him into the street, where they ripped at his clothes and stole his money. In the scuffle Bush was able to get away. In the wake of this attack, citizens were "anxious that the matter should come to trial."[50]

An unnamed person filed a complaint against the men, and Justice of the Peace Orlando Simons took Bush's affidavit. At trial no one spoke in his behalf. The *St. Paul Times* editorialized, "For want of interest on the part of the public, for the want of witnesses, aye, even for the want of a friend on the part of the black man, the case was dismissed and the law robbed of justice." The *Times,* an antislavery newspaper, then reported: "Yesterday morning that defenseless African left St. Paul, and as he passed our office he remarked, 'I am going to a place where there is a God in

Africa as well as in Israel. I am going to Chicago, where I know I can get justice done me.' . . . If the people of St. Paul will permit the law to be thus set at defiance, they will realize to their sorrow the fact that their property will depreciate in value and their city become famous for its mid-night assassinations."[51]

The episode reflected the volatility of race relations between black and white unskilled laborers—that blacks not only were rivals to be degraded and murdered but also were viewed as inherently too foul, too bestial, for human companionship. The episode also illustrated how middle-class residents of St. Paul dealt with such tensions. Although they tended to abhor violence in their midst, they resorted to threats if necessary. The social and political welfare of blacks was not their concern.

As this incident illustrates, the duty of mainstream St. Paul—like the shopkeepers' duty to defend Bush—ended with removal of an altercation to the street. The good citizens of St. Paul wanted only one thing—peace. If peace was possible as a result of blacks being excluded from the community, then so be it. If peace was attainable when blacks were integrated in society, that likewise was acceptable. Whatever promised peace had their support. Taylor and Farr rarely dealt with poor whites, and their successful barbering business brought them into contact with some of the territory's elite. They had no problems with their white neighbors.

Poor whites inhabiting the lower landing closely watched new blacks disembarking from steamboats, passing the hovels of Lowertown on their way up to St. Paul, where they could get steady work as cooks and porters and jobs that customarily went to laborers like themselves. They imagined these blacks might prove themselves the newest addition to what the Yankees referred to as "a useful class." If so, the blacks would realize the American dream in a way that the enfranchised white Catholics of St. Paul could not. There was recourse. Unlike the blacks, even the more "uppity" ones like Taylor who owned businesses, white laborers—even the lowest of their class—could vote.[52]

The reaction of white laborers—and the Irish, in particular—was potent, for their voting capacity was great. Legislators reflected their sentiment by arguing that the Mississippi was becoming a conduit for those expelled or fleeing from the South. These fugitives, the legislators insisted, would compete for jobs customarily held by unskilled whites—or would become paupers and wards of the territory.[53]

The sentiment was translated into action when in 1854 the entire St. Paul delegation in the territorial house supported Bill No. 34, "a bill to provide for the good conduct of Negro and mulatto persons." Modeled on the 1807 Ohio law, it required all blacks intending to reside in the territory to permanently post a personal bond of three hundred to five hundred dollars as a guarantee of good behavior, virtually barring people of meager resources from settlement. The bill failed, however, by a ten-six vote.[54]

Following the bill's defeat, St. Paul representative John H. Day, angry with St. Anthony–area legislators who opposed his bill, gave notice that during the next legislative session "he would introduce a bill to compel all the negro population of the Territory of Minnesota to reside in St. Anthony and Minneapolis." Dr. Day's segregation bill never materialized. Yet his threat illustrated an embryonic rivalry growing between Hennepin and Ramsey Counties on the issue of civil rights for black Minnesotans.[55]

In a larger context, Minnesota legislators had debated whether by enacting Bill No. 34 the territory was to join the diminishing number of midwestern states that continued to have black codes. By 1854 only Illinois and Indiana had such codes. Michigan and Wisconsin never did, and Iowa did not legally adopt one. Even Ohio no longer had one.[56]

But the Minnesota legislators did not debate what other states had done. When ultimately confronted with the question of whether to embrace a law penalizing blacks merely for being in the territory, Minnesota legislators were repelled. Legislator Robert Watson, of such a mind, was credited for successfully defeating the bill. In his memoir he wrote:

> The thing I took most pride in accomplishing was the defeat of [Bill No. 34]. . . . Indiana and a number of other western states had passed such laws, and in so doing were disgraced in the eyes of antislavery people who were then getting numerous. I saw [Joe] Roulette, [Peter] Roy, and [Donald] Morrison [mixed-blood legis-

lators from Pembina], talked with them about it and got their promise to vote against the bill. So with their help the free soil element in the House killed the bill on its third reading, and thus saved Minnesota the disgrace of putting a "black law" on her statute books.[57]

Roy, Morrison, and Rolette, described as "bright, quick, cunning and unprincipled," were seen as men of color from a part of the territory where no one perceived blacks as a threat. To them the exclusion law probably made little sense. Minnesota was becoming a strange place where people of European ancestry, who had lived in the region all of their lives, were not considered white.[58]

Paradoxically, as legislators defeated the bill, they did not consider repealing the exclusionary suffrage law. Their reasoning may have been that the denial of voting rights and civic participation did nothing to prohibit blacks from otherwise contributing to the commonwealth of Minnesota, whereas the black law would have effectively denied blacks and mixed bloods of African descent the opportunity even to be useful. Within this logic blacks who enjoyed the respect of the Yankee elite lived from 1849 to 1854 under a series of laws that increasingly restricted their civil rights.

Two years later, in an example of how the Yankee elite could not control the city's electorate, the target of discrimination shifted from black adults to black children. At that time the city's school board began efforts to segregate black children from their white classmates, relegating the black children to the worst facilities available.[59]

In fact, antiblack sentiment was so rigid that when school superintendent Benjamin Drew discovered that a boy who was one-quarter black was attending a white school, he told the teacher that "she had done wrong to receive him as [the boy] would not be allowed to remain." The teacher responded, to no avail, that the mixed-race boy—one-quarter black—"is no darker than many [mixed-blood Indians] who were here."[60]

What a different city St. Paul had become. In 1850 three schools were established to provide "ample means for the education of *all* the children in town." One of these schools was in the basement of

the Methodist church that Jim Thompson had helped to construct
and finance. Back then race had been incidental to educating children. Now, it was consequential, no matter how tenuous the link to
an African heritage. The segregation policy of the St. Paul school
board and Superintendent Drew's action, especially, may well have
been the reason that Old Settlers Jim and Mary Thompson moved
with their adolescent son from their beloved St. Paul—where
racism intensified as the city grew more "civilized"—to live in the
less-settled area of Shakopee.[61]

During this same period, while territorial leaders nurtured
commercial intercourse with the Catholic mixed bloods of distant
Pembina, St. Paul's Catholic community endured the suspicion and
contempt of the Yankee Protestant elite, some of whom conducted
business with the Red River mixed bloods. The town's underclass
was composed predominantly of the Lowertown Irish, French
Canadians, and mixed bloods. Yet the fact that these people, and
not men like William Taylor or Jim Thompson, could vote created
a peculiar imbalance. In any event, until 1855, when the steamboat
Dr. Franklin, which had transported fugitive slaves to Taylor's
home, sank and thereby ended the Minnesota leg of the Underground Railroad, Taylor's concern for his brethren was primarily
freedom from slavery. Suffrage could come later.[62]

By then the territory was embroiled in a bitter debate over slavery, ignited by the congressional passage of the Kansas-Nebraska
Act. Nowhere was the debate more heated than upriver in the twin
towns of St. Anthony and Minneapolis.

5

Shake the Dust from Your Armor!

BY 1854 a growing number of Northerners thought it foolhardy to believe slavery would stay in its place or that slaveholders could be contained within the legal fiction of boundaries. This was the frontier, where laws were as effective as the government's power to enforce them. Neither federal troops nor state militias were available to secure the borders against fugitive slaves or slaveholders who would inevitably, albeit illegally, move into a free-soil region if they felt the land was suitable for plantations. Far too many policy makers confused the slaveholder's ambition to acquire more land, enslave blacks, and reduce small white farmers to inveterate poverty with the slaveholder's constitutional right to "life, liberty, and the pursuit of happiness."

While Southern politicians came from a region with far fewer white males qualified to vote, they demonstrated a genius for getting their way with the federal body politic. Time after time they forced blustering compromises upon their Northern and Western colleagues to keep the peculiar institution alive. *Give us what we want or we will secede!* was the perennial Southern threat when the politicians of this great nation tried striking a balance.

The so-called Gag Rule most clearly demonstrated the arrogance of Southern power over the federal government. The rule saw that no petition submitted to Congress relating to the abolition of slavery was heard. Critics who persisted in arguing that the rule was in direct contravention of the constitutional right to petition were subject to censure, as was the case in 1842 with John Quincy Adams, venerable former president serving as the representative from Massachusetts. (The censure attack failed.) The Gag Rule exposed the dangers of slavery to Northerners as never before. As Paul Finkelman put it, "Slavery not only oppressed African Americans, but it threatened the political liberty of all free people, since supporters of the institution refused to allow opponents of slavery to speak."[1]

For the small farmer moving to the frontier of the Old Northwest Territory, survival meant fending off hostile Indian tribes, coping with harsh weather, and assembling political clout to forestall congressional duplicity with the slaveholder south of the Ohio River. Still, the climate and fertile soil of the Ohio River valley made the region attractive to slaveholders. The southern sections of Indiana and Illinois were geographically similar to Virginia and Kentucky, and they lay directly west of the two Southern states. Cairo, Illinois, was farther south than Richmond, Virginia, or Lexington, Kentucky. Some of the same crops with which Southern farmers were familiar could easily be raised in the region. In addition, salt mines near Shawneetown, Illinois, and the lead-producing region, which ran northward from Galena, Illinois, into southwestern Wisconsin, seemed attractive to slaveholders. But agriculture lured most slaveholders to the region. The nonslaveholding settlers were left to stanch the encroachment of slavery.[2]

Meanwhile, nonslaveholders began moving steadily into the region to join other settlers arriving from Pennsylvania, New York, and New England, where antislavery sentiment was strong. Together they established firm opposition to slavery. "As extreme individualists," historian Eugene Berwanger wrote, "they had a strong sense of democracy," and they considered the "haughtiness and pride" of the slaveholder toward those "who possessed no negroes . . . inimical to (democratic) institutions. Moreover, they feared political domination by the slaveholding class." Berwanger, quoting a commentator of the time, wrote, "[To them] the lord of three or four hundred negroes does not easily forgive the man who ventures to vote contrary to the will of such an influential being." Slavocracy was antidemocratic.[3]

Many settlers from the South, seeking broader economic opportunities, migrated to the Old Northwest Territories precisely because slavery was not permitted there. Assuming that the land was reserved for free labor, they had no intention of legalizing slavery and again establishing "a kind of monopoly of the United States land for slaveholders." In one act of protest in 1807, former Kentuckians went so far as to promise that unless Congress assured the prohibition of slavery in the region, they would prepare to "immigrate, to get free from a government which does tolerate slavery." Others threatened armed resistance. Such was the extent of their hatred for slavery.[4]

For future Minnesotans the restrictive article 6 of the Northwest Ordinance that banned the extension of slavery and the Missouri Compromise of 1820 firmly established Minnesota as free territory. Settlers streamed into the area, secure in the knowledge that they would not have to compete futilely with the voracious plantation system. This, plus the allure of twenty-one million acres of land that the federal government opened to white settlement, transformed Minnesota into a promised land.[5]

In this northernmost region of "settled" America, the tensions between the North and South seemed far away. Then the passage of the Kansas-Nebraska Act of 1854—which effectively repealed the Missouri Compromise by allowing settlers within those territories to be free or slave—essentially breached the wall of surrounding states and territories where slavery had been prohibited.

Minnesotans recognized that they, not the delegates who were supposed to represent them in Congress, would have to protect their interests—indeed protect the lofty principles of freedom. These Minnesotans would have to throw down the gauntlet. On March 18, 1854, the *Weekly Minnesotian* issued the call to arms: "We say to citizens, as did the immortal sage of Ashland upon a similar occasion, 'Awake! Arouse! Shake the dust from your armor as the lion shakes the dew drops from his mane, and march forward to victory.'"

In 1849 John Wesley North from upstate New York, a hotbed of antislavery, came to Minnesota with the passion of his mentor, Gerrit Smith, who believed that the two prominent political parties were "servants of slave power" and, as such, had virtually sold the soul of America to the devil. It followed, Smith held, that antislavery candidates nominated by either party must be "half-abolitionists." Further, he said, "An abolitionist who knew he must vote only for committed enemies of slavery must nominate them himself."[6]

Settling with his wife in the "delightful spot" of St. Anthony, North found a community of like-minded activists. On March 29, 1854, he joined a group of Hennepin County's leading citizens at Central Hall in St. Anthony to draft resolutions against the Kansas-Nebraska Act. This was the spirit that had helped defeat the "black code" bill during the previous legislative session and drawn the fury of St. Paul legislator John Day, who threatened to sponsor a residency bill restricting blacks to Hennepin County.

The draft resolutions condemned the act for opening all new Northern territories to slavery. Previous congressional enactments had divided the nation into free and slave regions, basically allowing Southerners to do whatever they wished within their own domain. But allowing slavery to extend into Northern territories was something else altogether.

To the argument that the new law ensured the true freedom of residents to decide on the so-called local matter of slavery, the Central Hall group expressed an understanding of the corrupting influence on governance of petty tyrants whose power came from the subjugation of human beings. As if foretelling the crisis to come in Bleeding Kansas, the group felt the ballot box would be but a mere formality when slave owners wanted a certain vote and minions were too impoverished to deny it to them. Minnesota opinion makers argued that slavery would make slaves of all but a few privileged souls. The act, they said, would permit slavery to "find entrance into that portion of our territory which is west of the Mississippi river. . . . [T]he 'peculiar institution' of the South [would] find its way into our very midst—a calamity to our Territory so great, that there could hardly be a greater."[7]

To reinforce the campaign against the act, on July 4, 1854, at the Congregational church in St. Anthony, a large crowd convened to mobilize all men "who value the liberty of their race . . . [and] who have had enough of the humbuggery compromises, and are prepared sternly to demand that Federal Government exercise its Constitutional powers always for *Liberty and Union,* and never for Slavery and a section." Hundreds attended.[8]

Although the gathering at the church was the precursor of the territory's first antislavery society, its resolutions did not make abolitionism the platform's centerpiece. Joining North as a drafter of the resolutions was Reverend Charles Gordon Ames of Massachusetts, a Free-Will Baptist minister who had come to St. Anthony in 1851 to do missionary work. Ames became the movement's voice as editor of the *Minnesota Republican,* a newspaper purchased for him by antislavery and temperance people. For the next year Ames railed against Whig duplicity with slaveholding interests and charged that both major parties were selling out free labor. He articulated a platform that would embody the founding principles of the new Republican Party.[9]

These two men, along with North's brother-in-law and fellow New Yorker George Loomis, created the driving force that stamped the St. Anthony Falls community as a veritable hotbed of abolitionism for the territory, a movement whose development coincided with the growth of the town itself.

When John North settled in St. Anthony in 1849, he was struck by the many fine opportunities at hand. Ann North, his wife, wrote to her brothers, "This is a very pleasant little village, and has grown amazingly since Mr. North was here before [1848]." To her parents she wrote, "Mr. North's business prospects, I think, are good. There is only one other Lawyer in town, and he is young, and rather light. The people all seem very kindly disposed toward us and we have already, I think, some warm friends."[10]

Located upstream from St. Paul on the east bank of the Mississippi River at the magnificent falls from which the town took its name, St. Anthony showed great promise of becoming the metropolis of the upper Northwest. John North could invest in properties that surely would increase in value, ones not being swallowed up by the large companies and established businesses in St. Paul. And as the town's only experienced lawyer, he could count on the mill company to bring him its business. Historian Lucile M. Kane wrote, "It had in the falls waterpower with so vast a potential that eminence in manufacturing seemed assured."[11]

Within a few years sawmills, flour mills, and a steady stream of new businesses all sparked a burgeoning economy. But it was a different community from St. Paul, one based on enlightenment and reform. Within two years a library association, a newspaper, and the University of Minnesota were established in the town. Full of optimism, Ann North wrote to her parents in New York: "We think St. Anthony is bound to be *the* town of the Territory. St. Paul is doomed."[12]

But before the town could do this—exploit the natural assets as well as the natural beauty of the area—the community faced major challenges. St. Paul had the advantage by virtue of its size and ability to bring in both settlers and money. Moreover, as historian Lucile Kane wrote, "The clamor of steamboats unloading freight and passengers at its two busy levees was a taunt to St. Anthony, for St. Paul could boast . . . that it was the head of navigation on the Mississippi. Although St. Anthony claimed that the falls marked the head of navigation, St. Paul pointed with unrestrained glee at the stubborn miles of boulders and low water that caused steamboats bearing cargo for St. Anthony to turn into the St. Paul landing."[13]

Realizing that resolving the latter problem would remedy the former, St. Anthony leaders called for eliminating the obstacles that robbed the town of its rightful place as the head of navigation by constructing roads and railroads and developing its waterpower, all for the purpose of attracting capital. St. Anthony was determined to win; the Mississippi would become the great central highway of the nation. St. Anthony as the head of navigation would be "the great manufacturing and commercial emporium for the country between Lake Michigan and the Rocky Mountains."[14]

But for all of its optimism, St. Anthony's immediate future was bound up in the fortunes of one group of businessmen associated with Franklin Steele, who controlled the waterpower on the east bank of the river and owned a great deal of property in the town. When Steele began having difficulties with his business partners in the East, he had trouble developing the holdings. Eventually, his position as an economic giant began to erode. As early as 1851, the Democratic *St. Anthony Express* characterized Steele's problems as "a mighty incubus" resting in St. Anthony.[15]

Unlike St. Paul, where giants controlled the economic and political agenda, St. Anthony was a place where power was more dispersed. Steele had influence but not the kind of control that the power elite held in St. Paul. North, for example, succeeded in being elected decisively to the legislature in 1850, despite the combined opposition of the fur company, the mill company, and the large numbers of French Canadian laborers who tended to side with their employers. North further irritated Steele when he opposed Henry Sibley, Steele's brother-in-law, for the post of territorial delegate to Congress. In St. Anthony one did not have to be a member of the power elite to further a personal agenda.[16]

In 1848, when Steele had bought the land and began to put his imprint on the town, it had an estimated population of three hundred. By 1850 the population had more than doubled, and five years later St. Anthony had approximately three thousand people. During the mid-1850s W. D. Babbitt, William S. King, F. R. E. Cornell, and Charles E. Vanderburgh, from the same area of upstate New York as North and Loomis, settled near the falls. These men later would figure prominently in one of the area's most momentous events—the 1860 slave trial of Eliza Winston.[17]

With the increase of new arrivals—largely Protestant northeasterners of English descent, professionally trained and avid for social reform—a new constituency took shape. North "confided in letters to his family that the day had passed when St. Anthony's founder [Steele] could assume he owned the town and pursue his interests without regard for others. With the motley group of French-Canadian and half-breed preemptors who had originally staked out the east side he might safely act the role of leader . . . but now St. Anthony had an articulate 'American population' that would not accept Steele's patronage."[18]

During the months following the passage of the Kansas-Nebraska Act, groups throughout the North met to protest the drift of federal policy toward shamelessly catering to slave interests. In Minnesota such activities were especially vocal. On March 23, 1855, a group of reformers met once more at Central Hall to draft four resolutions that would lay the philosophical foundation of the new Republican Party. One resolution was a call for "a law prohibiting the sale of intoxicating drinks," which reflected the "moral reform" influence on "the views and feelings" of this embryonic political organization. The last resolution, however, justified the new party as a response to "the present corrupt state of our National and Territorial politics." In a Faustian pact with slave interests, the reformers maintained, Congress and the Whig Party had sold their souls and, with them, all semblance of "public virtue."[19]

On March 29 and 30, 1855, two hundred men attended a mass meeting at the Methodist church in St. Anthony. William R. Marshall presided; John North convened the assembly; and W. D. Babbitt, C. G. Ames, and Congregational minister Charles C. Secombe facilitated various sessions. Three central issues drew them together—the abolition of slavery, temperance, and the commitment to stand up to Southern hegemony. The resolutions the delegates adopted, however, were a disparate mélange and included prohibiting the importation and sale of liquor, abolishing needless offices, paying no salaries for legislators other than for actual services done, limiting the taxation of revenues to the amount required for the necessary expenses of government, and extinguishing the public debt. The delegates resolved to extend a "cordial welcome to emigrants and exiles" in the New World, "but no welcome to banished paupers and criminals, or to those who plot the overthrow of the Republic," thereby elevating to high principle the intent to abolish xenophobic practices. Furthermore, they vowed to reduce land and ocean postage to the lowest possible rate.[20]

The briefest, albeit controversial position, appeared as Item 9 of Resolution 10: "No civil disabilities on account of color or religious opinion."[21]

For the first time since universal male suffrage was debated during the 1849 legislative session, a major gathering of Minnesotans considered and linked the abolition of slavery and the extension of rights to free black Minnesotans. Ames published the new Republican principles, which he titled "Circular Address of the Territorial Republican Convention," in the April 5 issue of his newspaper. In response the *St. Anthony Express* reported, "For a party which claims all the virtue, it was one of the most curious gatherings of pie-bald and mongrel politicians we have ever seen in the Territory." Remarkably, the editor hoped that the new party would be successful in saving Minnesota from "the clutches of slavery," but the newspaper made no mention of the proposal to extend civil rights to black residents.[22]

The omission was probably intentional since the newspaper was the Democratic organ of the city. The same sentiment was echoed downriver in the *St. Paul Times,* but it did not take root as firmly as it did in St. Anthony and Minneapolis.[23]

Nonetheless, the delegates were inspired by the success of the meeting, and they proceeded to organize a territory-wide convention to be held in St. Paul on July 25. The convention selected candidates to run in the fall elections, including William Marshall to oppose Democrat Henry Rice, then Minnesota's delegate to Congress. The convention "reaffirmed" in its platform the purpose of the Republicans "to array the moral and political powers of Minnesota, whether as territory or state, on the side of freedom, and to aid in wielding the whole constitutional force of the federal government, whenever we can and wherever we can, against the existence of slavery." The platform writers were adamant on the abolition of slavery and objected strongly to the nullification of the Missouri Compromise. They vowed that as officers of the territorial government they would keep slavery out of Minnesota.[24]

Prominent among the resolutions was the prohibition of liquor traffic throughout the territory, underscoring the strong moral as well as the political belief that "human slavery to liquor must be destroyed along with all other forms of servitude." Yet again, the platform included a proposal to extend civil rights to black Minnesotans.[25]

Even without such laws an inclusive social contract already existed for Hennepin County's black settlers. In 1856 in Medina township, the land protection association dragged a white claim jumper out of the cabin of an absent free Negro named Alfred. The reverence for the permanence of ownership and legitimacy of enterprise overrode considerations of race. Minnesota, as the reformers of St. Anthony fully intended, was to be the place where industrious, solid Christian black settlers were welcome.[26]

In 1857 Emily O. Grey, a black woman from Pennsylvania, arrived in St. Anthony accompanied by her first-born son, William, her husband's cousin Hamilton W. Grey, and his bride, Mary

Smallwood Grey. Her husband, Ralph Grey, had established his
barbering business in Minneapolis more than a year and a half earlier. They had not seen each other since he had first settled in the
town, and their reunion was joyful. Until they could move into
their own home, they occupied two rooms in the comfortable Jar-
rett House, which overlooked the falls. Emily found a community
where "civility and kindness seemed to be in the air. . . . You
breathed it in with every inhalation of the atmosphere."[27]

Soon they moved into their new home. Emily Grey described it
as "a small building . . . [which was] humble and unpretentious in
appearance." It had been converted from a barn into a comfortable
little residence with "floors put in, partitions and chimney built,
plastered, fences and a chicken coop erected. I papered it with my
own hands alone one day, as a surprise to my husband when he
came home that night." Together they began looking for "provisions and furnishings." She wrote in 1893:

> There were three furniture stores: one in upper town and two in
> lower town. . . . In those days there were not the establishments
> gotten up on the "installment plan" we have today. . . . An ordinary
> high-back rocking chair cost from eight to ten dollars; common
> basswood chairs painted black and varnished cost one dollar
> apiece. We were unable to purchase a bureau, so we patronized a
> home-made one, on account of our funds being short. It was made
> out of a large (store) box with shelves placed inside to answer for
> drawers and covered with calico.[28]

During the long hours while her husband worked, Emily Grey
received visits from their neighbors: "First one neighbor called and
then another, until we became acquainted and our visiting relations
were easy and smooth. Fashionable and formal visits were not much
in vogue, but the good, old-time neighborly calls . . . were more
generally indulged in. A grateful remembrance of the kind deeds
done for us by our new-made friends placed us in a lifelong indebt-
edness." They helped her "in domestic economy," showing her
"new methods of breadmaking and vegetable cooking . . . the art of
baking that toothsome New England dish of 'pork and beans' in the
same way they were cooked in the lumber camps," and preparing a

dish of "sauerkraut, part of the pickled backbone of a pig, and Irish potatoes. There was always some woman friend who would gladly be to me a guiding star to lead me out of the many little difficulties met within all households."[29]

One of Emily Grey's closest friends was Elizabeth Stone, wife of Alvin Stone, a house and sign painter. Emily described her as "an honorable woman, a true wife, a considerate and loving parent, a staunch friend, and a delightful companion." She wrote that another friend—Hannah Munson, wife of Luther C. Munson—was "of cheerful spirit, obliging in disposition, clear in judgment, readily discerning the true relation of things in the home sphere, invaluable to the neighborhood in assuaging grief, and well-fitted to bid defiance to discouragement." As the only black woman living in St. Anthony, she found "considerable warmth and support from her white neighbors."[30]

In the St. Anthony she knew, there were "several well-organized church societies" for Episcopalians, Congregationalists, Methodists, and Catholics. Although raised a Presbyterian, she eventually joined the Universalist Society located "in a plain looking, one story stone building . . . [situated just] north of the Winslow House" (which she characterized as "a pretentious structure"). She was drawn to the society for its "clear, certain, and significant antislavery teachings that flowed out from its portals."[31]

One afternoon she "received a visit from a gentleman and lady who introduced themselves as the Reverend Charles C. Secombe and wife," who came to invite the Greys to attend services at the Congregational church of which he was pastor. "It was a pleasant and profitable visit," Grey wrote. "The acquaintance thus begun was the means of opening up to me religious truths and their uses but partially revealed and making plain others unknown, so they could be brought into the concerns of everyday life."[32]

Seccombe, from New Hampshire, an ardent supporter of the antislavery movement, was that brand of controversial clergyman who blended the gospel with the politics of the times. Grey wrote, "His mouth was not muzzled in the pulpit when occasion required he should speak against the national crime of American slavery." His message spoke to her, a proud woman who upon giving birth to the city's first black child named him Toussaint l'Ouverture Grey, after the black Haitian who fought to free his people from colonial rule.[33]

Emily Grey's memoir reflects St. Anthony as a community in 1857 that both welcomed her and respected the natural rights of African Americans. "There has not been a moment in my life when I regretted that my feet had touched the soil of Minnesota. . . . Oh! The good neighborly fellowship, you can never forget!" she wrote. The St. Anthony she knew was composed of white northeasterners, who had come west having experienced life with a small, educated, and relatively assimilated black population, a population that, but for the color of their skin, was as worthy of citizenship as any white community.[34]

In 1857 as Minnesotans prepared for statehood and the newly formed Republican Party, which outnumbered the Democrats, readied itself to carry forth the standard of freedom and equality, the expectations of the reformers of St. Anthony and Minneapolis were high. They would learn that it was one thing to advance an agenda in one's community, quite another to do so throughout the territory.

6

Divided Brethren

THE DELEGATES FROM THE Democratic and Republican parties who gathered in St. Paul for the constitutional convention in preparation for statehood came expecting the worst. Charges of fraud over the election of delegates lingered over them, each party still smarting from the raucous, illegal, and, at times, violent efforts of men to give their parties an advantage. In St. Paul more than seven hundred illegal votes were cast, five hundred from one ward alone. In this ward a brutal mob seized the polls, remaining there and voting for their cohorts at will. Even the *St. Paul Pioneer and Democrat,* in its issue of July 1, 1857, reported that "irresponsible and unscrupulous men in the Democratic party" had perpetrated fraud.[1]

The Republicans, though less brutish, employed their own brand of chicanery—a tactic called "colonizing," which entailed conveying "wagon loads of voters" from one county to another. In one instance illegal voters were carried "from Rice county to Waseca on the day of the election, and at least two hundred illegal votes polled in the county." In the German enclaves of Mankato and New Ulm, Democrats accused Republicans of being Know-Nothings, referring to the anti-immigrant, antiliquor group that was hostile to that community. Republicans accused Democrats of being the party of slavery.[2]

Much was at stake. The handiwork of this convention—a constitution—would establish the very character of the new state. Despite efforts by some to place statehood above partisanship, the convention was expected to be a highly charged political brawl. As early as April, the *Daily Minnesotian,* a St. Paul Republican newspaper, stated, "It is idle to talk about having no politics in the convention. It will be all politics." The editor committed the force of his newspaper to achieve "this desirable end," meaning the vanquishing of the slave power.[3]

In the end the delegates came to St. Paul prepared to give the other camp no quarter. The Democrats proclaimed that they could not accept a convention dominated by the Republicans. The Republicans, for their part, were newcomers on the political scene. They knew that the Democrats controlled both the territorial government and the convention city and feared that the Democrats would cheat them of their victory, despite their fifty-nine delegates to the Democrats' fifty-five. The Democrats surely would have to employ unsavory tactics to outflank the larger Republican delegation.[4]

To play it safe, Republicans began to arrive in St. Paul several days before the scheduled opening of the convention. On Saturday, July 11, however, they were still uncertain of when the convention was to begin and unable to get a response from the Democrats. On Sunday, Republican leaders ran into Willis Gorman, former Democratic territorial governor, who said his colleagues were in caucus. In an effort to secure a commitment to open the convention at noon, Monday, they handed Gorman a slip of paper with a statement to that effect, signed by the leader of their delegation. Gorman accepted the paper and took it to his colleagues.[5]

Nothing else happened until 11:00 that night, when Gorman returned a statement to the Republicans that they would "meet at the usual hour for the assembling of parliamentary bodies in the United States." This note heightened the Republicans' anxiety about Democratic shenanigans, for as men with limited parliamentary experience, most were uncertain about the "the usual hour." The Republicans decided to spend the night in the council chamber at the capitol so as to be there when the Democrats arrived on Monday morning.[6]

Monday, July 13, should have been a day of profound historic significance. It was the anniversary of the passage of the Northwest Ordinance, executed seventy years earlier. As William Anderson has noted, under the provisions of the ordinance, Ohio, Indiana, Illinois, Michigan, and Wisconsin were carved from the wilderness to become sovereign states of the Union. The region remaining in the Old Northwest that had not yet acquired statehood was what the Old Settlers called Minnesota East, the land between the Mississippi and St. Croix rivers. Anderson wrote: "The first meeting of the constitutional convention might well have been given over to the solemn observance of the day and to the serious contemplation of its meaning. Partisan politicians, who had in the past few weeks already done much that was a reproach to the name of Minnesota, had other plans for the day."[7]

As noon on Monday neared, the Republicans were seated; they waited for the official opening of the convention, but not one Democrat had arrived. That morning the Republicans had elected John North to call the convention to order, but now he seemed uncertain—indeed, they all did—as to what to do without the Democrats present. They later learned that during their caucus the previous evening, the Democrats had reaffirmed their resolution to meet at "the usual time"—specified as midnight. The Republicans knew nothing of this.[8]

As the clock turned to noon, an employee of the Democratic-controlled territorial administration walked in with a ladder and without explanation climbed up to the large clock, removed the glass, and, as Republican delegate Thomas Foster recalled, "[set it] a-going according to their own time." The man left without a word. Sometime around 11:45 AM, before the time set for opening the convention, the Democrats filed into the chamber, approximately forty-five in all. Some, the Republicans later claimed, were not lawful delegates.[9]

As they entered, Democrat Charles Chase, secretary of the territory and a delegate with controversial credentials from St. Anthony, took the speaker's platform, stunning the Republicans. North scrambled onto the platform where Chase stood. Both men proceeded to call the convention to order. North quickly declared Thomas Galbraith the president pro tem of the convention, after the Republican delegates nominated and voted him into office. As the Republicans voted, Gorman, from the floor, moved that the convention adjourn until midnight the next day. Ignoring the Republicans' vote, Chase called Gorman's motion, which the Democrats passed unanimously. The convention, within just a few minutes after noon, had become a two-headed monster. Almost at the same time as Galbraith stepped up to the president's chair, the Democrats trooped en masse out of the chamber. This was the opening day of Minnesota's future.[10]

Throughout the summer Republican and Democratic delegates caucused separately in St. Paul to hammer out their respective drafts for the state constitution. The Democrats' draft, as the territorial constitution had done before, denied blacks all rights of citizenship. This single issue—whether the constitution should keep the racial exclusionary language of the suffrage provision—became the most volatile matter.[11]

Minnesota had to gain immediate statehood so that its senators could get to Washington—the balance of power between free-soil states and slave states was at stake. One problem, of course, was that there were now two constitutional conventions. Democrats and Republicans would not meet with each other, and the constitution that each caucus drafted reflected partisan interests rather than a joining of philosophic minds.[12]

While the delegates debated in their respective conventions, progress (or lack-of-progress) reports reached political leaders in the East. There leaders of both parties criticized their Minnesota brethren, pressuring them to reconcile, for they saw in Minnesota the circumstances that had led to bloodshed in Kansas. Some Minnesota delegates agreed. Willis Gorman feared the split could injure credit and "affect the capitalists of the territory disadvantageously."[13]

By early August delegates began talking about structuring a compromise committee to bring the two sides together and create one constitution for submission to the voters. Partisanship blocked progress, however, with black suffrage becoming the stumbling block to compromise. Passions reached such a pitch that delegates began doubting whether an accord could be reached. So tense were the exchanges that on August 25 Democratic delegate Gorman, who had just argued for compromise, and Republican delegate Thomas Wilson, who later served as chief justice of the Minnesota Supreme Court as well as in the legislature and U.S. Senate, confronted each other in the committee room, and Gorman broke his walking stick over Wilson's head.[14]

The specter of Bleeding Kansas was suddenly never more real.

Cooler heads viewed the outburst, however painful, as "a thunderstorm in clearing the air." As Anderson wrote, "It was unquestionably with a sense of shame and renewed determination that the committee . . . returned to its arduous labors."[15]

The first Republican delegate to stand and speak on the subject of black suffrage was New Hampshire–born B. E. Messer, formerly of St. Anthony, who argued:

> [There was] no reason . . . that class [negroes] should be deprived of this highest privilege under our government. . . . [C]olored men stood shoulder to shoulder with white men upon the battle-fields of the revolution. His blood, equally with that of the white man, enriches the soil of our common country. But while the white man was rewarded with pensions while living, and monuments of marble when dead, the colored man has been chained, fettered, and deprived of the dearest rights which can be enjoyed under this government—the right to suffrage. . . . If we attempt to barter away what we know to be right, for what we know to be wrong, I believe we shall be cheated.[16]

John North, who had recently left St. Anthony to resettle in Rice County, argued similarly: "I know of no principle on which our own rights are based that does not guarantee to every other class of human beings the same rights which we claim for ourselves. If there are exceptions to this rule . . . those exceptions cannot and do not exist in the nature of things as established by the Creator. The contour of the countenance, the complexion of the face which the Creator has stamped on human beings, does not give one class the right to inflict wrong and injury upon another."[17]

But the voices of Messer and North were in the minority. The majority of the Republican delegation opted to leave the extension of political rights to blacks for a later time. The voters, who would have to ratify the new constitution in its entirety, might reject black suffrage and, with it, the constitution. Dakota County delegate Thomas Foster reflected the tone: "I am willing to consent to admit the word 'white' in the Constitution, for I do not believe that the people are quite up to the highest mark of principle: the force of prejudice is yet so great among them. . . . Minnesota should not be delayed from coming into the Union at the earliest possible moment."[18]

Others argued that black suffrage would also result in splintering the Republican Party; freeing slaves was one thing, enfranchising free blacks was quite another. Many more held that blacks were unequal to whites, that blacks did not deserve political rights because the nation's social contract had not been drafted to include black people. In fact most delegates supporting equal suffrage did so because of the lofty ideals of the Declaration of Independence and the Constitution—not because they felt blacks were innately equal or had earned the right to vote.[19]

Indeed, the broader consensus reflected the sentiment of national Republicans in that, despite their stand on political rights, many Minnesota Republicans did not favor social equality with blacks. Rice County delegate and lawyer Oscar Perkins puts a face on the instinctive ambivalence with which Republican delegates viewed black Minnesotans. He supported black suffrage, and according to Gary Libman, his "impassioned plea for equal suffrage reveals that the power of intellect could overcome his prejudices against political rights but not social equality."[20]

Perkins stated, "I do not pretend that I should like to ask a negro into my family, and adopt him as a brother, but I know, after all, that the prejudice which I do entertain is a most miserable and contemptible thing, and ought to have no existence in my bosom. And when I come to vote upon any great question of humanity, in which that class are interested, I do not mean to be governed by those feelings." In any event, the majority decided that the question of black suffrage would have to wait for a later vote.[21]

In the Democratic version, "white persons of foreign birth . . . upon the subject of naturalization," persons of mixed white and Indian blood "who had adopted the customs and habits of civilization," and "persons of Indian blood . . . who had adopted the language, customs, and habits of civilization after an examination before any district court of the state" would get the right to vote. The sole objection within the Democratic caucus came from Sibley, who initially reasoned that the word "white" was unnecessary because the Supreme Court in the *Dred Scott* decision ruled that citizenship pertained only to white people. Fearing that the Republicans would succeed eventually in enfranchising black men, his caucus failed to find comfort in Sibley's interpretation of the decision. Federal law was one thing; this was an issue of states' rights.[22]

The word "white" remained in the text. In the end the Republicans agreed to adopt the Democratic language. All adult males residing in Minnesota, except "uncivilized" Indians and Chinese and black men like Ralph Grey, were now voting citizens of the state.[23]

The criticism from the Hennepin County Republicans of their political brethren was intense because they had not lived up to Republican principles of equality. The Hennepin County's *Minnesota Republican* accused delegates of having caved in to the Democrats' "base prejudice, born of slavery, which sneers at the black man's manhood." Declaring themselves "mortified and alarmed" at the convention's action, they called upon the rank and file to ensure that the party stuck to the "landmark" principle of justice enunciated at the first state Republican convention—that there be "no civil disabilities on account of color, birthplace, or religious belief."[24]

It did not matter to Hennepin County Republicans that the law of natural rights—"all men are created equal"—was a principle that the highest court in the land now deemed unconstitutional.

Earlier that year as Republican delegates prepared for the state convention, the U.S. Supreme Court had decided *Dred Scott,* in which a slave sued for his freedom based on his once having lived on the free soil of Fort Snelling. The Court held that he had no such claim. Blacks were not national citizens, and they could never have territorial or state citizenship. Furthermore, Congress had exceeded its jurisdiction by enacting the part of the Missouri Compromise of 1820 that banned slavery in the territories. If any doubt existed concerning the legal status of black people, the *Dred Scott* opinion dispelled it.

"This confusion is now at an end," said Abraham Lincoln, then a congressman from Illinois, "and the Supreme Court has defined the relations, and fixed the status of the subordinate race forever—

for that decision is in accord with the natural relations of the races, and therefore can never perish." It was indeed. "Now, my opinion," Lincoln noted during his campaign for the presidency, "is that the different states have the power to make a negro a citizen under the Constitution of the United States if they choose. The *Dred Scott* decision decides that they have no such power."[25]

The common perception of Minnesotans was that the decision was a two-pronged assault against black citizenship and the abolition of slavery, and in theory and law the decision should have ended the debate. "One of the first results of this decision will be to disfranchise all the negro voters in the free States. The decision pronounces this Government to be one of White men, and not Africans, nor Chinese. And no State law can make them citizens," reported the *Minnesota Republic*. But the Minnesota Republicans, according to that newspaper "the party of conservatism . . . devoted to the maintenance of Law and Order . . . [who] entertain a peculiar veneration for judicial tribunals, and especially the Supreme Court of the United States," nevertheless determined to keep the question of black citizenship open by placing the issue before the voters at a later date, as if the decision were still open for debate, as if such a referendum were indeed "constitutional." Despite *Dred Scott* many of Minnesota's Republicans felt that men like Ralph Grey could become citizens at a later time if the majority of Minnesotans so decided it.[26]

The more controversial issue was whether state law could ban visiting masters from bringing their slaves with them to the free soil of Minnesota. With the adoption of a new constitution in August 1857, the delegates guaranteed freedom to all inhabitants, expressly prohibiting slavery and involuntary servitude. The language was clear: article 1, section 2, stated, "There shall be neither slavery nor involuntary servitude in the State, otherwise than in the punishment of crime." In other words, slavery could not exist in Minnesota. This was a provision perfectly acceptable to the Democratic delegation. By agreeing to the language, they intended it to be narrow in scope: Minnesotans, in Minnesota, could not own slaves.[27]

But this did not end the controversy. Nothing in the new constitution prohibited masters from bringing their slaves to Minnesota, nor did it dissolve their slave ownership rights while they were visiting the state. In fact, *Dred Scott* was silent on this issue. Had the issue been presented, many observers expected the Taney Court to rule that Southerners had a constitutional right to take slaves into any state in the nation as long as the masters did not become residents of free states. But abolitionists, especially those from Hennepin County who also were leaders of the Republican delegation, felt that the mere presence of slavery in their midst degraded humanity. The stage was set for conflict.[28]

Slaveholders now visited Minnesota believing that *Dred Scott* protected their ownership of slaves—to the great consternation of antislavery Northerners. In St. Anthony, Ames editorialized bitterly, "Another result [of *Dred Scott*] will be, to bring among us, a great many of our Southern friends, *with their slaves,* to sojourn temporarily; to spend their money amongst us. . . . We should not wonder, if, within ten years, the shores of the Hudson and Connecticut rivers, and of Lake Winnepiseogee were lined with the residences of Southern planters, who will spend their summers in the North, and their winters in the sunny South."[29]

In St. Anthony, where merchants endeavored to structure a new form of commerce—tourism for vacationing Southerners—the very presence of human chattel forced the community to confront a fundamentally unprecedented dilemma. It was one thing to aid and abet fugitive slaves who had escaped from servitude in the distant South, as William Taylor and his friends and neighbors had done, and quite another to assist slaves while their masters were visiting in Minnesota. In St. Anthony helping slaves threatened the town economy.

St. Anthony merchants advertised the falls throughout the South as a place that provided a respite from the heat and humidity. During Minnesota's cool summers the supposed medicinal properties of the Chalybeate Springs at the falls and resort-like comfort of Winslow House, which overlooked the falls, attracted Southerners looking for relaxation. As plantation owners rode up the hill to the hotel, reported Minneapolis's *Lake Area:* "St. Anthony residents got their first glimpse at [their Southern guests], dressed in fine clothes quite different from the frontier homespun they were used to seeing. Another difference was the slaves brought along as part of their retinue."[30]

Within Minnesota's stronghold of abolitionism, the sight was explosive. "Let the free people of this country," Ames proclaimed, "keep their ears open and take heed of the result, whatever it may be. 'Eternal vigilance is the price of Liberty!'" Over the next three years abolitionists harassed the Southern tourists.[31]

Their methods infuriated many in their community as well as in St. Paul, for numerous residents had come to rely on the tourist trade of their Southern visitors. According to the *Minneapolis Sunday Tribune*, "In little groups, [abolitionists] would meet arriving steamboats at the St. Paul levee, booing and hissing Southerners who stepped onto the dock with black retainers bearing mountains of luggage. They would vilify and insult Southern visitors as they stepped into the four-horse stagecoach to be whisked to the Winslow House. At the hotel the lobby and halls were stealthily patrolled by small squadrons of the righteous emancipators, who set themselves up as ex-officio house detectives. . . . [They] had made such thorough pests of themselves."[32]

The good citizens of the area tried reassuring their Southern guests, said the *Stillwater Democrat:* "There was really no danger [of the intermeddling propensities of abolitionists] . . . since Minnesotans were law-abiding people and although there may be now and then an odious creature who would not scruple to invade the family circle, the Southerners were urged to come forth, bring their slaves, and enjoy themselves."[33]

A group of abolitionists gathered on December 2, 1859, at Woodman's Hall in St. Anthony to form the Hennepin County Antislavery Society. Spending its first weeks electing officers and drafting an organizational constitution, the society appointed two committees to lobby the legislature. One committee was to seek a personal liberty bill that "made it a penal offense punishable with fines and imprisonment for anyone to claim and attempt to exercise ownership over any human being within the bounds of the state." Antislavery societies in other states had tried the same tactics and, in some instances, were successful in enacting such bills.[34]

W. D. Babbitt, S. Bigelow, James F. Bradley, and Louis Ford

crafted the appropriate language. The second committee urged the legislature "to take the necessary steps for so amending our state constitution as to make no distinction of color in the enjoyment of the right of franchise." Neither initiative was successful at the legislature. James Bradley reported to the society "that there was no prospect of get[t]ing anything done by the present legislature as they seemed more interested in other matters and to care but verry little about the poor 'Nigger.'"[35]

On hearing this report, the society appointed a ten-member committee to circulate petitions among voters "urging the same subject" upon the legislature. On March 6, 1860, committee members reported excellent support for the petitions in various parts of St. Anthony and Minneapolis. Efforts once again were under way in the legislature to amend the constitution to provide equal suffrage.[36]

On March 7 a House committee introduced a resolution "earnestly" supporting such an amendment, declaring that it was acting upon a petition from 207 Hennepin County residents headed by Preston Cooper. The committee's majority report emphasized that it was contrary to the principles of humanity, the Declaration of Independence, and the Constitution "for the white man of Minnesota to disenfranchise its colored inhabitants, who help pay taxes, and submit to its government." It argued that "inspiration" and the Declaration of Independence taught that all men were created equal with certain inalienable rights while the Constitution was "a charter of universal suffrage" because it disenfranchised no man on account of color.[37]

After a brief debate an unrecorded vote tabled the resolution. Clearly, the members saw that it was not the right time to place the amendment before the voter; more important issues were at hand, and the legislature had only four days remaining in the session. The first clear objection, surprisingly, came from Minneapolis attorney David Secombe, a Republican who said he favored equal suffrage but "deemed the submission of such an amendment at this time would be inexpedient. It would be voted down by the people; the Democratic Party would vote in mass against it, and it would fail to obtain the votes of many Republicans."[38]

Another Republican, House Speaker Amos Coggswell of Steele County, said bluntly that he "hoped the bill would be indefinitely postponed. It was too late in the session to occupy the time of the members with the nigger question." Looking at Minnesota's population of 165,395 whites and 259 blacks, the Republican speaker—who when pressed proclaimed his affinity for James Buchanan, James Polk, and Andrew Jackson, all proslave, Democratic presidents—and other Republican leaders saw no political benefit in pursuing the matter.[39]

Although this appears to be a rejection of black rights, Coggswell's attitude reflected a legislature determined not to act on behalf of either side of black issues. On March 5 the state senate declined by a wide margin to act on a petition submitted by Democratic senator Charles Mackubin of St. Paul and signed by six hundred citizens of St. Paul, St. Anthony, Minneapolis, and Stillwater "praying for passage of a law" securing the right to slave ownership by Southern tourists visiting "for a period not to exceed the term of five months."[40]

But the abolitionists of Hennepin County were unimpressed with the legislature's decision to do no harm to the campaign for black rights. This was, in the final analysis, a Republican-dominated legislature. The constitution had been adopted, and Minnesota had achieved statehood. All reasons for expediency that had been argued before were now moot. There were no more excuses. Abolitionists felt a profound sense of betrayal at the legislature's persistent course of moderation.

At its next meeting the society passed a resolution condemning the Republicans for disgracing the state with their hypocritical stand on the suffrage issue. "That the odious distinction in our State Constitution," declared the resolution, "making the right of suffrage to depend upon the complexion, and the additional distinction between Indians and Negroes, invidious to the latter, is a disgrace to our state. That our Republican legislature [sic] have proved false to their professions of their abhorrence of the *Dred Scott* decision, in refusing to make provision for so amending the constitution as to extend the right of suffrage to all persons irrespective of color."[41]

In due course the society prepared further legislative initiatives to extend citizenship to free black Minnesotans. At the same time, insulted by the presence of visiting Southerners bringing slaves to their community, members of the society took direct action by facilitating the escape of these slaves.

Opponents of the abolitionists demanded action to stop "slave-napping." The *Minneapolis Plain Dealer* reported: "It is the duty of the people to put down the extremists everywhere. Let the conservative and true men of the South take care of the disunionists there, and the good and true men of the North take care of the Abolition fanatics here."[42] Historian Louis Filler could well have included the Minnesota abolitionists when he wrote, "In the eyes of less dedicated individuals he might well seem 'arrogant,' 'malignant,' 'belligerent,' and, above all, 'impractical.'" Even their fellow Republicans distanced themselves from abolitionist activity. Filler continued, "Whilst the Republican party has no concealment to make upon the subject of Slavery, regarding it as the giant evil of the age and uncompromisingly opposed to its extension into any territory or locality where it does not exist, still it has not undertaken, nor will not undertake [*sic*] to *force* freedom upon any human being, or to interfere in any way with the personal or private affairs of those who deem fit to visit us here from the Southern States."[43]

Sympathizers of abolitionism grew concerned at reports that some Republicans were calling for more drastic measures to curb such activities. A letter to the editor signed "Republican" stated, "We have even heard of some strong, active, enthusiastic, intelligent, high minded Republicans, talk of lynching those concerned in procuring the poor [slave] her freedom. Shame on such liberty-loving christians."[44]

But the abolitionists continued their campaign. The escalating tension finally came to a head in the summer of 1860 when visiting masters started losing their slaves. St. Paul and the twin towns of St. Anthony and Minneapolis handled these occurrences very differently.

On the evening of July 17, 1860, Henry Sparks, a body servant of Martha Prince, a vacationer from Mississippi, walked away from the International Hotel in St. Paul and disappeared into the night, carrying only a small bundle. Apparently, he had come into contact with blacks who worked at the hotel who told him that he was a free man because he was in Minnesota and encouraged him to leave his mistress. In any event, he succeeded in making his way out of town and finding temporary sanctuary at Farmer's House, a hotel on the road to St. Anthony, in the company of two free black men.[45]

A couple of days after his whereabouts became known, white men sent to retrieve Sparks entered the hotel and compelled him, allegedly by threatening to "blow his brains out," to leave with them. He was last seen aboard a steamboat sailing southward to the "silken patriarchal yoke of slavery."[46]

The *Minnesotian* reported that Minnesota abolitionists argued that Minnesota law had been violated: Southerners, "with full knowledge of our laws, and who receive our hospitality," had "trampled" on one and "violate[d] the other by kidnapping, by violence, and by force of arms, taking a *Man* from our State without color of law or the permission of the constituted authorities." Honor dictated that this "high-minded 'outrage'" not be "allowed with impunity." The men who kidnapped Sparks had to be brought to justice.[47]

Attorney George A. Nourse took the case and procured a writ of habeas corpus from Chief Justice Lafayette Emmett of the state supreme court, requiring Martha Prince, who allegedly was then depriving Sparks "of his liberty," to produce him in court. If this failed, as many supposed it would, the "dignity of the State" required that it punish the kidnappers, whoever they might be, "to the utmost of our laws."[48]

But this was St. Paul.

Responding to the writ before Judge Nelson Gibbs, Martha Prince claimed that she did not have Sparks in her custody, evidently true, considering that he was then on his way to Mississippi. She was released. The state then turned its attention to Sparks's "kidnappers." State's witness John Freeland, a free black man who had stayed with Sparks at Farmer's House, claimed that St. Paul police officers, including a police captain, forcibly took the fugitive away. The officers denied the accusation, insisting they

were elsewhere at the time, and Police Chief John O'Gorman corroborated the officers' claim. The defense even called Mayor John
Prince, who, having no material evidence to offer, attested only that
he had ordered the police not to "meddle with the case."[49]

The court determined that Freeland's claims were groundless,
the officers were released, and Freeland was tried and convicted of
perjury. This marked the end of the Sparks affair. Governor Ramsey, however, issued a reward for the capture and return of the
slave's kidnappers. And a week later Southern guests at the
Winslow House in St. Anthony had "an indignation meeting" to
discuss the propriety of leaving the state due to the turmoil surrounding the Sparks case. The decision would be made for them
in late August.[50]

A couple of weeks after the Southerners at Winslow House held
their meeting, Col. Richard Christmas of Mississippi, his wife and
child, and their slave Eliza Winston arrived in St. Anthony to stay
at the hotel. Christmas had never brought slaves on his vacations
in the North because of what he had heard about abolition activities, but in the summer of 1860, his wife was too ill to travel without her slave's assistance. In time Winston met Emily Grey and
through her communicated to local abolitionists her desire to be
free. Because Sparks had recanted after he was captured and sent
south, insisting that abolitionists had drugged and forced him to
flee from his mistress, Babbitt and his colleagues questioned Winston about her determination to be free. The credibility of the
movement in Minnesota depended on its members being viewed
as law-abiding liberators, not law-breaking kidnappers. Meanwhile, Christmas learned of Winston's plan and, to thwart it,
moved the family and the slave woman to a lodge on the shore of
Lake Harriet.[51]

Babbitt and Loomis went to court to procure a writ of habeas
corpus just as had the abolitionists in St. Paul. They were determined to show that they were obeying the law and that Eliza was
lawfully choosing to be free. But if the legislature would not enact
additional laws making her freedom possible, they would take her
case to court, as many abolitionists had done elsewhere.

As Finkelman wrote in *An Imperfect Union,* "By the eve of the

Civil War most of the North had strictly limited, if not abolished, any rights a visiting or traveling slaveholder might have," and the courts often took the lead: "The legal institutions of the free states reflected an antislavery attitude as strong as, and sometimes stronger than, that attitude among the general populace." More important, they wanted to place their actions on solid legal and moral grounds so as to distinguish themselves from the Southern slave catchers who kidnapped fugitive slaves and free blacks alike and sent them south.[52]

Judge Charles Vanderburgh ordered the sheriff to bring Winston to court, which was accomplished on August 21, 1860, with Emily Grey riding at the head of the posse. After a brief hearing in which Christmas's counsel, John Freeman, former New Yorker, former attorney general of Mississippi, and current vacationer at the Winslow House, argued that federal law preempted state law and that federal law—embodied within *Dred Scott* and the Fugitive Slave Act of 1850—protected Christmas's ownership of Winston. Winston's counsel, F. R. E. Cornell, who also was the law partner of the presiding judge, argued briefly that the Minnesota constitution prohibited slavery within the state and then rested his case.[53]

Just as succinctly, the judge held for Winston and freed her amidst an outraged crowd. Babbitt spirited her to his house with a mob in pursuit. Men angered by the decision and afraid it would threaten the Southern tourist trade stormed Babbitt's house, abolitionist editor William King's office, and Emily Grey's home before they were dispersed. In the days following the ruling, the streets of Minneapolis and St. Anthony were tense, with hostile words exchanged between abolitionists and those supporting the tourism trade. Still, Eliza Winston remained free.[54]

Partly because of this ugly mood, the lucrative tourist trade faded. Masters believing that their ownership of slaves would not be respected elected to stay away just as the abolitionists of St. Anthony hoped they would. The commercial vacuum left by the vanishing tourist trade made struggling merchants and dislocated workers anxious, for the local abolition movement had become an economic fly in their ointment. For weeks after the Eliza Winston case, men on both sides of the issue taunted each other in the streets. Violence seemed imminent. For a time St. Anthony and Minneapolis seemed to be, in the ultimate paradox, on the verge of civil war over the issue of slavery. Nevertheless, the society stepped up its campaign.[55]

By now the Hennepin County Antislavery Society had moved its base of operations across the river to Minneapolis. Convening at the Free-Will Baptist Church on October 12, 1860, the society, inspired by the Eliza Winston incident, resolved to act with "renewed diligence and labour in the cause of freedom and human rights." In this spirit the society appointed a committee to draft new petitions to the 1861 legislature, urging "the passage of a personal liberty bill and the striking out of the word 'white'" in the state constitution. It also instructed another committee led by W. D. Babbitt to call a mass antislavery meeting in St. Paul "as early as practicable."[56]

One week later, on October 19, Eliza Winston recounted to society members the events leading to her freedom, declaring that she was "satisfied with her present condition." The woman to whom she went and who set in motion her emancipation—Emily Grey—was not present. Indeed, all records of the society's activities indicate she was not a member, which was in keeping with the strange nature of the abolition movement.[57]

African Americans deserved freedom, their civil rights, and even a place in the social circles of abolitionists. They were unlikely, however, to be selected for leadership positions.[58] Nationwide, in the paradoxical manly world of abolitionism, women seldom shared leadership responsibilities with men. African Americans even more rarely held these positions, and African American women participants were virtually nonexistent.[59]

The Hennepin County Antislavery Society was no different. Out of some thirty members, four were women; none was black. "The Negro's most important function," wrote historian Leon Litwack about Northern abolitionist societies in a statement just as pertinent to Hennepin County, "was that of an antislavery lecturer, for 'eloquent' Negro speakers were able to draw 'in most places far larger' audiences than their white counterparts." This was understandable, for the very presence of blacks in close association with abolitionism could spark mob violence. In essence the personal relationships of abolitionists with blacks were inevitably complex. Emily Grey's dearest white friends were probably not antislavery activists.[60]

In the months before the 1861 legislative session, the society, inspired by the increasing number of Northern states that had passed personal liberty bills guaranteeing freedom to slaves entering the states, vowed to make Minnesota one of that number. Meanwhile, society member William S. King, editor of the Minneapolis *State Atlas,* warned area merchants against taking Southern currency that was as monetarily unreliable as it was immoral. He also published stories on increasing regional tension, on Southern legislatures that had recently voted to secede from the Union, and on the siege of Fort Sumter.[61]

Southerners were taking up arms. The rapid secession of Southern states took everyone by surprise. South Carolina had already left the Union on December 20. Then, on January 9, Mississippi left. Florida seceded the next day. Alabama, Georgia, and Louisiana all followed suit another day later. Texas and Virginia seceded within the week. The Union was indeed falling apart. War was inevitable. These events made the statewide abolition convention that Babbitt was attempting to organize virtually pointless.[62]

Still, during the first week of the new legislature, the society's legislative emissary, J. B. Bradley, reported that the petitions were ready for signature. No such petitions reached the legislature. Local merchants, however, intending to counteract the society's efforts, submitted their own petition "praying for a law guaranteeing the people of the Southern States their rights of property in this State." The Senate Committee on State Affairs declined to act: "In ... that the Constitution of the United States guaranteed to citizens of each State all the immunities and privileges of the citizens of every other State, *and that no legislation conflicting with this provision has ever been attempted,* the prayer of the provision was entirely unnecessary."[63]

This was not the only matter concerning slavery that the legislators faced during the session. The lawmakers had other interests. Even Eliza Winston's former lawyer, F. R. E. Cornell—abolitionist and legislator from Minneapolis—busied himself with legislation "to protect the people from circulation of worthless and depreciated money" and, as chair of the Railway Committee, labored to resolve the financing dispute that stalled the construction of a statewide railway system that would connect St. Paul, St. Anthony, and Minneapolis to all key trading points in the state.[64]

Indeed, lawmakers had determined to focus on the state's business, of far greater urgency than the interests of Minnesota's black residents. The war and, in time, a statewide referendum and three new amendments to the U.S. Constitution would take care of black rights and in doing so heal the breach among brethren. But in early 1861 the "trouble-makers" of Hennepin County knew none of these were on the horizon. All they knew then was vigilance, against what Minnesota Democrats were capable of doing, against what their own might do as well.

7

The Good Indians

BY 1860, two years after the constitution was ratified, article 7, section 1, still rankled the Republicans of Hennepin County, not only because race determined whether a person had the right of suffrage but also because one group of nonwhites, specifically "civilized" Indians—both mixed bloods and full bloods—could vote when blacks could not.[1]

The Republicans accepted that there should be incentives and rewards for Indians to leave their "savage" ways, to adopt the customs of the white man, of cultivation and harvest, of homesteading and Christianity, of civilization. But to *give* the right to Indians and not to blacks, who had built the nation, defended the nation, and enriched the nation, while Indians oftentimes were on the opposing side, was simply wrong. Hennepin County Republicans felt that the Republican delegation's endorsement of the provision, based essentially on the Democratic conference proposal, was the height of hypocrisy.[2]

The Democrats had a different agenda altogether. The suffrage provision would reward "business partners" who had helped to enrich the Moccasin Democrats. But worse—in the eyes of the Republicans—Indian suffrage would prop up the Democratic Party, whose power was diminishing, by infusing its numbers with a rural electorate who could, at worse, neutralize Republican power that largely came from the rural areas of the state and, at best, return the state to Democratic control. The first state gubernatorial election was extremely close until the count of ballots from two mixed-blood strongholds in the Pembina and Cass districts. After tallying the results, officials found that both districts voted unanimously for Sibley; Ramsey received not one single vote. Without the votes from the "good" Indians, the Democrats inevitably would become even more a minority party, a veritable political irrelevancy. With the new constitution those crafty Democrats would see a new day.[3]

This Republican perspective misread an essential aspect of Democratic thinking. The Democrats did not seem to feel they needed the Indian voter. The party of Jackson was better organized and more experienced than the Republican Party, whose large number consisted of tenuous alliances among competing interest groups and often suspicious ethnic groups. How Minnesota's party of Lincoln comported itself on its beloved issue of black suffrage illustrated the political paradox that size combined with inexperience leads to insecure and ineffective leadership. Let the Methodists, Baptists, and Lutherans, the Swedes, Protestant Germans, Norwegians, and Yankees, the reformers and bigoted Know-Nothings, and the merchants and farmers all fight it out.

Democratic power lay in such mixed-blood communities as the Red River Valley and in such reliable, bare-knuckled neighborhoods as Lowertown. By 1860 few full-blood Indians thought it desirable to be "white"; those who didn't think so ridiculed those who did. Besides, if the new state seal meant anything at all—it depicted a farmer plowing the land as an Indian in native dress rode away as if fleeing westward—the full bloods were, as many believed, a vanishing race. If denying blacks the right to vote was an act of racism, requiring Indians to speak English—when large numbers of enfranchised mixed bloods and foreign-born residents spoke little, if any—was a form of mockery and an empty political gesture.

But no one told this to the few Indians who still believed they could be citizens; who believed they could trust their white friends, some of the most prominent Moccasins of the state; who believed that truly civilized Indians could be equal to the mixed bloods, whose privilege in relation to the Indian was based solely on their white blood, equal even to the white man himself.

By the end of the territorial period, agriculture replaced the fur trade as a growing number of settlers moved into the region to farm, chasing away the animals Indians once hunted. For many Indians the white man was proving to be powerful, occupying land that the tribes had lost through treaties, clearing away trees, building houses, tilling soil, domesticating livestock, and putting up fences, all under the protection of the white man's army, the way of the future. The old ways were dying out. The white man's god had stronger medicine.

For some, "whiteness" was redemption, a chance to become a member of a preferred people. Within this group men cut their hair, wore pantaloons, converted to Christianity, and took up farming. In 1851, in return for the transformation, the Moccasins extended civil rights to certain Indians and to their mixed-blood family members, creating what Whig-turned-Republican Alexander Ramsey called "peculiar, quasi citizens," a people otherwise difficult for Anglo-American arrivals to understand.[4]

By 1858, though mixed bloods largely remained enigmatic to whites, their commercial importance had diminished. In this new world being "quasi" was a political handicap. Being fully enfranchised meant being a citizen without conditions, and full citizenship required one to be "white-like." Thus, achieving whiteness through the designation of powerful white men became critical. This essentially was the story of the Indians of the Hazelwood Republic.

The republic was only a small experimental part of a larger initiative to civilize the Dakota Indians of Minnesota. Since Taliaferro's experiment with Eatonville, Indian agents and missionaries had been interested in the problem of how to get the wild Dakota to adopt the ways of the white man—to become civilized.

Stephen and Mary Riggs had been missionaries to the Dakota for seventeen years by the time they followed physician Thomas Williamson from Lac qui Parle to the junction of the Yellow Medicine and Minnesota rivers in 1854. Riggs started the Hazelwood Mission, located along the Minnesota River, about five miles above the Upper Sioux Agency. Organized as an agricultural and educational center for the Dakota near the agency, it encompassed nearly "6,000 souls" from the Wahpeton, Sisseton, Mdewakanton, and Wahpakute Dakota bands.[5]

Some of the Sisseton and Wahpeton Dakota were willing to take on the ways of the white man and give up their Dakota habits, customs, and beliefs. They desired to form themselves into a separate band recognized by the Indian agent assigned to the Dakota and known as the "Hazelwood Republic." The year was 1856. Riggs saw the band as "a gathering up of our missionary efforts for the last twenty years." He wrote that it was established on the "principle of education, labor and the adoption of the dress and habits of white men." He said it would need help and encouragement from the government along many lines but particularly in the matter of education.[6]

The band adopted its own constitution, which required the election of a governor, a secretary of state, and three councilmen, and it contained seven articles. The first recognized the existence of One Great Spirit and His claims to the love and homage of all men. The second provided that those who joined the community must abandon Dakota customs, adopt the white man's dress, and seek to improve their condition by labor. The third set forth their esteem for education and their determination to build a schoolhouse and employ a teacher. The fourth expressed the intent to build houses, keep cattle in large fields, and properly punish anyone trespassing on their property. The fifth promised obedience and subjection to the U.S. government. The last article requested treatment of its members as if they were white persons. Harriet Bell, writing on the Hazelwood Republic, observed that the constitution was one in name only; it was really more a request for and pledge of allegiance to the government and values of the white man.[7]

On July 30, 1856, the Hazelwood leaders presented the new constitution in both English and Dakota and read it in Dakota to Indian agent Maj. Richard Murphy, who assured the leaders he would regard their governor and other officers as fully as he did any leader of the Dakota nation. The sincerity of the new governor—Paul Mazakutemani—about the ideals of the Hazelwood Republic was evident. In a passage in his narrative about his own conversion, Mazakutemani—a full-blood Dakota who would later rescue white captives of the Spirit Lake massacre and oppose the Dakota War—wrote: "Nearly forty of us at one time cut off our hair and put on the white man's dress and formed ourselves into a separate community of which we elected me chief; and our separate band was at once recognized by the agent, Major Murphy. This was in 1856. The agent was well-pleased with our onward movement, and said, 'If all Dakotas would do it, it would be well.' It was well. I liked it."[8]

The St. Paul *Financial Advertiser* editorialized:

> Away up on the head waters of the Minnesota, some forty miles above Fort Ridgley, in a corner of a miserly strip of Territory of which the usufruct was reserved to the Dakotas . . . in the wilderness home of some seven thousand shiftless savages, the very Hades of Indian barbarism, yet dim with ghostly songs and legends, the philosophers of France and the poets of European regeneration have been outstripped by the Dakota hunter and a veritable Republic, organized, representative, free, with a written Constitution and a code of laws has been established on the banks of the Yellow Medicine.[9]

Dakota agent Joseph R. Brown—appointed to the position by Governor Sibley in 1857 and who, according to Riggs, "[kept] Indian women"—said that the moral courage displayed by having their hair cut and their clothes changed in the face of jeers of their people was "unsurpassed in the annals of Christianity."[10]

In August 1857 as Republican and Democratic delegates worked on partisan drafts of the soon-to-be state constitution, Riggs spent five days in St. Paul trying to obtain favorable consideration of a petition for full citizenship for "our Hazelwood people." The level of divisiveness existing between the caucuses frustrated him. "It is a great shame that it should be so," he wrote in a letter to former missionary S. B. Treat, "but both parties are to blame, in my opinion. The Republicans, who are greatly in the majority, should not have been afraid of the political tricks of the Democrats."[11]

Nonetheless, it seemed to him fortuitous that the petition had reached the hands of the Democrats since, as he wrote, "so many of them are half-breeds and the fathers of half-breeds that they will look kindly on this class of persons." Accordingly, "several influential members" had assured him that civilized Indians would be brought under the same category: "In other words, they propose to make a new dictionary meaning of the word 'white' so that it shall include all mixed bloods of Indian descent and civilized Indians."[12]

While the Republicans supported striking "white" from the

constitution, a proposal favoring the Hazelwood Indians, the delegates feared that universal enfranchisement, which benefited blacks, mixed bloods, and civilized Indians alike, might endanger ratification of the final draft because white Minnesotans had grown hostile to Indians. Riggs does not appear to have considered that many whites might equally hold animus toward blacks: "[Republicans] don't dare to act out their own convictions of duty. I found here a great deal of prejudice against Indians, owing chiefly to this Spirit Lake affair." He referred to a raid led by Inkpaduta, a Dakota band leader, earlier that year, in which most of a settlement of whites in Jackson County was killed.[13]

At a crowded meeting at the First Presbyterian Church in St. Paul, with "a number of Republican members present," Riggs explained that the Hazelwood Indians deserved citizenship because they had participated in rescuing white women and children and bringing some of the warring band to justice. He soon returned to the mission "with the expectation that a section securing the rights of our people" would be introduced in the Republican constitution.[14]

His optimism was quickly dashed: "It seems as if this Spirit Lake massacre is doing immense damage to our operations. All improvements are stopped. Neither government nor individuals have done any thing this summer; even the crops have not been half taken care of. The white people have become very much prejudiced against the whole Dakota nation, and now talk loudly of having the reserve taken off. I fear that this will be the result."[15]

In other words, despite the activities and beliefs of the Hazelwood Indians and their willingness to embrace "the habits and customs" of civilized white men and to sever connections with friends and family who stayed with the old ways, white society still saw them as savages in white disguise. Even Riggs, whether championing race-neutral citizenship in talking with Republicans or advocating for an expansive definition of "whiteness" in debating with Democrats, could not erase from his mind that race was determinative: "The present and prospective state of things among us brings up several questions. Can Indians who are made citizens of Minnesota, for instance, hold land in fee simple?" In other words, could Indians *really* own their own parcels of land? "And can they be made citizens of the United States without altering the [U.S.] Constitution?" These were the Indians whites had said they wanted. Yet their skin color was immutable. They were Indians no matter what they did. They could never be white enough to be equal.[16]

When Riggs placed the Hazelwood petition with Democratic delegate Charles Flandrau, he assumed the delegate, who the year before had been Dakota agent and supporter of the Republic, would be a powerful champion for civilized-Indian suffrage. But during debate Flandrau, though expressing high regard for the work at Hazelwood as well as for the Indian signatories he knew personally, said that when "Indians like these desire to become civilized . . . the least we can do is to give them all the encouragement we can *with safety to ourselves.*" Further, he said, "While it is just and right that we should accord them these privileges, we should take care not to jeopardize our own rights."[17]

His concern was that Indians through deception could adopt outward manifestation of civilization without their conversion being sincere: "All a man has got to do who wishes to manufacture votes is to take a wild Indian, dress him up, bring him in and pass him off as having adopted the habits and customs of civilized life, and then strip off his clothes and let him return to his tribe. I submit that we ought to guard ourselves against the perpetration of such frauds."[18]

Flandrau argued further that Indians, especially, must be closely watched: "When an Indian has really become civilized, and desires to possess the privileges and immunities of the citizen, let him present himself to some tribunal in which the people have confidence, which will protect the rights of the citizen, and let them extend to him the same rights, if he is capable of enjoying them."[19]

This is a far cry from what Flandrau wrote years later: "The first act necessary for initiation as a citizen of the republic was cutting off the long hair universally worn by the Sioux, and if any act could be taken as indicative of sincerity, this one seems to be conclusive."[20]

Nonetheless, in 1857 Flandrau was skeptical. He argued that if

Indians satisfied "special scrutiny," Minnesota had a duty to extend suffrage in compensation for their exploitation at the hands of white men: "An Indian who desires to become civilized, and who has made sufficient progress in civilization, is as much entitled to vote as any other man. They were the original possessors of our soil. They have suffered at our hands, and if we can extend to them any suffrage as compensation for what we have taken from them, and it can be done without danger to ourselves of introducing an element into our politics which may give rise to corruption and fraud, I trust it will be done."[21]

Adopting the language of civilization and replacing one's native tongue was a sure sign of commitment to civilization. No longer could one shroud the utterances of one's true thoughts with the veil of the Dakota language. But considering that white men lied all the time, this position was disingenuous. The numerous 1857 incidents of election fraud committed against the Democrats in St. Paul while selecting delegates to the constitutional convention prove the point. Even the Democrats' newspaper admitted as much. The Republicans were just as guilty. It was all the work of civilized white men. Nonetheless, on the issue of Indian suffrage during the convention debate, Flandrau concluded, "I trust gentlemen are not so prejudiced against the Indians as to prevent them from receiving justice at our hands."[22]

At the constitutional convention Democratic and Republican delegates agreed on the suffrage language concerning civilized Indians, jointly approving a provision that required not only that the class adopt the "customs and habits of civilization" but also that they demonstrate facility in the English language. The provision would prove an insurmountable obstacle for many of the converted Dakota, and the Moccasins, from their years of experience trading with and living among them, had to know this. The Republicans, on one hand, especially those living in west central and southern Minnesota, would not grant anything to a class they feared might murder them in their beds. The Democrats, on the other, were interested in conducting commerce with Indians, not in making them citizens. Men like Paul Mazakutemani, who had converted to Christianity, adopted the white man's customs, farmed, become literate in the Dakota language, and helped white refugees escape or worked for the military, could never be citizens—because they never learned to speak English.[23]

Dr. Williamson, seeing the Democratic farce, predicted in an 1857 report to the American Board of Commissioners for Foreign Missions a growing alienation among the former partners of the Moccasins: "The influence of the American Fur Company, which has thrown more impediments in the way of the improvement of the Dakotas than almost everything else, is fast waning among them, and can never again be what it has been."[24]

Riggs pressed forward, however, as if the logic of justice could preempt the logic of racism. The new state constitution, he wrote, "requires them to have adopted the language as well as the habits and customs of civilization. As there is no specific language of civilization, it is our purpose to bring the Dakota language under that category." In other words, article 7, section 1, only required that citizens speak "the language . . . of civilization," of which white English-speaking American civilization was only one. Any culture whose language was written, and as such required literacy, qualified as a "civilization."[25]

The Hazelwood Indians studied the Bible, the Ten Commandments, the hymnbook chosen by the American Tract Society, *John Bunyan,* and later, the newly ratified state constitution, all written in Dakota. But reading these texts in their own language was not proof enough of their commitment to a civilized life, nor was facing the hardship of meeting the otherwise simple task of dressing white. Riggs wrote: "Last week two young men had their hair cut off and afterwards put on pantaloons. When an Indian wants to change his dress and put on white man's clothes, the question is how to get them. To meet this question, our Republic men have fallen into the habit of helping every one to get his first clothes. This way may be burdensome. But at present they do it cheerfully."[26]

In the Dakota world the cutting of a man's hair was tantamount to severing him from his Dakota identity. Thus it was the most important part of the civilizing ceremony because, as agent Brown noted, "No Sioux will go on the warpath without a scalp lock."

These Dakota accepted the duty of working a farm and performing tasks demeaning to men in traditional Dakota culture. The Hazelwood Indians embraced such commitments knowing not just that they severed themselves from their heritage but also that they invited derision, the "mischievous teasing and petty larceny by the 'blanket Indians,'" who stayed with the old ways. Folwell wrote, "From the beginning of the experiment the 'blanket Indians' had ridiculed and tormented those who were adopting the life of the white men, whom they stigmatized as 'white men' and 'dutchmen,' thus likening them to the unwarlike German settlers in the [Minnesota] valley."[27]

Yet their willingness to face these adversities and others was an insufficient sign of commitment. The only thing that mattered was that Indians speak English. Riggs wrote encouragingly about the Indians' efforts to start English-speaking schools at Hazelwood, though he was skeptical of the sincerity of government officials who praised the Indians for their efforts: "Our people here chose to have an English school this winter and elected as teacher John McCullough. So we have two English schools at Hazelwood. Mr. McCullough has been teaching for three weeks. I doubt whether it will be of as much practical utility as a Dakota school. Still as much may be expected of an English day school *here* as in any place in the Dakota Country. And the government officials all profess to want to have English taught. I am inclined to think that in most instances the *real want* is to have nothing."[28]

He was specifically critical of agent Brown who, Riggs wrote, "profess[ed] to be desirous to start a school at every village, and yet he has stopped some schools that were intended to go into operation."[29]

Considering that the matter had been resolved in the earliest days of the territory, the issue of mixed-blood suffrage was surprisingly volatile among the Democrats. Convention delegates wishing to continue restrictions on mixed bloods as well as foreigners struck some of their own colleagues as wrongheaded.

George L. Becker of Ramsey County argued: "Sir, when I have seen the Indian half-breed baring his bosom for the protection of the white man; when I recollect that from the earliest days of our settlement we have found our strongest protection in this class of people, and that the captives taken by hostile Indians have been rescued and returned by those half-breeds, I say that to make a distinction against them in respect to the rights of citizenship, is monstrous. No discrimination whatever should be made against those men and our own white citizens."[30]

"We all know," argued Henry Sibley, one of the leading and oldest Moccasins of Minnesota, now joining the debate, "that these mixed bloods as a class occupy in ninety-nine cases out of one hundred entirely different positions in respect to civilization from the Indians." Becker insisted that the offending provision "presupposes that these mixed bloods are not civilized." Sibley responded that the language was used because a "certain portion— a very small portion [of mixed bloods]" who "reside among the Indians, and have not adopted the customs of civilized life."[31]

In other words, the actions of a few were to determine the civil rights of the many. In any event, mixed- and full-blood Indians, unlike blacks, at least had a chance—however qualified, however unrealistic—at the franchise.

In contrast to their position on the mixed-blood and full-blood Indian suffrage provisions, the Democrats were far more liberal than the Republicans on the matter of alien suffrage. In this class of new arrivals, the Democrats saw their political future. Their proposal called for any alien to be able to obtain voting rights simply by declaring his intention to become a citizen and providing proof of one year's residence in the United States and four months in the state. The Republicans proposed limiting alien suffrage to those who resided in the state at the time the constitution was ratified or who had resided in the state for at least two years. No one had to speak English to qualify for citizenship. Although the convention adopted the Democratic proposal, the Republican Party realized it could benefit from white, foreign-born voters as well.[32]

Notwithstanding the intent of these Democrats to impose burdensome qualifications on Indians, Riggs worried about a new Minnesota falling under what he viewed to be anti-Indian Republican rule and its implications for the Hazelwood Indians, in particular. First, there was the residual problem of so many uncivilized

Indians in their midst, the consequence of Democratic rule. With too many forces at work to erode the integrity of the great experiment of the Republic, the Republicans easily concluded that what opportunity there once may have been to civilize the Indian had passed. Second, the white and Indian cultures, even of the civilized Indians and mixed bloods and white, farming settlers, were at opposite ends. The whites believed in rugged individualism, a philosophy the Indians could hardly espouse considering their reliance on annuities, federal supplies, and assistance in building their homes and sawmills. In this sense "farmer" Indians could never be Republicans. They relied too heavily on the government for support.[33]

At the same time, the Republicans felt that tribalism and communalism were too much within the soul of the Indian, and this made him un-American. This, too, was the fault of the Democrats, for exploiting an economic system that enabled uncivilized lifestyles. "The legislature of Minnesota," wrote Riggs, "is this year largely Republican—and the Republicans have talked so much about the *Moccasined* [sic] Democracy that I fear that many of them will not be well disposed to do justice to the Indians."[34]

In December 1859 the newly elected Governor Ramsey requested from Riggs information on what other states had done in reference to "citizenizing" Indians. Riggs felt that nothing would come of it. In a letter to Treat dated January 30, 1860, Ramsey acknowledged receipt of a copy of the Massachusetts Indian citizenship law that he would forward to the appropriate legislative committee. But he did not see it as pertinent to Minnesota: "Unfortunately, in a frontier country where the number of wild or uncivilized Indians is as large as here, and where their depredations upon, and annoyances to settlers are great, it provokes such a prejudice against the whole race, as to delay proper action, even in the case of those Indians who may entitle themselves to an advancement to all the rights of citizenship."[35]

During the legislative session of 1861, Riggs again drafted a provision for Indian citizenship that included Dakota as a civilized language and engaged Gideon Pond, one of Minnesota's oldest missionaries and most respected Whig statesman, who also created a Dakota-English dictionary, to lobby for its passage. Though

Pond reported "there was little doubt but it would succeed," the bill, as Riggs anticipated, failed.[36]

In June 1861 Riggs tried to expand the law by bringing forth the applications of citizenship for nine full-blood Dakota men from Hazelwood to the district court. The court and attorneys examined each applicant; Riggs acted in their defense. While all the men dressed as white men, "presenting quite a neat appearance," only one of them—Lorenzo Lawrence—possessed knowledge of the English language, and he was the only one granted citizenship.[37]

Advancing the claims of the other eight men, Riggs argued that the Dakota language was not a barbarous language, "as it had been reduced to a system and was capable of use in the printed books, in writing, and for all other practical purposes." Once the Dakota of the Hazelwood Republic adopted the habits, customs, and pursuits of civilization and lived "together in a community separate and distinct from the remainder of the tribe," even though they retained their native language, by definition they became a community "living in every respect as white or civilized people." The judge disagreed, holding that "Sioux was a barbarous language" because it "was not a language or literature by which these people could gain knowledge of *our* system of government," the Dakota translation of the state constitution notwithstanding.[38]

It was established: "civilized" meant "white," and "white" meant speaking English. The Christian farmer Dakota of the Hazelwood Republic, who wore short hair and pantaloons and lived in houses separate from the so-called blanket Indians, were only *nearly* civilized. Because they did not speak English, they had lost ground toward citizenship, unlike the German speakers of New Ulm, who could vote. Thus, no longer "quasi citizens" as Governor Ramsey had once called them, the Hazelwood Dakota were after statehood quasi civilized.

These "good" Indians, 125 families living on farms in 1861, were isolated from but surrounded by some 7,000 hostile "blanket" Dakota who stole pigs, drove off cattle, and raided cornfields, as well as by Indian traders who opposed the civilization experiment and may have imported whiskey with which to tempt them "to their old life." The *Henderson Democrat* editorialized that "good

Indians" were as "the evil contact of the day." Yet neither Brown nor his successor, Thomas S. Galbraith, was able to obtain military protection for the Hazelwood Republic.[39]

Tension came to a head between the "blanket" and farmer Indians when warriors struck at the Hazelwood mission on the Yellow Medicine River in the Dakota War of 1862. Even though the Republic was wiped out as its residents fled from the Dakota, who destroyed all of the buildings along with their labor of many years, when it was time for white retribution, the innocence of the good Indians was obscured by the villainy of the bad. In August 1862, when the conflict began, Minnesota—indeed the nation—was at its most vulnerable.[40]

By the fall Lincoln had not yet transformed the war for unity into a war for emancipation. Even so, many in Minnesota realized that the interest of black men was bound up with the source of national conflict. Republicans suspected Democrats, long noted for their antiblack sentiments, of inciting the Dakota attack on white farmers.

Even before the Dakota conflict, as the Civil War raged, many Republicans in Minnesota were suspicious of mixed bloods, particularly since many had descended from territorial Democratic traders. The nature of the times was to be distrustful of Democrats. The greater number of settlers arriving between 1855 and 1857, coming primarily from New England, New York, Pennsylvania, and the old Northwest, settled on "treaty lands" west of the Mississippi, opened to settlement in accordance with Indian treaties of 1851, between the northern boundary of Iowa and the Minnesota River. In their political views the settlers generally became Republican, though because the northern part of the territory was under the control of the Moccasins, many of them felt "politically impotent and isolated."[41]

The apportionment of 1855, which occurred before the large influx of immigration, left no possibility of equitable representation for southern Minnesota. As William Anderson noted, "The capitol at St. Paul was almost inaccessible to the southern population at certain seasons of the year. It was easy under the circumstances to imagine all sorts of political trickery going on at the capital." Further, he wrote, "Men living in southern Minnesota did not have to be Republicans to grow suspicious of St. Paul; many undoubtedly joined the Republican party because it promised early to be strong enough to break the power of the St. Paul–Stillwater region, the stronghold of the territorial Democracy."[42]

The seeds of distrust, already sown by the late 1850s, sprouted and bore bitter fruit on the eve of the Dakota War. In the midst of the Civil War, as the North suffered defeat after defeat, Republicans knew that while every Democrat might not be a traitor, every traitor was indeed a Democrat. Few were above suspicion.

Even though during the summer of 1862 government officials failed to distribute annuity payments, offering "no advices and . . . only . . . vague excuses," Republicans felt that the suspicions and anxieties of the Dakota were "heightened and inflamed" by the "behavior and language of whites and half-breeds among them." Further, "the traders had generally belonged to the old Moccasin Democracy of the territory and state and had no expectation of better times under 'Black Republican' rule. Altogether there was a considerable 'copperhead' element on the reserve." Not so subtly, the message was simple: Indian annuities and black freedom were incompatible. Galbraith reported that literate mixed bloods kept the Dakota informed of the progress of the Civil War as well as the defeat of General George McClellan at Gaines' Mill and the poor outcome of the Peninsular Campaign in Virginia. Folwell wrote: "The Great Father, they were told, was whipped—'*cleaned out*'— and '*niggers*' would get the money due the Indians."[43]

Thus stirred the belief that the Dakota viewed all blacks as their enemies. The fact that Dakota warriors during the earliest days of the conflict attempted to kill Jim Thompson and destroy his property reinforced this belief.[44]

With time came rumors that secessionist emissaries working among the Dakota "poisoned the minds of the warriors." Such rumors were baseless, but Indian agent Galbraith nevertheless believed "rebel sympathizers did all in their power to create disaffection among the Indians." An editorial in the *St. Paul Press* said,

"That the secession sympathizers and agents have been instrumental in causing the difficulty with the Indians is evident." Even Senator Henry Rice, a Moccasin Democrat, in a letter to the editor of the *St. Paul Pioneer* wrote, "The Sioux Indians were induced by rebels and traitors to make war upon our people." Riggs, who spoke out against the mass executions in Mankato, suggested that "men of the opposite political faith were not careful in their conversation" and "that they kept the Indians informed of the disasters of the Union Army . . . with some exaggerations," which "was a political sin."[45]

Such sentiment illustrated the small regard that these white men gave the depth of grievance held by the Dakota. If the "chief cause" for the war was to be "found in the insurrection of the Southern states," the cause was one of expediency and timing—to attack when their enemy was most distracted by rebel forces. By late summer of 1862, the Dakota simply did not need conniving whites to trigger their attacks. The Dakota, who had been promised food and supplies in 1851 in the Treaty of Traverse des Sioux, now starved. But those who had little meaningful contact with Indians had only a superficial understanding. The Dakota—all of them—were not to be just defeated but annihilated, and this was to be carried out by civilized men. While the offer from presumably unpredictable Ojibwe warriors to fight the Dakota was "tactfully declined by both Governor Ramsey and Major General Pope," christianized Ojibwe—full and mixed bloods—served in Minnesota's Ninth Infantry, Company G, to fight both the Dakota and the Confederates.[46]

Another Indian unit—the Renville Rangers—fighting against the Dakota consisted, paradoxically, of Dakota mixed bloods. Named for the county from which most enlistees came, the Renville Rangers initially organized to fight the Confederate army during the desperate months of 1862. As Chief Eagle wryly said of the unit, "The Indians now thought the whites must be pretty hard up for men to fight the South, or they would not come so far out on the frontier and take half-breeds or anything to help them." Though headed to Fort Snelling for their deployment south, they were instead ordered to defend Fort Ridgely. There they fended off the attack of Big Eagle and his warriors, meeting them again to defeat the chief at the battle of Wood Lake.[47]

Meanwhile, the black men of Minnesota could not fight for a national cause that would result in their freedom and political equality.

Carol Chomsky has written that the extent of killing and disruption caused by the Dakota and the brutal nature of their attacks on a settled community further explains the American response. Hundreds of settlers were killed, and more than ten thousand fled their homes fearing for their lives. The Dakota destroyed homes and storehouses, and the settlers knew they would have to face the winter without sufficient supplies. Many Minnesotans personally knew someone who had been killed in the fighting, and the attack came at a time when Minnesota and the nation felt particularly vulnerable as a result of the Civil War. Add to this the widespread though unfounded belief that most of the Dakota committed wholesale rape and mutilation and the outpouring of rage and disinclination to view the actions of the Dakota as justifiable, and warfare becomes easier to understand. Furthermore, by treating the Dakota as criminals, the United States could remove all of the Dakota from the state, thereby opening up to settlement much land that the Minnesotans had coveted for years. But the rage was sincere.[48]

The U.S.-Dakota Conflict had stirred hatred among Minnesota whites toward the Dakota, and in the aftermath of the fighting most argued that the "bad" Indians—those convicted of killing settlers—be punished and the "good" Indians—those found innocent of wrongdoing—be removed. At least one strong voice argued for conciliation for both moral and strategic reasons. Thomas S. Williamson, the respected missionary among the Dakota, held that banishment was tantamount to extermination of the entire Dakota nation: "Nothing would please Little Crow better than to be able to make the Sioux who are at large, generally believe that those who have surrendered to us have been, or will be destroyed. For they will say and think: The Big Knives have destroyed those of our people who defended and delivered their captives. They are determined to kill us all if they can catch us. There is no hope for us. Let us fight and plunder while we can."[49]

As early as September 9, 1862, in a message delivered to the legislature while the fighting was in progress, Governor Ramsey declared, "The Sioux Indians of Minnesota must be exterminated or driven forever beyond the borders of the State." Later, both houses of the state legislature approved a memorial to be sent to President Lincoln and Congress urging that all Indians, not just the Dakota, be banished from the soil of Minnesota: "This terrible blow has fallen not alone upon our present prosperity and happiness as a people, but upon our hopes for the future, unless it shall be put in our power to say, 'The Indian is gone from Minnesota!'— *not one Tribe or two Tribes, but all—ALL*—in consequence of and in atonement for August, 1862. Can Minnesota ask less? Indian removal, immediate and total, is the universal prayer of the people of Minnesota."[50]

Still others wanted more extreme measures taken, for they accepted nothing less than the extermination of the Indians. Predictably, those who held no ideological humanitarian beliefs, who witnessed the slaughter of white families or lost relatives, or who simply felt vulnerable to attack or clung to a racist motivation to hate Indians were inclined to support the bloody policy of vengeance. That some who strenuously embraced freedom and equality for black people simultaneously supported the extermination of all Indians is curious; extending grace and citizenship in a magnanimous effort to include those elected few into the fraternity of civilized men was foolhardy. In 1862 liberal Republican editor Thomas M. Newson wrote to General Sibley, "Of what avail now all the teachings of missionaries?—the parental regard of the national government?—the false sympathy and partiality of our State in granting them the right of suffrage to the exclusion of the free intelligent black? Look at the result. The indiscriminate slaughter of our hardy pioneers and their families, one of whose lives is worth more than a dozen of these infernal devils, every one of whom should be hunted down with the same feeling of intense, absorbing hate as they tread upon the poisonous reptile."[51]

By the end of the conflict, Jane Grey Swisshelm—editor, feminist activist, and a prominent abolitionist in Minnesota—was demanding that the Dakota be removed *and* exterminated, encouraging the legislature to authorize it. In her article "Scalps," she wrote,

"It is folly to fight Indians as we would European soldiers. Let our present Legislature offer a bounty of $10 for every Sioux scalp, outlaw the tribe and so let the matter rest. It will cost five times that much to exterminate them by the regular modes of warfare and they should be got rid of in the cheapest and quickest manner." In a later article—"The Indian Wrongs"—she wrote that the Dakota had "by all laws human and divine forfeited their right to life." In response to the stories of atrocities, she wrote, "A Sioux has just as much right to life as a hyena, and he who would spare them is an enemy to his race."[52]

As historian Sylvia Hoffert wrote, "Within a few months, Swisshelm switched from a relatively evenhanded treatment of white-Indian relations to one that rejected the rule of law (authorizing due-process protection to Indians) and advocated frontier vigilantism." With fellow abolitionists Swisshelm shared the view that Indians were victims of white exploitation and violence, but she philosophically departed from it when Dakota reprisals threatened the promotion of business, white settlement, and white civilization. In the end, by mid-1863, all the Dakota would be removed from the state.[53]

Folwell reported that the shipment of thirteen hundred Dakota to Crow Creek on the Missouri River in Dakota Territory in the early summer of 1863 left some two hundred Dakota remaining at Fort Snelling or unaccounted for. He wrote, "About that number who had been steadfastly friendly to the whites had been allowed to depart for their old homes on the reservations." Some, presumably, were members of the Hazelwood Republic.[54]

This was the moment in which Minnesota fully embraced the identity emblazoned on its state seal: as the civilized man plowed the earth, the savage on bareback fled west.

The act of March 3, 1863, providing for the exile of the hostile Dakota bands further authorized the secretary of the interior to relocate meritorious Indians on tracts of eighty acres on their own reservations. "This benevolence," wrote Folwell, "was utterly futile. The settlers swarming in advance of survey and sale and after would not tolerate Indian neighbors. As outcasts these Indians wandered about." The Indians who were not sent into exile—the "good" Indians—nonetheless remained homeless. The language-exclusionary state policy made citizenship unreachable for most Indians. Federal policy and its reservation plan now made citizenship almost unimaginable. Paradoxically, if civilization was to come to the Indians, it would have to be in the absence of contact with white settlement, for, as the *Henderson Democrat* had editorialized before the war, "contact with the white has rather depressed than elevated [the Dakota]."[55]

Recognizing the inevitable friction between Indians and whites, especially as white settlement spread across land that had been Indian country, the government pursued policies intent on separating the two races. Commissioner of Indian Affairs Charles E. Mix wrote in a report dated October 31, 1863: "As the end and object of all governments should be the happiness and welfare of the governed, so the object of all our efforts in behalf of the Indian should be *the improvement of his condition,* and to that end the adoption of that policy which promises the most rapidly to increase his intelligence, promote his happiness, *and finally affect his civilization.* The plan of concentrating Indians and confining them to reservations may now be regarded as the fixed policy of the government. The theory of this policy is doubtless correct."[56]

He saw a problem in the plan, however. Although reservations were established "outside and beyond the limits of our settlements," it was inevitable that the tide of emigration, "which, in this country, is advancing with such wonderful rapidity," would engulf the areas in which the reservations were located. "The result," Mix observed, "is found to be most disastrous to the Indians."[57]

By the end of 1863, as the United States approached its third year of civil war, a perverse sense of achieving Indian "civilization" came to mean absolute separation from white civilized life. John Otherday, Paul Mazakutemani, and Lorenzo Lawrence—the only Dakota of the Hazelwood Republic community to become Minnesota citizens—all spent their latter years on the Sisseton Reservation in Dakota Territory. Gabriel Renville, the Dakota mixed-blood farmer who urged Williamson to escape after reporting to the missionary on the killing at the Redwood Agency, negotiated the Treaty of 1867 that established the reservation and became its first leader.[58]

Where missions and Dakota villages were once situated along the Minnesota River, settlers moved in to start new farms. The state seal depicting a farmer plowing up the rich earth as an Indian rode away was more than emblematic of white sensibilities—it was prophetic. The only good Indian was a removed Indian.

On May 5, 1863, fugitive slave Robert Hickman and his Pilgrims, refugees from Missouri, disembarked from the *Northerner* at Fort Snelling. Only hours later, 540 Dakota men, women, and children were marched aboard the same steamboat and sent to their permanent exile in the West. They were the last to be removed from Minnesota, guilty of the crime of being Dakota, a people who had conducted war against white settlers during a time of national calamity.[59]

Six months earlier in Washington, Caleb B. Smith, secretary of the interior, had recommended to the House Committee on Indian Affairs the removal of the Dakota to some point in the Missouri Valley and furnished a draft of the act for that purpose. The act of Congress of February 16, 1863, annulling all treaties with the Dakota including the specified demarcation of Indian Country effectively left the tribe homeless. The subsequent act of March 3, 1863, following the recommendation of Secretary Smith, provided for the removal of all Dakota then in the custody of the government to someplace outside of the state. President Lincoln selected an area on the Missouri River within a hundred miles of Fort Randall, where the Indians "would be secure from the intrusion by whites," an area for a possible reservation that had "good soil, good timber, and plenty of water."[60]

The Indian office did not wait for the selection of a specific tract of land to be assigned to the exiled Dakota but "prepared to ship them off like so many cattle." Missionary John P. Williamson, son of Thomas S. Williamson, who had grown up among the Dakota, chose to go with them downriver. In his account of their departure, he wrote: "The last one was counted on just at dusk, after which, an escort of soldiers being brought aboard, we shoved off. . . . We are, however, hardly under way when from all the different parts of the boat where they are collected, we hear hymns of praise ascending to Jehovah. . . . Then one of them leads in prayer, after which another hymn is sung; and so they continue till all are composed; and drawing their blankets over them, each falls asleep."[61]

These were the "good" Indians, as the *St. Paul Daily Press* referred to noncombatants in the Dakota War. But even though they were "good," they were not quite "civilized," and they were being removed from the state, ostensibly, because of it. The question became whether or not the government could remove them safely past St. Paul.[62]

One day earlier, on May 4, the *Davenport* had left the fort with 770 Dakota likewise making the river journey to St. Joseph, where the steamboat would meet the others who would arrive by rail. Of this number there were only "about fifty men in the entire company." About half an hour on its way, the steamboat stopped at the St. Paul levee to take on freight, and there a crowd gathered. Some in the crowd, urged on by a soldier wounded at Birch Coulee, the site of some of the most bloody fighting of the Dakota War, hooted and threw stones at the Indians, easily hitting their tightly packed targets on the boiler deck. The *Daily Press* reported: "Some of the squaws were hit upon the head and quite severely injured." To restore order, Capt. E. C. Sanders of Company G, Tenth Regiment, commanding the guard consisting of forty men, ordered the crowd to desist or "he would order his men to charge bayonets among them."[63]

The next time the *Davenport* arrived at St. Paul, on May 14, a mob assembled to focus its wrath on the arrival of the second contingent of "contraband" blacks.[64] The next day, however, after returning from Fort Snelling, the steamboat landed at the St. Paul levee bearing 417 Winnebago Indians before departing for St. Louis. No mob assembled to assault this new collection of human cargo. Instead, according to the *St. Paul Daily Press,* as the boat docked for three hours, large numbers of citizens came to "view the Native Americans and make purchases of Indian trinkets." One observer found that "the Indians showed their shrewdness by taking advantage of the demand and charging exorbitant prices. Bows, such as they sold at the Fort for twenty-five to fifty cents, brought one dollar and a half and two dollars quite readily. Ten cent arrows at the Fort were twenty-five cents at the levee, and two dollar strings of beads five dollars." These Indians, along with the last contingent scheduled for exile, were called "red christians."[65]

At Hannibal, Missouri, the Dakota on the *Northerner* disembarked and were loaded onto railroad cars and carried to St. Joseph. There they waited some days for the arrival of the *Davenport*. As Folwell noted, "There was not room enough for all to lie down at night and they were forced to sleep by relays." The weather was hot, and the rations of pork and hardtack were moldy. He continued, "The steamer laboring against the powerful current of the Missouri did not reach its destination until May 30. As a result of that 'middle passage' the hills about Crow Creek were soon covered with graves."[66]

Those Indians who survived the trip grew hostile toward the authorities, reflected in a dispatch requesting immediate reinforcements to "meet the threatened Indian troubles." Several of the Indians had pitched their camps within the grounds of the fort and "insolently" defied the troops to remove them. As the *Daily Press* reported, "It should be borne in mind that these are the Indians who were so 'good' and humble when surrounded by United States bayonets at Forts Snelling and Mankato. Their christianity needs the constant incentive of muskets, to make it efficacious for their salvation."[67]

Thus, some opinion makers viewed the policy of removal as a more humane solution than extermination to the so-called Indian problem. Minnesota, rid at last of its Dakota inhabitants, and reasonably certain the Ojibwe would remain far away in the northern woods, could now pursue its quest to be the white farm state it was destined to be. The focus of Minnesotans could now return to preserving the Union.

Despite deeply rooted animosity toward the Dakota and widespread suspicion of Indians in general, Indian suffrage survived as a constitutional right. Meanwhile, the politically dominant state Republican Party, in full support of a Republican president in a war effort that evolved into a crusade against slavery, chose not to extend the same rights to a class of people whose condition was largely the basis for its founding.

8

Trouble on the Levee

ON AUGUST 22, 1862, President Abraham Lincoln wrote: "My paramount object in this struggle is to save the Union, and is not either to save or destroy Slavery. If I could save the Union without freeing any slave, I would do it; and if I could save it by freeing all the slaves, I would do it; and if I could do it by freeing some and leaving others alone, I would also do that."[1]

Complicated by the monumental task of waging a victorious war was the cumbersome task of preserving unity within the increasingly fractious North. Unimpressed with lofty notions of national unity, the members of poor white and ethnic communities who filled the ranks of the labor class saw freed slaves as a direct threat to their livelihood and the conflict as "a war for the nigger." Others, like segments of the sizable merchant community of New York City, who viewed their commercial interests as interwoven with Southern trade, called outright for secession as early as 1860 and continued their campaign well into 1864. But so far these rumblings were rhetorical, localized, and relegated to fringe elements; acceding to them would make the dissolution of the Union inevitable. Lincoln performed a delicate balancing act on an ever-narrowing fulcrum of moderation.[2]

The steady attrition of Lincoln's armies, which had seen more losses than victories, forced him, even while mindful of his critics, to abandon his moderate stance as he focused on defeating the Confederates: it was all-out war. Wanting an army that wanted to fight—the enlistment of dissenting civilians might undermine military capability—Lincoln realized that freeing slaves had strategic value. He seemed to take to heart the sentiments of abolitionist preacher Henry Ward Beecher: "Let our armies, as a 'military necessity' and strategical [sic] act, declare 'freedom' to all, and in a moment we will have an army of 4,000,000 human beings on our side—allies in every house and on every plantation. The enemy is demoralized. Panic sweeps through the Southern land. Here is a foe more dreadful than Northern armies." Simply put—an army of freed slaves could pose a threat to the rear flank of the rebels.[3]

But until the North won a decisive battle against Lee, it would remain a white man's war. Federal law had prohibited free blacks throughout the North from enlisting in federal and state militia units from the war's inception. In contrast, Indians and mixed bloods could and did enlist, as illustrated by Minnesota's Ninth Infantry, Company G, and the Renville Rangers. Free blacks were not yet a part of the larger military plan. In September 1862, following the Union army's repulse of Gen. Robert E. Lee at Antietam, Lincoln issued a preliminary proclamation of emancipation promising that on January 1, 1863, slaves in states still in rebellion should be "thenceforth and forever free." He promised that the army and navy would "recognize and maintain the freedom of such persons."[4]

"Thank God that the word of Freedom for the slave and salvation for our country has come at last," acclaimed Jane Grey Swisshelm, abolitionist editor of the *St. Cloud Democrat,* who also expressed wariness about fully trusting a president whose commitment to emancipation appeared as deep as expediency allowed. Most Minnesota politicians, however, shared her sentiment. Even conservative Democratic senator Henry Rice approved the president's proclamation, much to the consternation of his party's leadership in the state.[5]

On January 1, 1863, Lincoln issued the Emancipation Proclamation: "Upon this act, justified as a 'military necessity,' he invoked 'the considerate judgment of mankind and the gracious favor of Almighty God.'" But the proclamation applied only to those slaves in rebel states, excluding those who lived in parts of Virginia and Louisiana as well as other slaveholding areas then under federal control. In 1863, although it was the site of unrelenting guerilla activity by proslavery forces, Missouri nonetheless stood under the Union banner. Accordingly, emancipation did not extend to slaves there. But to certain Missouri slaves the legalism was nothing more than a distinction without a difference. For them the president had freed the slaves. They were now free to go wherever and do whatever they wished. Their desire, as free men and women, now superseded the president's wartime design.[6]

Robert Hickman was an unusual slave. Born in Missouri in 1831, this man of great physical strength, developed from years of working as a rail splitter, possessed intellectual talents impressing everyone who knew him, especially his master, who had permitted him to learn to read and write as well as to acquire a license to preach the gospel. Hickman showed leadership qualities that most other slave masters would have viewed as a threat. Hickman remained through most of his life in the same master's service; he was a valued slave. Hickman was also strong willed. Despite warnings from his master, he often stole away to visit his family working on a neighboring plantation. Upon being returned after one such venture, he was restrained by four men and beaten by the overseer. That did little to discourage him from pursuing his ultimate goal— escaping with his family to free soil. Inspired both by the exodus of self-emancipating African Americans crossing into Iowa and the desire to assert a right that the president of the United States now acknowledged was his, Robert Hickman made plans to leave.[7]

With fellow slaves from the Boone County plantation, Hickman worked nightly to construct a river raft. Traveling by water to the promised land, rather than going overland where there was always the chance of capture by proslavery guerillas, increased their odds of success. Moreover, by 1863 the Mississippi River, which Northern steamboats frequently traveled to connect St. Louis to ports upriver, was under Union control. The raft offered their best chance for freedom.[8]

Upon the raft's completion on or about May 3, Hickman and the men of the group gathered their families—forty men, ten women, and twenty-six children—and set out on the river. On a moonless night they crowded with simple provisions onto the raft to depart. But Hickman and the others had failed to equip the raft with oars, sails, or any device that could propel them northward, and the raft simply drifted on the black waters of the Mississippi.[9]

On the following day a steamboat carrying mules and wagons for the government churned northward from St. Louis to St. Paul. Somewhere in the vicinity of Jefferson, Missouri, the *Northerner,* owned by the Galena Packet Company and commanded by Capt. Alford J. Woods, came upon the strange craft and its occupants, drifting helplessly in the center of the wide Mississippi. Hickman explained to the captain that he and his followers wanted to go north where they could live and work as free men and women. Whether the captain's next action was primarily motivated by humanitarian impulse or by the knowledge that his employer wanted to bring "contraband" to Minnesota to address the severe labor shortage remains uncertain.[10]

In any event, Captain Woods ordered that the raft be tied by a strong cable to his boat and towed the floundering raft northward to his home port. Neither the captain and his crew nor Robert Hickman and his followers anticipated the reception they would receive at the levee in St. Paul's Lowertown.[11]

On May 5 the *Northerner,* with the raft of black passengers in tow, approached the levee in Lowertown. A crowd gathered and grew restless and then boisterous as it became apparent who the new arrivals were. Men in the crowd—primarily Irish laborers—became so threatening that Captain Woods ordered the *Northerner* to bypass St. Paul and steam upstream to Fort Snelling, thus relieving city authorities of the need to appease the mob. As a Republican newspaper, the *St. Paul Daily Press,* reported: "The police were very much alarmed at the appearance of such a thunder cloud, and thinking they were to be landed here, proposed to prevent it on the ground that they [Hickman and his followers] were paupers. The Irish on the levee were considerably excited, and admitted by their actions that the negro was their rival, and that they fear he will outstrip them. On finding [the Negroes] were bound for the Fort, [the Irish laborers] resumed their whiskey and punches with great equanimity."[12]

On its face the reception of the *Northerner* was peculiar. First, in an effort to contain the disturbance, the police seemed intent on arresting the blacks whose presence incited the troublemakers instead of arresting the troublemakers themselves. This stance was not uncharacteristic of mob containment in Northern cities; blacks typically were arrested while being assaulted by antiblack mobs. In other instances, and equally commonplace throughout the antebellum North, police simply permitted riots to run their course provided they could be contained in poor communities.[13]

By the spring of 1863, the labor shortage in Minnesota had become acute. The war effort had drawn many of Minnesota's men to military service in the Civil and Dakota Wars. Thus farmers were forced to reduce the acreage under cultivation because of the difficulty of planting, harvesting, and transporting their produce without help. The *St. Paul Daily Press* reported: "Since the absorption of so much of the laboring class in the army, many of our farmers have found it necessary to reduce the quantity of land under tillage from the sheer want of putting in their usual crops, and even then, much of it has gone to waste from the deficiency of help at harvest time."[14]

The federal troops at Fort Snelling were also under severe pressure. In an effort to free soldiers for other military activities, General Sibley contracted for contrabands to be brought from St. Louis for work under federal supervision. Contrabands also could alleviate the labor shortage in the private sector. Although Hickman did not know about Sibley's desire for contraband labor, he probably would have welcomed it: work meant opportunity.[15]

Regardless of the obvious shortage, state legislators and opinion makers from St. Paul condemned the enterprise, for, they argued, the Mississippi would become a conduit for blacks and mulattoes streaming northward, bringing unfair competition for jobs normally filled by poor white laborers. This was their stance as early as 1854.[16]

The concern revived in 1859 when legislators introduced a bill to prevent the migration of free blacks and mulattoes into the state and require the registration of those already in residence. Like their predecessors, these legislators insisted that blacks would compete for jobs customarily held by poor whites, thus denying that class of citizens a livelihood. Moreover, whites unwilling to work with blacks might resort to violence. At worst, the legislators argued, black people would become paupers and wards of the state.[17]

As late as February 1863, citizens opposed to the use of contraband labor were circulating petitions on the streets of St. Paul requesting that the legislature again consider the issue. Even persons sympathetic to the black migrants wondered out loud about the efficacy of Sibley's plan. Under the heading "What Will He Do with Them?" the liberal editor of the *St. Paul Daily Press* wrote:

> General Sibley sometime since made arrangements to have some contraband sent up from St. Louis for teamsters. The first installment made their appearance on a barge that was brought up by the Northerner yesterday. . . . This was rather more than was bargained for, and the question arises, what will be done with them? Women and pickaninnies will not render material assistance in driving mule teams over the plain, and they would probably show very large whites of their eyes on such an occasion. We presume they will be left to garrison the Fort, while the head of the family goes roaming among the mules.[18]

Despite the vast acreage in the state to be tilled, black labor seemed of uncertain value rather than an answer to an agricultural need. This is on first impression quite odd, considering that most freed slaves and fugitives—men, women, and children—who came to Minnesota had been field hands on Southern plantations.

In contrast, white settlers intent on farming, and having the resources to do so, were well received. The state's population surged from 172,023 in 1860 to 250,099 in 1865, an increase of 45 percent. Minnesotans seemed to welcome the new arrivals, both American- and foreign-born. The *Daily Press* reported on May 9:

> We record with much satisfaction an unmistakable increase of immigration to this state. For a number of days we have observed, on the landing of the packet boats here, an unusual number of passengers on board, and on enquiring of the clerks, have been informed, in each instance that they travel upwards with larger passenger lists than for two or three years past. . . . The class of immigrants is another gratifying circumstance. They are nearly all agricultural and are all of a solid, intelligent and well-to-do class, who will make good settlers. Nearly every family has its horses, cows, etc, and have [*sic*] evidently "come to stay." The proportion of children is

unusually great. . . . On a recent trip the McLellan left La Crosse with 98 bright-eyed little boys and girls, to become the future legislators, farmers, and merchants of Minnesota.[19]

Three days after the *Northerner* arrived at St. Paul, the *Daily Press* pronounced the arrival of a large contingent of "Hollanders" (meaning Germans) as laudable as that of the earlier group of immigrants, for they, too, were a "hearty and industrious looking people," likewise in possession of farming implements, household gear, "and plenty of money—regular 'shiners' too, and nothing else." Possessing their own equipment and money distinguished these European settlers from the new black arrivals, for the Hollanders would be self-employed while the penniless, low-skilled former slaves could only be employed by others.[20]

Key to understanding the racial tension reflected on the levee is that the prejudices and interests of "a number of gentlemen of this city" ran counter to the prejudices and interests of the mob, for whom the lowest of menial tasks provided the only means of work. The "gentlemen," many of whom employed Irish laborers, were numerically in the minority, and their hold on city matters was distinctly tenuous because the political voice of the city was fast developing a brogue.

As the majority of St. Paul residents—which had maintained a solid antiblack Democratic lock on city hall—and the legislative delegation clamored for a restrictive black immigration law, "intelligent farmers" and the city's gentleman class argued that the importation of five or ten thousand blacks would be a great advantage to the state. "We happen to know," wrote one opinion maker, "that in agricultural occupations, as indeed in many others, hired negro labor is, on the whole, more efficient, and more tractable and docile, than the class of white labor which is usually available for such purposes."[21]

In this context the "white labor" deemed to be less efficient were the "low Irish." The *Daily Press* observed:

This fact, which is established by experience, is further corroborated by the testimony of our Celtic "hewers of wood and drawers of water," who, by the intense savage hostility which they have everywhere manifested to the introduction of negro labor, virtually confess their inability to compete with it in the lowest functions of industry, and thus frankly acknowledge themselves the inferiors of their Black competitors. . . . The negro contrabands, who have recently arrived here, furnished another proof of their superiority over their Kilkenny persecutors by the favorable contrast of their spirit, civil and inoffensive manners with the brutal insolence of the savages who assailed them with insults, and even bodily violence.[22]

Whoever provided the cheapest labor would get the work, and to the gentlemen of the city, "it was almost impossible to get respectable white servants now at any price." It is, therefore, understandable that St. Paul's white laborers—and Irish laborers in particular, the majority of whom were Democratic voters—felt a need to close ranks against the Republicans, the cursed abolitionists, the new black arrivals, and even some affluent fellow Democrats like Henry Sibley, who had been hailed by their Republican enemies for showing a "great deal of good sense" by bringing black contraband to the state.[23]

A year earlier the St. Paul and Galena Packet Company, along with the La Crosse Company, dispatched agents to St. Louis "to engage Negroes as deck hands on the steamboats" after their white deck hands struck for higher wages. Sibley, in addition to his other accomplishments, was a founder and director of the Galena Packet Company, which enjoyed government contracts and employed black strikebreakers. This was war, and it was being waged on two fronts—against the Confederacy in the South and the Dakota in Minnesota—and these hostilities compounded the need for steamboats carrying supplies for troops to operate unimpeded by aggrieved laborers. The financial vitality of St. Paul and the gentlemen of the city who benefited from it likewise depended on unhampered steamboat service.[24]

Indeed, prosecuting the war effort was steeped in duplicity. Sibley's plan to bring contraband labor to Minnesota, which relied on freeing slaves from the federally controlled state of Missouri, at least in spirit contravened the executive order of his commander in chief. At a time when work went to the labor force willing to accept

the lowest wage and skin color was irrelevant, at least where un-
skilled labor was concerned, all "gentlemen"—Republican and
Democrat alike—were capable of acting against the interests of
Irish laborers.[25]

To heighten tensions further, the Conscription Act, passed in
March 1863 by the congressional Republican majority in an effort
to bolster the flagging induction rate of volunteers for the army, exacerbated the sense of Irish subservience to black emancipation.
Under the act white males between the ages of twenty and thirty-
five and all unmarried white men between thirty-five and forty-five
were subject to the draft. But an explosive provision of the act permitted exemptions for draftees who presented an "acceptable sub-
stitute" or paid three hundred dollars, thereby shifting the burden
of service to poor white males. In cities with a large immigrant
underclass—New York, Philadelphia, and Boston, as well as St.
Paul—the act virtually forced the Irish to fight for the freedom of
the people they most despised and feared, and this circumstance
led them to riot in Northern cities.[26]

Anticonscription riots occurred in several states, marring the
jubilance of the Union victory at Gettysburg, reviving anti-Irish
sentiment, and prompting an outpouring of rage against the Irish
even more virulent than that displayed during the height of the
anti-Catholic, anti-immigrant, Know-Nothing movement. "Some
insisted," wrote historian Tyler Anbinder, "that once the North
subdued the Southern rebels it would have to subdue its Irish inhabitants, as well." While the Irish were deemed a menace, for they
rioted in a number of states, the cheap labor they provided made
them a necessary menace. Nonetheless, the riots themselves, man-
ifesting an ever deeper cleavage between classes, between native-
born and foreign-born Americans, between whites and blacks, intensified debate about declaring federal martial law to be
administered by an army that was largely Republican. The St. Paul
Irish laborers felt no differently, for later that summer their many
threats to resist the act compelled the state to post a provost guard
in the city for weeks.[27]

The cultural experience of Irish Americans faced an even

greater paradox. They knew of racial oppression as experienced in their own country, where many sympathized with American blacks and condemned American slavery. Yet they became, once settled in America, stridently antiblack. Ireland's Great Liberator, Daniel O'Connell, expressing frustration at learning that his fellow Irishmen in America had turned their backs on abolitionism, said that they had been changed by "something in the 'atmosphere' of America."[28]

There was something in the atmosphere, as illustrated by the incidents on the St. Paul levee on May 5 and one week later. On May 15, one day after the *Northerner* transported the "good" Indians past the levee, a second barge bringing freed slaves from St. Louis arrived in St. Paul, and the reaction of the mob meeting the transport was as threatening as before. The steamboat *Davenport,* escorted by chaplain J. D. White and a rather passive contingent of soldiers from Company C of the 37th Iowa Regiment, towed the newest black arrivals, numbering 218, to Fort Snelling, where they could safely disembark. In a newspaper account entitled "Insolent Nagurs," which dripped with sarcasm and mockery of the Irish yet foretold a new breed of black pride, the editor of the *Daily Press* wrote:

> On the last trip of the Davenport, a deck hand insulted one of the contraband women on board. Her husband overhearing the affair gave the brute a sound thrashing. Another deck hand sassed the colored steward of the boat, who had gone out to see what was the matter, when the latter polished him off in good style. These "nagurs" [sic] must be put down. What right have they to defend themselves from insult and abuse against the gentlemanly and intelligent deck hands and wharf rats who dislike them so? That's what's the matter, a brudder [sic] Bones says at the show.[29]

In the end high-minded citizens viewed Minnesota as the beneficiary of the newest arrivals. General Sibley received praise for his "best judgment for the good of the service in availing himself of the excellent quality of brawn and muscle which has been placed at his disposal in the persons of the numerous refugees from slavery." Farmers were to prosper with the "hired negro labor." One observer wrote:

It was impossible, for the impartial spectator, who witnessed the scenes on the levee . . . not to assign the negro to a higher type of civilization than the white barbarians who howled around them as if, like beasts of prey, they thirsted for their blood. . . .The people of the State are prepared to welcome a large accession of negroes to our laboring population; and unless there should be a great and rapid improvement in the manners and minds of the kind of people who now mainly monopolize the menial branches of industry and claim the monopoly by right of race and natural status—not even the rigorous laws of climate will be sufficient to withstand the more potential law of demand, or prevent such an influx of negro emigrants as may be necessary for the instruction and civilization of the now dominant element of our lowest laboring class.[30]

Minnesota's untilled fields awaited their arrival, their industry. But instead of bearing arms against the Southern armies as Lincoln had planned, harvesting Minnesota's crops as Sibley's Republican boosters had hoped, or even driving mules over the plains for the army as Sibley had desired, the greatest number of black emigrants remained in the city's poorest neighborhoods to create the newest underclass. Two days after the arrival of the *Davenport,* the Republican *Daily Press* ran the advertisement, "Colored Servants for Hire."[31]

While some of the black emigrants settled near the fort, where they found employment as teamsters and laborers, most looked beyond the trouble on St. Paul's levee to see the city as a place where they could realize their ambitions. One such man, coming to Minnesota as contraband, settled into his new St. Paul life, and he had a dream. Robert Hickman, with his followers, who took the name "Pilgrims," quietly labored to establish a church that would later evolve into a major institution of religious and civic activity in the city and a setting in which cultural identity could flourish. Still, their lives would not be easy.[32]

Throughout the spring of 1863, merchants watching the impact of the war on a changing economy from their shop windows could see the beginning of the end of the fur trade and, with it, much of their own businesses unless they adjusted to the new reality of an agricultural economy. By summer the only mixed bloods passing through St. Paul were captives being transported to Fort Snelling before being removed from the state altogether. Tensions among the white labor class were exacerbated when Robert Hickman and two steamboats of black contraband approached the levee, further agitating those who despised the handiwork of Lincoln's black Republicans.

It was true: Minnesota was Republican. But St. Paul had remained a Democrat stronghold. Loyal to the Union, St. Paul's residents nevertheless continued to elect entire Democratic slates to local office.[33]

And Democratic politics meant Democratic law. In February and March black men were arrested, tried, and fined for sleeping with white women. Which law had been violated was not clear. Nevertheless, the unapologetic double standard of prevailing social custom had been breached, and for this the black men and white women offenders deserved punishment. In the early days when Moccasin Democrats, many of whom had become civic, political, and business leaders, had sexual relations with Indian women, they were simply acting as prudent businessmen, solidifying their trade relationships with tribes. Now, when white women were arrested for having sex with black men, the Moccasins deferred to the social convention of the day, which considered these women racial traitors. The times were filled with moral duplicity.[34]

At the same time, sentiment against the Dakota in Minnesota was virtually universal, and it was no different in St. Paul. Many whites had personally experienced the trauma and savagery of the war or knew people who had. For those who did not, animosity toward the Dakota intensified because the fighting occurred during a time when the Union seemed most vulnerable to defeat and when Minnesotans were seeing their young men slaughtered on the battlefield on faraway battlefields in the South.

The blacks arriving in St. Paul in May 1863 shared none of these experiences. They had just slipped away from a lifetime of slavery and made it to the promised land. They had not seen threatening Indians as they steamed up the Mississippi. Only those who had known William Taylor and mourned his murder in the U.S.-Dakota

Conflict knew how dangerous and unpredictable the countryside could be. St. Paul was safer than where they had been.[35]

Yes, there was racism in the city, but the war kept slave catchers away, and the Dakota were now gone. The chief concern of black residents was to find a way to make a place in this new urban world and, in time, come to share the particular brand of Republican bias of their political patrons. The great abolitionist Frederick Douglass captured the new sentiment in a speech he delivered at the twenty-sixth annual meeting of the American Anti-Slavery Society, when he addressed the theme of acceptance and integration of the black man in America:

> The only reason why the Negro has not been killed off, as the Indians have been, is that he is so close under your arm that you cannot get at him. If we had set up a separate nationality, gone off on the outer borders of your civilization, right before your bayonets and swords, we should have been pushed off, precisely as the Indians have been pushed off. . . . The Negro is more like the white man than the Indian, in his tastes and tendencies, and disposition to accept civilization. . . . He loves you and remains with you, under all circumstances, in slavery and in freedom. You do not see him wearing a blanket, but coats cut in the latest European fashion.[36]

Whether the Indians to whom Douglass referred were good or bad was immaterial. His message was a justification of Republican patronage and a call for black aspiration.

9

In Relief of the Reproach of Unjust Discrimination

THE YEAR 1865 offered a tumultuous swirl of events. Four terrible years of civil war had come to a close. Abraham Lincoln was reelected president only to be assassinated a few months later. As Radical Republicans in Congress prepared to enact a series of reconstruction laws, they jousted with Lincoln's successor, Andrew Johnson of Tennessee, a Democrat and former slaveholder whose prickly temperament prompted fighting between the executive and legislative branches of the federal government. In a matter of months, Americans were faced with a new kind of uncertainty, and black Americans, though exhilarated by the end of slavery, waited to see whether freedom could be translated into full citizenship.[1]

The Republican Party of Minnesota was equally watchful. In 1866 the Republican-controlled state legislature adopted a series of resolutions expressing the belief "that Southern traitors, vanquished in arms, were still hostile." Thus the legislature demanded that freedom and civil rights be granted to all people, regardless of race, declaring that Minnesota would look to Congress for the true policy of Reconstruction.[2]

Not since Minnesota's constitutional convention in 1857 had black suffrage been seriously debated. Republicans, to the chagrin of many supporters, determined that joining the ranks of antislave states was of higher urgency. As the business of statehood grew more pressing and war seemed increasingly inevitable, Republican legislators, who by 1860 controlled both houses, were on a course of determined moderation, deferring neither to their abolitionist colleagues nor to promoters of trade with slaveholding visitors.[3]

After the United States finally declared war on the Southern states, holding together to preserve the union far overshadowed voting rights for the smallest handful of the state's residents. Like most Northerners, Minnesotans were not ready for the measure, and even the few Republicans who wanted to introduce the issue refrained from doing so to avoid alienating Northern Democrats, whose support was essential to the war effort.[4]

Not until 1865 did the Republicans bring the issue before the state. This time they were of one mind. In a vote strictly along party lines, Republicans in both houses of the legislature passed a bill that proposed a referendum to strike "white" from the suffrage provision. Despite strong opposition from the Democrats, the bill passed by a large margin.[5]

Charles Griswold, a clergyman from Winona County, was the prime mover and defender of the bill, leading an extensive petition campaign and introducing three petitions from Winona, Hastings, and Rochester favoring black suffrage. He was joined by F. M. Stowell, who submitted a petition of 150 residents from Anoka, and Charles Taylor, who presented a petition from Rice County.[6]

Most notably, however, on January 10 the House received a memorial signed by members of the Golden Key Club, a literary organization for black men in St. Paul. This action marked the first concerted effort by Minnesota's black population to secure its voting rights. R. T. Grey, M. Jernigan, and Ed James, three of the principal signers, would become officers in 1870 of the Sons of Freedom, Minnesota's first statewide black civil rights organization.[7]

With such support Griswold believed that the electorate was ready to pass a referendum for black suffrage during the November elections. In a speech delivered on the floor, he said, "The fortunate moment has arrived. If we do not improve it now, it may never come again."[8]

The Democrats then posed a new ploy: they proposed joining a woman's suffrage question with black suffrage, knowing that Democrats and Republicans alike would oppose it. J. M. Gilman of St. Paul recommended eliminating the word "male" from the constitution, arguing that the same reasons for advancing black suffrage applied to women as well—women paid taxes, obeyed laws, were as intelligent as blacks, and had fought for the Union by performing various services during the war. Supporters of black suffrage objected, insisting that the two questions be submitted

separately to voters. They also knew that women's suffrage was unpopular. Gilman's amendment was soundly defeated, 21–10, along
party lines. Gilman returned with a new amendment that limited
suffrage to those who could read and write, insisting that "ignorant voters" were becoming "the prey of politicians" and debasing
the ballot. Once again the Republicans defeated the measure.[9]

On February 7 the Republican-dominated House passed the
bill, 31–8, along party lines. Two weeks later, on February 21, under the leadership of Levi Nutting of Rice County, the Senate approved the bill, 16–4, along party lines. It was settled; the voters
would decide on black suffrage in November.[10]

With the black population of Minnesota only a fraction of 1 percent of the total population, the issue was one of principle, not political expediency. After the bill passed both houses, a delegation of
fourteen black men called on Nutting in his hotel room, presenting
him with a gold-headed cane in appreciation for his work. The
Chatfield Democrat distorted the style and substance of his remarks
of gratitude: "Udder states will, I doubt not, foller the scent of
Minnesota, and 'stend to all de poor white folks de same bribilege
dat you is goin' ti 'stend to the peoples of Minnesota as de nex' 'lec-
tion, and we will lib to see de day when da will be neiber white nor
black, but de beautiful yaller . . . cas da know how improbin it am
to misseginate wid de cullered folks."[11]

Through the summer the debate between Republicans and
Democrats grew more heated across the state. An increasing number of prosuffrage newspapers began linking voting rights to literacy, thus joining the significance of a good education with citizenship. By the time of the Republican conventions, however, the
papers joined their brethren in focusing exclusively on support for
black suffrage. The already strident Democratic press grew ugly
as it turned its campaign into a personal attack on Griswold. The
Mankato Weekly Record called him a "Negro at heart" and con-
tended that because he devoted "his exclusive time and talents to
legislating for the Negro, we shall not be surprised to learn . . .
that he has painted himself black and become a Negro. . . . [A]
change of skin color was all that was necessary to complete his
transformation."[12]

In all-out war, the Democrats exploited the deepest prejudices and fears—civil equality meant social equality, and that meant miscegenation. Three days after the Democratic convention, the *Chatfield Democrat* colorfully drew the connection:

> The people of this country should not deceive themselves in one of the most important issues now before them. Negro suffrage . . . means much more than the simple fact of conferring the right to voting upon the released slaves of the South, and their little less enlightened brethren of the North. [The intent] is to place them with you in the jury box, beside you at the table, along with you in bed, to make them your father-in-law, your brother-in-law, your son-in-law, your uncle, your aunt, your niece, your nephew, your equal in everything and your superior in patriotism, blackness and flavor.
>
> It don't [*sic*] mean that the privileges of Sambo are to cease when he shall march to the polls and offset your vote with his, but you must take him to your home, have your wife wait on him, let him kiss your sister, set up with your daughter, marry her if he wants her, and raise any number of tan-color grandchildren. You will be called on from the Congo as a candidate for Congress, the legislature, and all other offices of honor and profit.
>
> Negro suffrage is but a steping [*sic*] stone to universal equality in everything, even to the detestable and God-forbidden principle of miscegenation. In it is covered up all the hideousness of amalgamation. It is loaded with the footed breath of mongerlism [*sic*] and carries with it the putridity that will blot from earth the white race of this continent.[13]

Other papers published similar views—stories suggesting interracial rape was the logical product of black suffrage.[14]

Black performance during the war, argued editors, by no means earned them the ballot. Blacks, according to the *Chatfield Democrat,* had become soldiers "through compulsion . . . and could never be relied upon to bare their bosoms to the enemy's shot and shell, without being under the protection of gallant white men."[15]

In rejecting black suffrage, Americans were showing support for President Andrew Johnson, a fellow Democrat then enjoying the sentimentality of succession in the wake of the martyrdom of Abraham Lincoln.[16]

In rejecting black suffrage, Minnesotans were protecting the employment of white laborers.[17] Foreign-born voters would lose their influence on state government. The wishes of the heroic Civil War veterans, "none of whom supported black suffrage," would be repudiated. The assault only strengthened the resolve of such leading Republicans as Gen. Christopher C. Andrews, Congressman Ignatius Donnelly, outgoing governor Stephen Miller, and gubernatorial candidate William Marshall, a leader of the first gathering of Republicans in St. Anthony ten years earlier. Notably absent in their outward support, as noted by Chief Justice Salmon P. Chase, were Senator Alexander Ramsey and Congressman William Windom, and they were roundly criticized by party brethren.[18]

The time had come for the people to decide. By a vote of 14,651 to 12,138, the suffrage amendment failed. William Marshall easily won the governorship, and the entire Republican slate won its respective seats. But a majority of the people, quite simply, was not ready for the black men of Minnesota to enjoy what every white and mixed-blood man enjoyed.[19]

In January 1866 Republicans renewed their commitment to black suffrage. Republican legislator Stephen Hewson proposed a strategy to coordinate the amendment campaign statewide with local campaigns led by party leaders. The party's enthusiasm was, however, more tempered. In his inaugural address governor-elect Marshall declared that, while he was in favor of black suffrage and that public support for such an amendment had increased, he would let the legislature decide whether the time was right for the question to be submitted to the people. Outgoing governor Miller was even less supportive, urging the legislature to submit a qualified suffrage amendment enfranchising all males who could read and write, who held property valued at least at three hundred dollars, or who had received an honorable discharge from the U.S. Army.[20] The House Republicans voted 24-8, however, to kill a qualified suffrage amendment. According to one reporter, the 1865 defeat had dampened Republican resolve, and support of any form of universal suffrage might mean political suicide: "Some few of the men voted against the bill on the professed ground that the question of Negro suffrage, having been so recently decided against, it was not expedient to bring it up in any shape at present." The events in Washington also concerned them. President Johnson, having troubles with the Radical Republicans, was forming the Conservative Party, a coalition of Northern Democrats and conservative Republicans who strongly opposed black suffrage.[21]

Minnesota Republicans watched anxiously as some of their leaders—men like Senator Dan Norton and state attorney general William Colville—left their ranks to join the new party. Many other Republicans accepted endorsements from the Democratic Party in 1866. The Republican Party appeared to be on the verge of falling apart.[22]

Minnesota Republican support for black suffrage was at its lowest in 1866, revitalized only by the results of the national 1866 elections. Despite the president's strong efforts to campaign against the Radical Republicans, voters nationwide returned overwhelming Republican majorities to Congress in a clear repudiation of the president's policies. As a result many moderate Republicans began supporting radical efforts to enfranchise blacks in several locations. In January 1867 Congress enfranchised blacks residing in the District of Columbia as well as all federal territories and insisted that black suffrage be a requirement of statehood for Nebraska. In March, Congress required black suffrage as a condition for readmission for former Confederate states. Minnesota Republicans themselves experienced a splendid victory when they decisively won two congressional districts against candidates supporting President Johnson.[23]

The party acted with renewed vigor when Governor Marshall called for the legislature to submit a suffrage bill to the people. Representative B. F. Perry sponsored and guided a bill through the House and Senate, where it met virtually no resistance. Democratic opposition was weak and demoralized until October, when candidates and speakers began their attack. As in the 1865 campaign, they appealed to the same racial prejudices of foreign-born Minnesotans and laborers, shocking supporters with stories of rape and miscegenation, arguing that America belonged to the white man.[24]

Through it all the Republicans stepped up their campaign. This time, however, they strategically identified the amendment not expressly as a black suffrage amendment but cryptically as the "Amendment to section one (1), article seven (7) of the Constitution," evidently to avoid repelling unknowing, antisuffrage Republicans. The *St. Paul Daily Pioneer* described the provision's language as a "Republican sugar coat of the pill so that voters may not know its character" and an "elegant euphemism."[25]

In the end the referendum failed, but this time by a smaller margin. After losing by 2,513 votes among 26,789 cast in 1865, the proposal was defeated in 1867 by 1,298 votes among 56,220. Perhaps the most significant cause of the defeat, more than the "indifference and lukewarmness [*sic*] of [Republican] backsliders," was that the state central committee had failed until late into the campaign to direct county committees to place the question on the *general* Republican ballot. Consequently, the committees in key Republican counties, due to timidity, indifference, or "very general misunderstandings," placed the amendment on a separate ballot—overlooked or ignored by voters who otherwise supported the Republican ticket. "Thousands," reported the *St. Paul Daily Press,* "voted for the general and local tickets without thinking anything about the amendment, and so cast no vote on that question, or were confused by the multitude of amendments and cast no votes on them." It was a painful lesson to have lost by votes they could have won. The Republicans set their sights on 1868.[26]

On January 10, 1868, Governor Marshall fired the opening salvo in the new campaign for black suffrage in his annual message to the state House and Senate. In that speech, appealing heavily to the principle of Republican values, he argued that Minnesota was ready to support black suffrage. Referring to the election returns of 1865 and 1867, he insisted that public opposition had declined. The black man had served his country well and was being taxed without representation, and Republicans had a duty to protect the rights of oppressed people. His comments were warmly received.[27]

Three weeks later state senator Hanford L. Gordon, insisting that the denial of such a right would lead to a tyranny of the majority and class warfare, sponsored a bill to place black suffrage on the November ballot. He recommended that the amendment not be identified in arcane parliamentary language as it was in 1867.

Learning from the party's mistake in 1867, he proposed that the question be placed on the general Republican ticket rather than on a separate ballot. With a large Republican turnout expected for the presidential election, Gordon and his colleagues believed the provision would draw enough new votes to guarantee the amendment's success.[28]

Perhaps one of the most principled stances came from congressional candidate Morton S. Wilkinson, who, despite the possibility that his position could result in his defeat, insisted that black suffrage was more important than personal political gain. To him it was the duty of Minnesota Republicans "to work for it and talk for it, and urge your neighbors to vote for it." Other prominent Republican congressional candidates like Christopher C. Andrews agreed, insisting that his candidacy not be separated from the amendment: "I would rather be defeated a dozen times over than have the suffrage amendment lost." These leaders so intricately interwove their campaigns with the amendment that to vote for one was to vote for the other. The strategy succeeded. The amendment passed with a wide margin. In November more than 90 percent of votes cast for the Republicans supported the suffrage amendment.[29]

Minnesota's accomplishment preceded congressional ratification of the Fifteenth Amendment by two years. In 1870 outgoing governor Marshall sent a special message to the state legislature urging it to ratify promptly and unanimously the federal amendment, a request with which they complied.[30]

The Republican Party expected only strict adherence to moderation and decorum of the new black citizens, for Minnesota was in the business of promoting personal industry, and the black leaders of Minnesota were determined to show themselves worthy. If the inception of this new age can be demarcated in time, the conven-ing of the Colored Citizens of Minnesota meeting on January 1, 1869, was the marker, for there the emerging black political and social elite expressed party loyalty, created the first statewide civil rights organization, and displayed semblances of economic patronage. The concept of "civil rights" became increasingly and exclusively a matter of black-white race relations.

On Friday evening, November 13, a group of men prominent in St. Paul's burgeoning black community met in the room used for worship by the Pilgrim Baptist Society to discuss what manner of public demonstration could best commemorate the recent referendum extending voting rights to Minnesota's black men. After remarks from Maurice Jernigan, Robert Hickman, David Edwards, and Thomas Jackson, the group decided to plan for a mass convention to celebrate the victory and show gratitude to the politicians who had championed the cause. The group appointed a committee to make the necessary arrangements, selecting Jernigan, Jackson, and Williams, all of whom were from St. Paul, to lead it.[31]

After the meeting they joined Seibert's Band, which they had employed for the occasion, and, climbing into wagons and carriages, set off to serenade some of the Republican leaders who had championed their cause. They first stopped at Governor Marshall's home, where the band played the governor's favorite tunes. After brief speeches the governor invited the group inside, where he served them refreshments. The governor then requested that "one of the newly made voters" sing "Old Shady."[32]

Taking their leave, the men next visited the International Hotel, where Senator Morton Wilkinson was staying. Jackson stepped forward and expressed gratitude for Wilkinson's political courage, pledging loyalty to the Republican Party: "Though quite unpopular, the issue was manfully sustained. You took the ground at the risk of defeat, and maintained it until at last your efforts have been crowned with success; and to you we return our hearty thanks. We have long watched the efforts of our friends. We know them, and shall ever remember them. And to you, as one of the leaders of this great principle, we pledge to the party our hearty and undivided support. The battle has been fought. The victory is won, and to the victor belongs the spoils."[33]

In other words, black votes henceforth would be Republican votes. Indeed, included in their plans for the evening festivities of January 1 were efforts to restrict admission to "specific guests and colored folks," presumably, as the liberal editor of the *St. Paul Press* wrote, "to keep out Democratic ward politicians, for they would swarm among the new citizens in multitudes greater than the locusts to Egypt."[34]

Acknowledging their loyalty, Senator Wilkinson tied their victory to a moral victory for all Minnesotans: "It was not for you alone that I labored during long and weary years to produce this grand result. It was for humanity that we labored. Not for the American, nor the foreigner, nor the white, nor the black, but it was for man that this great battle was fought. The success has elevated the people of our State to a higher plane, and a loftier platform, than they ever occupied before."[35]

At this, the gathering gave three rousing cheers for the senator and then proceeded to visit, first, *Daily Press* publisher and editor Frederick Driscoll and, second, physician Jacob Stewart, mayor of St. Paul, who received them into his home for a buffet of refreshments. Again, Jackson spoke:

> We, your colored friends, have taken this occasion to call on you this evening, not as the mayor of the city, for that would not express to you our real feelings toward you; but as the friend of the oppressed; as the advocate of right against might. But more especially, have we come to give vent to our pent up feelings. . . . I must tell you sir, the wires and mails have [brought] us glorious and gratifying intelligence that at last the good people of Minnesota have granted manhood suffrage to the black man, have really taken it to their hearts to be just, to grant to the intelligent black man a right to vote for the assessor that places value on his property. As God created us all free and equal, it was a grievous wrong done to us in being burdened with all the venom of malicious cruelty and injustice. And why? Because our skin was a little darker. You must indeed, excuse us, sir, for taking this pilgrimage tonight to see you and shake the hand of an honest friend. We come, to be sure, with a shout and a noise, but as I said before, did we not open our mouths and pour out our soul this evening; we should have lost the opportunity of voting for you in the next Congressional election.[36]

The revelry at Stewart's home ended shortly after midnight, "with cheers for our worthy and liberal-hearted mayor."[37]

Five days later the committee convened to adopt a resolution calling for a state mass convention, assembling in St. Paul on January 1, 1869, the sixth anniversary of the Emancipation Proclamation and the freeing of four million slaves. Committee chairman Maurice Jernigan appointed subcommittees to organize the banquet and invitations. Meanwhile, as further inducement to attract a large gathering from around the state, the general committee requested that all railroads and stage lines running to St. Paul carry black people at half fare. The travelers would pay full fare coming but return home at no cost. A subcommittee rented Ingersoll and Odeon Halls for the occasion. Another invited Frederick Douglass to the meeting. The planners anticipated a crowd numbering between three hundred and five hundred people.[38]

On Thursday, December 31, the newly enfranchised citizens of Minnesota began to arrive in the city: "Every train and every stage during the day brought in small squads from different parts of the state; but with the evening trains came special cars from over the Hastings and Minnesota Valley and Central Roads, filled to overflowing." On January 1 the morning train on the Pacific Road, carrying residents from Minneapolis and St. Anthony, "brought down two well-filled cars."[39]

Minnesota's capital city, which had turned in the largest vote against black suffrage, found itself assembling the largest gathering of black Minnesotan voters ever. As the hour approached for the convention to begin, leaders of the movement met in the home of chairman Jernigan, where they spent the morning organizing the Sons of Freedom, later to become the first statewide civil rights organization. At about noon the leaders left for Ingersoll Hall.[40]

Inside the hall the growing numbers of attendees delighted in the display of flags and pictures of President Lincoln, generals Grant and Sheridan, abolitionists William Lloyd Garrison, Gerrit Smith, and Frederick Douglass, and others. Draped over the stage was a large banner emblazoned with the word "Emancipation." On the side of the stage hung one of the pikes used by John Brown at Harpers Ferry in West Virginia. The assembly was predominantly black, "a good size and respectable audience," and a large number of spectators also attended, among them several prominent Democratic politicians sitting in the back row. As more people entered the hall, the Great Western Band took position at the front of the gallery "and played several inspiring airs."[41]

At 12:45 PM chairman Jernigan called the convention to order, and secretary Thomas Jackson read the official call for the convention. Those attending sang the hymn "Freedom and Truth," with the band's accompaniment. Afterward the assembly selected permanent convention officers. Robert Banks of St. Paul, the sixty-two-year-old barber from Missouri who had served as the patriarch of St. Paul's black community, was unanimously elected president. On taking the chair, he spoke about the new nation born when black men were granted citizenship and, invoking the words of Daniel Webster, expressed hope that the day would come soon when "there should be no North, no South, no East, and no West; when all men shall have equal rights, and citizens of Minnesota or of Georgia, could each visit the other State, and all the States of the Union with the same rights as here at home." He then called on Reverend Robert Hickman to lead the audience in prayer.[42]

In his introductory remarks, which set the tone for the convention and voiced the aspirations of the new black citizenry, Banks enjoined his brethren "to be sober and orderly," for "they could not afford to be riotous." Banks admonished further: "They should read the papers—read both sides—and strive to be well-healed on national affairs. They should teach their children good manners, and to be respectful to old age. . . . [T]hese things would be a great help to them throughout life. They should keep out of debt: it was easy to get into debt, but hard to get out."[43]

According to the record of the *Proceedings,* Banks was even more definitive on the subject of politics:

> Let there be no resolution of a milk-and-water character: let there be no see-sawing; no compromise between the two parties. "Here," said the speaker, "is a man of whom you can say, 'Here is a genuine old Black Republican!'"[44]

This last remark drew great applause. When it died down, Banks told the story of noble former general Andrews, whom he praised as one of the heroes who had placed his political future at risk on behalf of the suffrage question and become a model for party leadership. After criticizing the Democrats, Banks challenged the party of Lincoln by saying, "Give us men to lead us! When you give us drunkards and gamblers and political shysters, I swear I'll desert!" Again, the convention erupted in applause.[45] He then called for the selection of officers and committees. The remaining officers elected were carefully chosen from communities throughout the state, although the larger number came from St. Paul, in consequence of the majority of blacks present being from the city. The convention then adopted the new constitution of the Sons of Freedom. The organization was to consist of the "colored men of the whole State," and no fees would be charged for membership. Its objectives were to help blacks in as many ways as possible, particularly in their jobs and trades, to keep population records of blacks both in and out of school, and to look after their personal property and real estate if necessary. After these formalities it was time for the speeches.[46]

The first to speak was the governor of Minnesota, William R. Marshall, who in a keynote address frequently interrupted by applause reminded the audience that, while more than seventy thousand voters went to the polls to resolve the issue of black suffrage, the forty thousand voters who supported the measure deserved the gratitude. He said:

> In the name of forty thousand free electors of this commonwealth, I welcome you to liberty and equality before the law. In the name of the State of Minnesota, which has relieved itself of the reproach of unjust discrimination against a class of its people, I welcome you to your political enfranchisement.
>
> By the voice of the people—in this case most truly the voice of God—you are endowed with the highest privileges of American citizenship. Your enfranchisement, by the voluntary act of those who before had the exclusive right to the ballot, is a great moral victory—a great triumph of Republican principles. It is the full embodiment in our laws of the great truths of American Independence, that all men are created free and equal, and that all just governments derive their power from the consent of the governed.[47]

Mayor Stewart then spoke, underscoring the duty that black voters had to support the Republican Party: "The same struggle that which triumphantly put General Grant in possession of the White House, put the Black Man in possession of the ballot. The same voice which said to the turbulent South—'Peace be still'—said to the Black Man who chooses to make his home in our towns and on our prairies—'Hereafter you may vote.'"[48]

Stewart chided the Democratic politicians seated in the rear of Ingersoll Hall: "There are those who denounced Negro suffrage, who have written against it, and resolved against it, and spoken against it; but the Republican party did not shrink from advocating it, even when, as the event proved, it was unpopular in its own ranks. There are those who have sought bitterly and strenuously and have fought to the very last to withhold Negro suffrage, but the Republican party have been just as determined to grant it, and *it has done it.*"[49]

Then he cautioned black voters to be suspicious of their new-found but false Democratic friends who would advise them in how to use the ballot:

> Those who never uttered any protests when the colored man was in bonds, but insisted that that was the right place for him; others who cried out in sorrow and stern denunciation when Abraham Lincoln went down and whispered "Freedom" in his listening ear—those who, after he was liberated, tried still to make him a mere menial and serf in a land of freeman—these will never weary of advising the colored man. Very high and pure too will be the standard of citizenship which they will hold up to his gaze. Very likely they will shut him out from the schools, but they will insist, with pathetic emotion, that he is intelligent, and if, perchance, a colored man is found who couldn't read his vote, what a hue and cry would be raised. Very likely it would be but a sorry provision of straw which they will help to furnish in the way of openings and opportunities for work; but they will not fail to exact the full tale of bricks; and if, perchance, a colored man should happen to be found indulging in idleness, what holy horror would be expressed, and what lugubrious essays there would be on the sin of *colored idleness!*[50]

Pointing to the hypocrisy of Democratic politicians, he added:

Very likely their own habits would keep them from exposing a great amount of whiskey with which to tempt colored men into drunkenness; but if, perchance, a colored man should happen to be seen reeling up and down the streets, what gallons and gallons of cold water would be poured on the poor fellow's head in the way of touching temperance lectures! And when a colored man breaks the law and commits a crime, into what agony of emphasis will the types swell that he and all the world may see how much worse it is in him to lie and steal, and rob and murder, than for others![51]

These Democratic friends, Stewart warned, might even feign such an interest in the colored man and become so solicitous for his welfare as to occasionally set him up for office—but without the true powers of office.[52]

After the mayor spoke the audience called for state senator Nutting. Noticing that the Committee on Resolutions had just entered the room, the former state senator from Rice County, who in 1865 had spearheaded the suffrage campaign through the legislature, reluctantly approached the podium, promising to keep short his remarks and calling on this audience to vote with conscientiousness rather than from Republican loyalty. He reminded the audience of so-called recent converts to black suffrage whose interests were surely contrary to their own. They would find plenty of men ready to tell them how to vote; a leading paper opposed them and that same morning had changed its tone so as to speak of them as "our colored fellow citizens."[53]

When the crowd began shouting the name of the offending newspaper— *"Pioneer! Pioneer! Pioneer!"*—Nutting quieted them: "Probably, they will be claiming you as blood relations before the spring elections."[54]

Nutting concluded by observing that a good deal of advice would be given—he would only say, "Vote justly, vote rightly." They should vote for the Republican Party if they thought that was right, which prompted a cheer, but they should not degrade themselves by forming a colored man's party. They were American citizens, a statement that again drew cheers, and they should vote as such without regard to color or position.[55]

The extended cheers for Nutting as he returned to his seat portrayed a gathering, however, that had committed itself to one political party. And in one of its resolutions, the convention expressly committed black loyalty to the Republican Party:

> *Resolved*, The Republican Party is due our grateful acknowledgement for the many and diverse changes in our condition, from the hound-hunted species of property, who for nearly a century had no rights which a white man, possessing the same physical nature, the same gift of the Five Senses, the same love and affection, was bound to respect; for giving to brutalized, skin-browned man his rights to life, liberty and the pursuit of happiness; and we pledge to that party, as a unit, as long as it shall maintain honest men and honest measures, our hearty support.[56]

Two additional resolutions pledged "reverence and gratitude to the memory" of Abraham Lincoln and "valor, fidelity and privations of the Union army and navy, who, had they not been successful in overthrowing the most gigantic rebellion ever inaugurated, would have found us today the helpless and unprotected victims" of the slaveholding Confederacy.[57]

The fourth and final resolution called upon Minnesota's black population to ensure quality education for their children:

> *Resolved*, That we enjoin upon all colored citizens, with especial solicitude, to foster and encourage those moral duties which build up such traits of character as integrity, wealth and intellectual culture. The liberality with which the State has placed the means of acquiring an education within the reach of all, makes it our bounden duty to keep our youths in regular attendance in the public schools. A neglect of this amounts to a crime. The necessity of it must be apparent. Republican institutions lose all hopes of perpetuity where ignorance prevails among the people. It thus becomes us to give to the cause of education all the encouragement of which we are capable. We must educate—EDUCATE—our youth, if we expect them to possess these fine distinctions of mind and character arising from a well-cultured and firmly adjusted moral nature, and make them what an American citizen should be.[58]

At 4:00 PM the convention adjourned. It reconvened at seven that evening when "the floor of the hall and gallery was both densely packed, a large number of white people being present." Chairman Banks introduced Reverend A. H. Paterson of St. Paul's Episcopal Church to lead the audience in prayer and song. Convention secretary Jackson read congratulatory letters from Gen. Christopher C. Andrews and Representative Charles Griswold, both of whom had labored to place the suffrage question before the voters. The convention again sang "Freedom and Truth," after which the speakers of the evening—Senator Morton S. Wilkinson and Congressman Ignatius Donnelly—were introduced.[59]

The senator, who in 1868 tied his election prospects to passage of the suffrage referendum, joined previous speakers in reminding the assembly of the great sacrifices that early abolitionists endured in behalf of black freedom. Then he shifted his message to the political accomplishment recently achieved by the black people of Minnesota and prescribed their duty to attain complete freedom. Only the black people themselves could achieve social and economic equality. The only impediment was their resolve:

> So far as Minnesota is concerned, we have done our part in the enfranchisement of the colored race. The solution of that question remains with you. It has been said that the white race were the dominant race of the world, and with some degree of truth. The white race have been dominant, and the solution of that is to be found in the single word WORK.
>
> The right of the franchise cannot elevate you to respectability among men. If you would be respected in the sight of the nation, you must work; if you will be respected by good man, you must hew out your own fortunes. . . . [Cheers.]
>
> You must carve your way through the solid rock, as the Caucasian has done, and rise to be dominant among the nations of the earth. It is work that will do it. Do not be content to be barbers and porters in hotels, but be men, hard-handed, laborious men. It was for such men that the homestead was passed.[60]

Wilkinson's prescription lay in agricultural redemption, not the occupations to which blacks had been limited, not the profession of barbering, in particular, that had allowed blacks—many of them seated before him—to acquire a toehold in the urban Minnesota economy. Barbering had given most of the black leadership their contact with Minnesota's power elite. Wilkinson's sentiment did not apparently dampen the mood of the assembly, for they cheered his next comment:

> When I first went to Congress, in 1860, there was an administration in power which I thank God, soon went out which allowed no place for you in the Homestead law; no homestead for the black man; but through the influence of some of those heroes who rules the hour, this distinction was wiped out, and now there are homes and homesteads for you and your children, as well as for me and my children. . . .
>
> Now, my fellow citizens, I hope you will take these things into consideration, teach your sons that this broad domain is for you, as well as for the white man; make your children mechanics, make them blacksmiths, make them home builders, make them stone masons—and be assured that through labor, and *through labor alone*, you are to be honored and respected among men.[61]

Senator Wilkinson had prescribed the agenda later espoused by the great Negro leader Booker T. Washington, who championed education and training, emphasizing mechanic over liberal arts.

After a prolonged cheer the senator concluded his remarks, having planted the notion that the city of residence for the large majority of those seated in the hall could never be a place where they could view their neighbors as allies. His words served as an invitation for them to relocate to the farmlands of Minnesota, where they would be among friends, or to rely on those friends for political support. If the majority in this city was against you, then grand agricultural people were for you.[62]

Over the next two decades the clarity of alliance dimmed, for as laws enacted by the Republican-controlled legislature strengthened banking, milling, and railroad interests against those of the farmer, the interests of Minnesota's black community increasingly centered on the political, legal, social, and business matters of the urban experience. Nonetheless, the principles of hard work and industry associated with farming were the same by which black people would be judged.

"Your race is on trial in this country," said Ignatius Donnelly, speaking next: "*On trial,* I say, at the bar of public judgment. The eyes of the American people are upon you. Every step you take is marked. You cannot, any of you, degrade yourselves without degrading your race! . . . The white people of this country watch you with varied emotions and ask, 'What will this people do? Will they work out an honorable destiny among the nations of the earth?' I feel you will."[63]

Donnelly explained that the black race could survive as a people even though other races had disappeared because of their intimate contact with white people:

> I recollect, my friends, that you are the only race on this earth that ever came in close and intimate contact with the white race, and did not perish before it. See how the Finnic [*sic*] people disappeared from the face of Europe. Once it occupied the continent; now it is found only upon the remote capes vastnesses of the North—in broken fragments of Lapland tribes. As they came in contact with the white man they disappeared. Look at the Indian of our own country. As the white man advances, the Indian perishes. He is rapidly becoming like the deer and the bison, a thing of the past—fast disappearing from the face of the earth. Why! Because he has not the *civilizable characteristics of the colored man.*[64]

To Donnelly patience was one of the black man's most "civilizable" characteristics: "The eloquent gentleman who preceded me said that the basis of civilization was work, patient work, patient industry. He was right. Men have mocked you because you have been so docile, so patient, so long suffering, so long enduring under all oppression. It is not a proper subject for jeers and mockery. I am proud of it. . . . Those men who would mock you for your patient virtues, forget that the endurance of suffering is the highest evidence of manhood."[65]

He then focused on the final most important endeavor toward ultimate equality:

> My friends, in the future as in the past, be patient, be forbearing, be gentle, be peaceful, be industrious. . . . Seek every opportunity for education. . . .
>
> Do all you can to give a thorough education to your children, and if any one of the children of your race shows a special aptitude in any one direction press him forward in the race of life. If your people will produce a single Shakespeare or a Burke, it will stand redeemed in the judgment of mankind.[66]

The political sentiment of the convention—from the introductory remarks of convention president Banks to Donnelly's final speech—was decidedly pro-Republican, and the victory for black suffrage was a victory for the Republican Party.

The convention served several functions. First, it provided a political show-of-force to the Democrats, displaying a union between the state's newest voters and the state's predominant political party. That the convention occurred in St. Paul was logical, since the city was the capital of "free, young, noble Minnesota," as well as the site of the largest concentration of black residents. But the irony of holding such a meeting in the city where, as Senator Wilkinson said, "the majority was against you" could not have been lost to anyone present.[67]

Notwithstanding the Republican mayor at the time, St. Paul remained the stronghold of the Democratic Party, as it had been since territorial days. Its legislative representatives had routinely argued against black suffrage since 1849, promoting a "Black Code" in 1854 intended to discourage black settlement. Throughout the 1850s and 1860s, the white population was increasingly foreign born, filling the ranks of the least skilled and least assimilated peoples of the city. The poor whites saw black people as their most dangerous socioeconomic rivals. Poor whites became a considerable political force in the city.[68]

After 1865 the growing black population was increasingly restricted to residence in the Lowertown neighborhood, owing to antiblack sentiment throughout the city, thereby minimizing the prospect of acculturation of former Southern slaves, who were increasingly the newest black arrivals. Holding a convention in St. Paul that commemorated the emancipation of slaves and the enfranchisement of black men was a celebration against the convention of St. Paul antiblack sentiment. "Aye, my friends," Congressman Donnelly said, "we live in a glorious and wonderful age."[69]

The convention also showcased the "civilizable" attributes of Minnesota's black people. The liberal *St. Paul Daily Press* depicted the Southern freedmen arriving in the state: "They are among the most industrious, useful, and well-behaved of our citizens and a large proportion of them are highly intelligent. It is safe to say that in every moral and intellectual qualification for exercising every right of citizenship, they are as a class superior to the large majority of those who compose the Democratic Party in this State."[70]

But the greater number of white people, as Donnelly had stated, would watch the new voters "with varied emotions" and wonder how black people would comport themselves while participating in the governance of the state. The colored race was indeed on trial. The success of the convention presented the best opportunity to assuage concerns by showing that black citizens could be as responsible as their white compatriots. News reports, therefore, became crucial. The Republican and Democratic press alike commented positively on the event. The *Daily Press* reported:

> The meeting was in every respect a great success. It was characterized by great earnestness and unbounded enthusiasm, and at the same time with a degree of order, harmony, and an exhibition of parliamentary knowledge . . . and also by a universal courtesy and sobriety, from which the Democratic demagogues who have been so loud in denouncing the ignorance of the negro, may well take lessons in conducting their own meetings.
>
> Indeed, even the anticipations of the warmest friends and advocates of the rights of our colored citizens were more than satisfied with the good order, sober earnestness, harmony, courtesy, sterling good sense, wisdom and appreciation of the demand of the hour, manifested throughout the Convention.[71]

Even the *St. Paul Weekly Pioneer,* which had campaigned against black suffrage, commented positively about the blacks present: "The colored people filled their part well. They did all things decently and in order. They were temperate, considerate, and high-toned, and gave, throughout their proceedings, many evidences that they are worthy of the possession of their new rights and franchises."[72]

After noting that black enfranchisement in state and local elections was ultimately inconsequential, the paper turned its wrath against the "white trash" and "political shysters" who spoke to the assembly. The *Pioneer* reported: "The display of the piddling politicians [white] who assumed all the glory of the movement, and claimed to be its authors, were contemptible in the extreme. . . .

They extorted, now and then, a laugh, and procured a noisy applause from their susceptible auditors, and they cracked their whips over the newly made voters, dictating to them what should be their future political actions."[73]

Intending to compliment the black leadership of the convention, the *Pioneer* reported that President Banks, "the venerable colored chairman of the meeting," accused the Republican Party of "uncommon demagoguery" instead of challenging it, as he had, to continue providing good leadership: "There was not a sensible negro in the audience who believed the balderdash of Donnelly, that the black race was superior, originally, to the whites. [White speakers] insulted the good sense, and all the ideas of common decency that are cherished by both races, in partisan zeal, smutty jokes, and bad stump oratory."[74]

The message to St. Paul's Democratic readership was both partisan and clear: white Republican leaders, who had real political power, were the enemy—not the new black voters, whose electoral power was negligible, albeit potentially useful. Perhaps in time even these citizens could be brought within the Democratic fold. The *Minneapolis Tribune* characterized black voters as no different from white:

> The gathering of our recently enfranchised citizens was in every respect a most credible affair. There was nothing in about the proceedings to distinguish it from a convention of intelligent white men. . . . There is, in fact, nothing to distinguish the colored voters of Minnesota from the average white voters except the color of their skins. If there be among them who lack education or are deficient in natural intelligence, they can be easily matched by white men of equal ignorance or stupidity. Human nature is human nature, under whatever outward semblance that exists, and the differences between men are, after all, more attributable to circumstances and associations than to natural distinction.[75]

To the extent that success meant positive press coverage, the convention was successful.

The convention was a joyful expression of freedom and equality, but it was also an occasion upon which black citizenship was explained to Minnesota as the embodiment of opportunity for the improvement of a sober, patient, and hard-working people, determined to contribute to the commonwealth through the development of farming skills and the mechanic arts. The portraits of generals Grant and Sherman and President Lincoln gracing Ingersoll Hall suggested that black citizenship vindicated the noble sacrifice of Minnesota's fathers and sons who had fought in the war. The advent of black citizenship made Minnesota as great as the everlasting promise on which the nation was founded and enhanced a sense of regional pride.

As Mayor Stewart had said: "It ought to heighten the satisfaction we feel today to remember that that same November hour which put the ballot into the hand of the negro in Minnesota, armed him with the same potent weapon of self-defense and freedom in our sister State of Iowa. By judicial decision it was already his in Wisconsin. So that henceforth the great Northwest is to stand a solid unit for human rights."[76]

As evidenced by his "civilizable" character, the black citizen was also superior to other racial and ethnic peoples who had not succeeded in acculturating themselves to an Anglo-American Protestant ethic. He was superior to Indians because he was a Christian and superior to Catholics because he was a Protestant. Thus the black citizen was more like the growing population of hearty Anglo-American and northern European settlers who made the state their home—*he* but for the color of his skin was *us*.

Unshackled by "the reproach of unjust discrimination," the black citizen now was free to be self-sufficient, a threat to no one but a master, nonetheless, of his own fate. Such a man could only contribute to the bright future of Minnesota. All that remained to make this so was to improve his education and the education of his children. As the last adopted resolution of that convention read: "Republican institutions lose all hopes of perpetuity where ignorance prevails among the people." Laws that relegated black children to an inadequate education must be abolished. Ignatius Donnelly had given the most prominent voice to his party's next critical initiative.[77]

10

The Attainable Destiny

ON OCTOBER 4, 1864, a "wild Irishman" named Cooney stormed into the Walnut Street School, and upon seeing a black child in the classroom, "his virtuous indignation boiled over," ranting that his children were not going to school with "naygurs . . . he'd be 'domned' if they should." The teacher summoned a policeman to escort Cooney away.[1]

The *Daily Press* reported: "If he had behaved himself he would not have been arrested, but he had 'naygur' on the brain so bad that the Captain pronounced him his prisoner, to which he demurred quite forcibly, but was brought to his sense by a slight compression of the windpipe. At the City Hall his pocketbook was compressed to the amount of $15, and now we suppose he won't be appeased until he has murdered some 'domned naygur.'"[2]

Such was the state of race and education in St. Paul schools in 1864. From 1857 the school board had attempted to segregate black children from the larger student population, but the high cost of the Civil War and the Dakota War made sustaining a black-only school impossible. In fact, acting on their own, some teachers—like the one who in 1859 taught a child who was one-quarter black in her class against the wishes of Supt. Benjamin Drew—allowed black children into their classrooms, ignoring the mandates of the school board. This was the situation Cooney found at the Walnut Street School.

In any event, in October 1864 the school board, just a day before Cooney's tirade, reaffirmed its commitment to segregate black children for the remainder of the school year with whatever resources it saw fit to invest, deferring, no doubt, to constituents like Cooney who saw black adults as a threat to themselves and black children as a threat to their future. The board had noted at its meeting that seventeen black children were attending the school in the Adams Division, "and many [white] parents were taking away their children on that account. It also led to difficulty between the white and black children." Something had to be done. Over the objection of Supt. Brewer Mattocks, the board resolved to segregate black children by establishing for them a separate school.[3]

By the end of the school year, black parents were growing frustrated at the abysmal conditions of the black-only school. Finally, on August 10, 1865, a group of black veterans who had served in units of the U.S. Colored Infantry published in the *Daily Press* a pointed, strongly worded petition criticizing the St. Paul school board and its chairman, Col. Daniel Robertson, for the appalling quality of education that the city offered to black children and the consequent exclusion of "their black children from public schools." How many signed the petition is unknown, but explicit in their demand was the assertion that as self-sacrificing veterans of the war for freedom, they were prepared to withhold their payment of school taxes "upon the twelve or thirteen thousand dollars worth of real and personal property held by us in the city."[4]

Despite the petition, in October 1865 the public received official notice that a "School for Colored Children" would open in Morrison's Building at Ninth and Jackson Streets in St. Paul. A Miss Morrow would receive a monthly salary of thirty-five dollars to teach the classes. According to the board's report, forty-five black school-age youth resided in St. Paul at the beginning of the academic year of 1865–66. On average twenty students attended classes. Soon after classes began, the board of education discovered "problems of maintaining and operating" the school. Not until two years later did the superintendent of schools announce that "the colored school will not be opened until further notice."[5]

But in 1865 the *St. Paul Daily Pioneer* called for improvement to the colored school: "Some more comfortable place should be provided than the building at present occupied, and it seems to us that a small expense might very properly be incurred in furnishing *this school* with a few maps and other pieces of furniture, similar to that which is provided for the white schools. . . . The windows would not lose anything by being filled with glass instead of pine boards. We hope that those whose duty it is to tend to these matters will visit the school, if they have not done so already, and remedy the evils complained of." The plea fell on deaf ears, and the school limped on until 1868 despite dim lighting and decreasing attendance.[6]

In contrast, by 1865 white students attended three elementary schools, each valued at more than eight thousand dollars, a respectable sum for a publicly built facility. And in 1865 a new school—Franklin Elementary—was constructed at a cost of $16,969.65, which included "the site, furniture, fence and outbuildings" and eighteen classrooms. Its enrollment was 2,111; the total operating expense, $13,875. Although separate, Miss Morrow's "colored school" clearly was not equal to Franklin Elementary.[7]

The veterans' petition marked the advent of a concerted lobbying effort by black parents to address these issues, its sentiment shared by Minnesota's most fiery and controversial congressman later that year. In Washington on December 14, 1865, four days before Congress ratified the Thirteenth Amendment abolishing slavery in America, Ignatius Donnelly introduced in Congress a resolution calling for the creation of a national bureau of education. Six months later, on June 5, 1866, James Garfield introduced a bill to establish such a bureau and allowed Donnelly to make the opening address on its behalf.[8]

Looking to the great European nations that had taken the education of their peoples under the care of the state, Donnelly called for America to follow their example. With English philosopher Francis Bacon's dream of a "university with unlimited power to do good, and with the whole world paying tribute to it," he argued that education promoted civility and peace and eradicated social structures that kept one man subservient to the other.[9]

Donnelly's was the vision best providing the opportunity to heal the war-torn nation, separated by region, race, and class; he had articulated it in Congress on several occasions. In a speech on February 1, 1866, for instance, he advocated for an amendment to authorize the commissioner of the Freedmen's Bureau to provide a common school education for all refugees and freedmen who applied for it. Because local governments could not be trusted to facilitate a quality educational system, Donnelly believed the nation must undertake the effort.[10]

Although Donnelly was arguably Minnesota's most controversial political leader of the nineteenth century—his actions and policies sent Republicans and Democrats alike into apoplexy—his notion of providing a common school for freedmen was not generally condemned.[11]

But when the substandard nature of such schools was revealed, Donnelly realized that government-sponsored schools did not ensure a good education. Safeguards to assure quality could exist only when the children of empowered parents shared classrooms with disadvantaged children whose parents were less privileged. When a white parent gained benefits for his child's school, all children enrolled similarly benefited. Conversely, when a school had parents with no influence over the delivery of resources, the school received nothing. More important, black children denied contact with the dominant race could never assimilate into the larger community and instead became adults restricted to quasi-alien status. Segregated black schools inevitably made their students different and therefore inferior. Donnelly, therefore, called for an end to the practice of school segregation.[12]

His colleagues in the state legislature, who could see the result of local control within the city in which they convened, reached this conclusion as well. On November 30, 1867, the *St. Paul Daily Pioneer* called attention to the dilapidated condition of the building set aside for black students:

> The colored children of this city are excluded from the free schools which are located in convenient and comfortable buildings, well-supplied with maps, charts, blackboards, and the usual equipments of such institutions, and are placed in a separate department, which is devoted to people of color. . . . Some of the windows have been broken out, the plastering is falling off and the keen air of winter will find entrance through many a crack and cranny. To keep out a part of the cold that would otherwise find entrance, the windows have been partly boarded up, so that while the benefit of increased warmth is attained, the disadvantage of a decrease in light has to be submitted to.[13]

In such conditions learning was all but impossible. The city fathers of St. Paul could not be trusted with the educational welfare of black children. Indeed, the spirit of long-sought equality so proudly enunciated by Republican leaders at the Convention of Colored Citizens compelled them to abolish school segregation. They called for legislative action that went beyond simple compliance with article 13, section 1, of the state constitution: "The stability of a republican form of government depending mainly upon the intelligence of the people, it is to be *the duty of the legislature to establish a general and uniform system of public schools.*" The state would henceforth withhold funds from any school district continuing to segregate children on the basis of race.[14]

Not even the black leaders at the convention had specified this. They called for parental diligence in getting their children to school, and in the new constitution of the Sons of Freedom they mandated the recording of student attendance. But integration seemed an unattainable goal. The leaders of the Republican Party felt differently.

The St. Paul school system, the only school system in the state with a policy segregating black students from white, offered an abysmal facility. Regardless of where they lived in the city, black children had to go to the segregated school. They could not possibly compete educationally with white students. By the end of the legislative session of 1869, three months after the convention adjourned, the Republican-controlled legislature passed a law discontinuing school segregation in St. Paul, the city with the largest concentration of black residents and the stronghold of Minnesota's Democratic Party. The campaign to desegregate public schools, primarily a St. Paul story, was another frontal assault on the influence of the rival party.

On Saturday, February 27, 1869, state representative William H. C. Folsom sponsored "a bill to amend section 39, title 1 of chapter 39 of the General Statutes, regarding education," or "Bill No. 198."[15] Despite its cunningly understated name, the bill held major implications for the St. Paul school system, for it sought to deprive school districts "in corporate towns" of school funds when black children were denied admission because of their race. If made into law, the bill would effectively destroy school segregation, and it clearly applied to St. Paul.[16]

School desegregation had been a matter of concern for Republicans since 1865, when they relaunched their campaign for black suffrage. On January 10 members of the Golden Key Club filed a petition with the Republican-dominated House. They argued that the middle-class virtues of industry, intelligence, and sobriety were the "cardinal elements" upon which black people could "erect good citizenship" and added that better education would awaken in blacks "integrity and moral worth" as fine as in the most enlightened and intelligent whites. Legislators linked literacy and citizenship as one.[17]

John Kellet, a commentator writing in the *Mankato Union* who signed his articles only with the initial *W*, offered one of the most persistent voices emboldening the legislature to extend civil rights to black Minnesotans. He wrote that environment, not heredity, was the cause of any degradation among blacks. In his essay on March 17, he added, "[Blacks] never have had the advantages of an education. They have for centuries been taught their inferiority and stupidity. But the day is dawning when they will show that there is stamped upon their race the image of the same all-wise God." Over the next four years those views deepened.[18]

When Folsom presented his bill to the body on February 27, 1869, Democratic representatives J. L. MacDonald and J. J. Egan of St. Paul spoke against the bill to no avail. The bill passed with a large margin. One week later, after a long discussion, the bill won approval in the Senate and was enacted into law. With the words, "There shall be no classification of scholars with reference to color, social position or nationality by any school trustee without consent of parent or guardian," the state forced St. Paul to end school segregation. Thus, black children—the majority of whom were poor, illiterate recent arrivals from the South—were legally free to attend the same educational facilities white children did.[19]

But the voices of concern were many. The *St. Paul Daily Press* reported: "[The black children] will have to take their chances in our already overcrowded schools. The greatest difficulty will be in classifying them, as even the full grown colored boys will have to go to the lowest primary classes, where the desks are arranged for children six to ten years old."[20]

For white families with deeply held antiblack sentiments, the image of "full grown colored boys" seated next to younger white schoolchildren was profoundly unsettling. Despite being urged to enroll, only thirteen black children did so by the spring of 1869, due in some quarters to "a strong deterrent in keeping many Negroes away from the schools they were legally entitled to enter." Nonetheless, six of these thirteen black children enrolled at Franklin Elementary, to enjoy amenities that did not exist in their former school.[21]

Segregation in St. Paul schools probably would have lasted for a long time without the state action. Many whites convinced themselves that desegregation was in fact bad for black schoolchildren because more of them had been enrolled in the black school than were now attending white schools. The editor of the *St. Paul Daily Pioneer,* sharing the views of the superintendent of schools and the mayor, wrote: "The fact stares us in the face that nearly all of the colored pupils in this city are deprived of the means of obtaining an education through the public schools, by this law. It would seem that every evidence as this would be sufficient is warranted to openly repeal. [The law] was impertinent and worse than unnecessary in its inception, and is wholly wrong and injurious in the operation. It really deprived the colored people of this city of the opportunity of educating their children and that is sufficient cause to warrant its repeal."[22]

The notion of desegregation as depriving black children of an education is curious. Some black parents may have agreed that their children would be best educated in all-black classrooms far removed from the hostility they anticipated in predominantly white schools. Moreover, some black parents, feeling the stigma of their race, which relegated them and their children to the lowest socioeconomic rungs of society, may have concluded that education, regardless of its quality, was pointless. Both notions are, of course, speculative. Nonetheless, that only a fraction of school-age black children enrolled in predominantly white schools seemed to vindicate the opponents of desegregation as positive proof that the new policy had failed.

In his address to the board of education on April 19, 1869, Mayor James T. Maxfield expanded on this view when he insisted that the black parents preferred separate school facilities for their children. Seeing no reason their wishes for a separate school should be denied, he hoped that the legislature would cooperate in the matter.[23]

The black parents of St. Paul should have the choice of sending their children to all-black schools. In championing the wishes of black parents, the Democratic mayor spoke on behalf of *their* desires, not those of the antiquated forces of unredeemed bigotry. The mayor was giving voice to his city's newest voters, and the voters' (which undoubtedly included a multitude of white parents) interests were his interests. This, as the mayor insinuated, was a reformed St. Paul acting responsively to *all* its citizens, regardless of race, creed, or color.

The speech seems more tactical than strategic in the sense that it was intended for a St. Paul audience and not necessarily to serve as a springboard for legislative change— it did not appear in petition form to the Republican governor or appropriate Senate or House committees, nor even to the sympathetic, though politically weak, Democratic legislators who represented his city. Rather the mayor delivered his speech before the school board, which had long supported school segregation. Since there was no concerted effort to initiate a repeal of the law or even an amendment, the mayor seems simply to have been preaching to the choir—the board members and the supporters in attendance. His speech seems to have reflected the urgings of a conscientious public servant in words designed to cast his administration—indeed his city—in the image of true reform.

This, at least, was the sense that St. Paul did not just belong to the mayor but to the city's entire Democratic machine, fostered by an action that had occurred three weeks earlier in the court of common pleas.

11

"Your Race Is Now on Trial!"

ON DECEMBER 28, 1868, Willis P. Harris, "a bright, intelligent-looking colored man " of twenty-two (or three) years and an unemployed laborer, allegedly entered the boarding room of another black man named Andrew Jackson, on Roger's Block, and stole from him a small sum of money.[1]

After he was arrested and brought to police court, Harris was held to answer the charge in the Court of Common Pleas of Ramsey County. After his indictment by the grand jury, the court scheduled his trial. Nearly three months after the alleged crime, he had his day in court. The day was Tuesday, March 23, 1869—one week after the legislature passed the school desegregation bill, five and a half months after the black men of Minnesota received the right to vote, and three weeks before Mayor Maxfield called for school resegregation before the St. Paul school board, of which Sheriff Daniel A. Robertson was chair.[2]

What young Harris saw as he entered the courtroom had to be unnerving. The offense was serious but nothing to warrant the kind of attention the trial evidently drew. As he scanned the gallery of white spectators, Harris noticed their attention riveted elsewhere—not on him but on the jury box. What he saw there was truly a surprise, but not the last one in this case. Here he was, a poor black man, defended by one of Ramsey County's prominent trial lawyers, Isaac V. D. Heard—former city attorney, former county attorney, future state senator, and noted chronicler of the Dakota War. And on the twelve-man jury that would decide his guilt or innocence were five black men—the first in Minnesota history to serve in this way.[3]

Jury selection had taken up the whole morning. Thirty-six talesmen, or men summoned to act as jurors from among the by-

standers in the court, and all white, were examined in voir dire—
the preliminary stage of a trial in which the respective attorneys
question prospective jurors to determine their ability to hear a case
objectively. Only one man, James Pendergast—the only one expressing no racial bias—survived the cut.

By noon, when the court was adjourned, Judge William Sprigg
Hall had directed Sheriff Robertson to summon twenty more talesmen to the opening of the court in the afternoon. By the appointed
time the sheriff assembled twenty more, all waiting for examination. Five of these men were black, "presenting almost every shade
of color, from the deepest black to the most delicate white."[4]

Eleven more jurors were selected, including all of the blacks.
Given more than 3,500 white voters in Ramsey County eligible to
serve, the five black jurors are unlikely to have been selected by
happenstance. Whether the judge ordered or fellow Democrat
Sheriff Robertson—a man of considerable political and civic
stature, having been the publisher of the *Minnesota Democrat,* a
mayor, a state representative, as well as being a current chairman
of the St. Paul school board—took it upon himself to summon the
five blacks is uncertain. But the selection of the county's first black
jurymen would surely create a stir, and Robertson was unlikely to
do anything that would disrupt the court of Judge Hall without his
knowledge and permission. More likely, the sheriff and the
judge—indeed the leadership of St. Paul—selected them to send a
message.[5]

Evidently, they also intended the message to create a stir. During the two hours in which Sheriff Robertson was to find and deliver new talesmen, word spread rapidly that black men were being
considered for jury duty. When court reconvened at 2:00 PM, the
gallery "presented an unusually animated scene." The public stir
caused by the jury selection led the *Minneapolis Tribune,* a Republican newspaper, to make this rather colorful observation: "Our
neighboring city of St. Paul has been greatly agitated over the fact
that colored men have been allowed to sit on a jury there for the
first time. It created an excitement only equaled by the advent of a
tribe of wandering Arabs, and so aroused the refined and delicate

sensibilities of the goodly citizens of St. Paul as to fill the court-room to overflowing, and furnished the principal theme of conversation upon the streets, and in the drawing rooms and parlors of this aristocratic metropolis."[6]

Then, drawing from a deep reservoir of contempt for its long-term political rival, the *Tribune* tightened its rhetorical screw: "It is indeed in the new order of things for that Democratic city, and in fact the whole State, and it is no wonder that some of her citizens stand aghast, and are shocked at such a terrible proceeding. St. Paul is truly advancing with the popular will, and there is hope yet that she may redeem herself. Next they will be electing negro aldermen, and then a negro mayor, and perhaps a negro 'governor of St. Paul!' What a spectacle it would be for such a Democratic stronghold."[7]

In restrained contrast the Democratic *Weekly Pioneer* reported simply: "The colored citizens looked dignified and anxious; the 'white folks' curious." As the power elite of St. Paul cautiously reached out to the leaders of the city's newest voting class, Minneapolis mocked them.[8]

The first few talesmen summoned by the clerk were white; since each said he had formed an opinion about the case, all were excused. At last the clerk read the name of R. J. Stockton, the first of the black men summoned. Stockton came forward, answered all the questions satisfactorily, and was sworn in. "The agony was over," reported the conservative *Weekly Pioneer*. "The first colored juryman ever in Minnesota was in the jury box." Indeed, he was the first black man since 1840, when Jim Thompson was deposed in the Deniger trial, reported to participate in a legal proceeding. In turn the remainder of the jury, including the four remaining black talesmen—Maurice Jernigan, Thomas Jackson, Henry Moffitt, and Robert Hickman—was sworn in.[9]

All five black men had cooperated in organizing the Convention of Colored Citizens, and all had worked together in their respective enterprises, further suggesting their selection was not happenstance. Jernigan was a highly successful barber whose emporium resided in the Merchant and the International, two prestigious St.

Paul hotels catering to Minnesota's political and business elite, some of whom may have been Democratic leaders. His partner was R. J. Stockton, also a barber. Hickman was a preacher of the Pilgrim Baptist Society, the church in which the constitution of the Sons of Freedom was drafted. He worked with Henry Moffit as a white-washer. All five men lived in the Third Ward, densely populated with white native-born and foreign-born neighbors representing every socioeconomic level from unskilled laborer to professional.[10]

With the jury now sworn in, the trial proceeded. After about two hours, the jury retired and deliberated swiftly. In less than half an hour it rendered a verdict of not guilty. On a motion from defense counsel Heard, his client, Willis Harris, was discharged. The trial itself was not newsworthy, but the presence of black jurymen raised the hearing to historic proportions. Ramsey County, noted the *Press,* had taken "the lead in conferring upon colored men one of the privileges of citizenship granted at the last election." In a self-congratulatory tone the Democratic *Weekly Pioneer* expounded: "It is a noticeable fact that the first colored jurymen that acted in the State, were summoned by a Democratic sheriff, in a Democratic county and Democratic city, in a court presided over by a Democratic judge, and where the county prosecutor was a Democrat."[11]

Despite St. Paul's history of antiblack sentiment, the seating of the state's first black jurymen did indeed occur in that Democratic stronghold. The question, of course, is why? Was this a demonstration of St. Paul's newfound enlightenment regarding its newest citizens or an experiment designed, perhaps cynically, to determine whether blacks could act responsibly in exercising an important aspect of the franchise?

Perhaps the selection of black jurors was a gesture of civic inclusion that the city would no longer discriminate because of race, color, or creed or, more pragmatically, an action to attract blacks to the Democratic fold. Perhaps, it was to show Minnesotans whose menfolk had fought and died in the last great war that St. Paul Democrats were not the party of slavery, disunion, and racism. In fact, the level of invective that the city's Democratic leaders and newspapers advanced against the campaign for black suffrage stood in high contrast to the congenial discourse that uniformly characterized the blacks who assembled in Ingersoll Hall on January 1 and the jurymen who heard the trial of Willis Harris. The Democratic leaders were realists, fully intending to make good of a bad situation—the good lay in attracting to the fold any voter who otherwise would vote Republican. Thus a political establishment that had long resisted black equality selected blacks for jury service. Perhaps the Democratic Party faced a dim political future in the wake of the Civil War, one all but assured by a statewide reverence for unionism and a martyred president. To survive, the party had to attract as many disaffected Republicans as possible.[12]

Though the black vote was miniscule in 1869, pragmatism dictated two guiding principles. First, the Democrats recognized a simple fact of life—namely, that blacks could vote whether anyone else liked it or not. This perhaps also explains why some Democratic leaders attended the Convention of Colored Citizens in the face of gentlemanly ridicule. Second, taking a lesson from the Republicans of the late 1850s, the Democrats—with enough of a coalition—might someday reach a majority. The Republicans had done that in the 1850s, stitching coalition to coalition with a carefully tailored set of principles.[13]

To build on this theme, the Minnesota Democrats began in January to accuse the Republicans of hypocrisy, as reflected in an article in the *St. Paul Pioneer* concerning the failure of the "radical party" to appoint blacks to legislative clerkship positions: "Not a single colored man has been nominated for any office. The radical party, that has conferred upon the colored people the right to vote, and which demands the votes of the colored people for their candidates, did not give them a single office—not even that of a common messenger or fireman. . . . They will be very glad to get the votes of colored citizens, but they have no offices—not even the cheapest and meanest—for the colored voters."[14]

The *Weekly Pioneer* was more pointed, referring to the Republicans—especially those who had attended the convention—as "uncommon demagogues," "political shysters," "piddling white radicals," and "white trash." But the paper assured its white readers and whatever black readers there might be: "The colored people filled their part well. They did all things decently and in order. They were temperate, considerate and high-toned, and gave, throughout their proceedings, many evidences that they are worthy of the possession of their new rights and franchises."[15]

Yes, the Democrats were now saying to the new black voters, the Republicans freed and enfranchised you, but we gave you *real* opportunity, *real* power by extending the privilege of that franchise, the power to judge your neighbors. In selecting black jurors, the Democratic Party seemed to tell black voters it was giving them a viable choice that would be lost if they remained unquestioningly loyal to the Republicans. In other words the act of selecting black jurors might weaken the Republican hold over them: doing nothing would surely secure the Republican's lock.

This, at least, was Sheriff Robertson's concern. In a letter to his son years later, Robertson argued that whereas the Civil War was just in ending slavery, extending the vote to black people could only serve to perpetuate racial strife through the North and South. Worse still, he argued, the black voter would forever be indebted to the Republican Party, permitting that party's continued dominance of national and regional power. With such dominance all checks of accountability would melt away, inviting even the most generous of Republican spirits to descend into corrupting absolutism.[16]

Perhaps prompted by echoes of speeches equating black citizenship with undying Republicanism at the Convention of Colored Citizens, Robertson may have concluded that such a course could be averted if the Democrats departed from their tradition of racial exclusion and gave black voters a reason to change parties. Protecting a citizen's right to choose: this was what Minnesota Democrats stood for. Not letting the political and economically privileged class dictate to the "common man": this was the hallmark of old-fashioned Jacksonian Democracy. This indeed was the spirit of Mayor Maxfield's speech to the St. Paul school board three weeks later, for the mayor represented all his constituents, especially a small number of black parents wishing to send their children to an all-black school.

But there was a problem. A Democratic sheriff had investigated the alleged crime of the defendant. A Democratic county attorney had found probable cause to prosecute. An all-white grand jury—probably composed predominantly of Democrats—had indicted Harris. The verdict was obvious: black men and Irishmen were always guilty. The question was, of course, would black jurymen—the best that St. Paul's black community had to offer—find in favor of law and order as administered by Ramsey County Democrats or find in favor of race?[17]

The Harris trial provided the opportunity to find out. The stakes were relatively low: the crime alleged was minor, and both principals—the defendant and the alleged victim—were black. No record exists of how the jury polled, but when the verdict of not guilty was announced, to the Democrats the answer was in. The blacks had apparently voted for the black. The reaction was markedly restrained. No Democratic opinion maker of Ramsey County outwardly criticized the outcome of the trial. The verdict stood on its own, a judgment *for* the defendant and *against* the jury. Blacks could not be relied on to protect Democratic justice, let alone the security of the community.

By 1870 the perception that blacks made up the most felonious criminal class in the city intensified. In a county in which they were .9 percent of the total population, they constituted more than 13 percent of those charged with theft, nearly seventeen times their number in the population as a whole. Sociologist Joel Best has observed that 10 percent of arrests resulted in jail sentences or felony trials, but for blacks the rate was 60 percent. Moreover, blacks generally received harsher sentences than did whites charged with similar offenses. "Such discrimination occurred within an atmosphere of racial prejudice."[18]

Newspaper reporters used ethnic epithets freely and presented blacks as frequent lawbreakers. "The police court room," reported the *St. Paul Pioneer,* "was filled yesterday with the nicest, blackest, most savoriest, cluster of colored niggers ever gathered together in that room." According to Best, "this atmosphere must have made police officers quick to arrest blacks whenever they came under suspicion." In fact, the St. Paul police were praised when they arrested criminals. Crime was to be deplored, and newspapers seldom took the side of anyone charged with a crime. Best found that no one protested "if the police roughed up prisoners" or used other "questionable practices."[19]

Within this atmosphere the Harris verdict was rendered, and the white people of the city took it all in. As Congressman Ignatius Donnelly had warned blacks during the Convention of Colored Citizens, "Your race is now on trial in this country. On trial, I say, at the bar of public judgment. The eyes of the American people are upon you. Every step you take is marked." The white residents of St. Paul watching this "step" probably conveyed to their political leaders their own verdict on this jurisprudential gambit, with a reminder that they, the white constituents, were the bulwark of the Democratic Party and not the handful of "colored citizens." The Democratic leadership of St. Paul apparently agreed, for decades passed before blacks again served on Ramsey County juries.[20]

Two months after Harris was acquitted, he was charged with larceny for stealing $180 from the store of M. Koch. On April 6 he pleaded guilty and was convicted and sentenced to two years and four months at the Minnesota State Penitentiary at Stillwater. His jury, this time, was all white.[21]

Donnelly's sense of the trial the black race had to endure encompassed more than the Harris verdict. To be sure, the distinguished manner exhibited by the black jurors during voir dire, the hearing, and the deliberations fully embodied what Donnelly called the "dignified position which [the black race] now occupies as equal citizens of our nation."[22]

The reverence that the blacks showed the judge and the proceedings positioned these leaders in a good light, for despite recent history, they showed respect to those who had participated in a system of exclusion. These were the character traits referenced in Donnelly's expansion on the standard by which the black race would be judged: "The history of the world is a history of the working out of [Christian] principles, changing the minds and hearts of men, and lifting them to the proud level of doing justice to the humble and the helpless."[23]

Indeed, everything that black people did and accomplished would be judged. He told them to show courage and never forget the duty that came with knowing whence they came:

As you have come up from the Red Sea of bondage with the foam still upon your garments, always, everywhere stand true to the great principle of liberty which has lifted you up. *Wherever you find an oppressed people, hold out your hand to them. Allow no prejudice, no argument, no sophistry, to turn you aside,* but under that great blazon of "Emancipation" which you unfurled today . . . be everywhere the missionaries, the apostles of liberty and progress in this land. *Everything there is of you—your long suffering, your liberation, your entire history, point you forward in that direction.*[24]

Here it was: Donnelly called on the black citizens of Minnesota, from the city whose political leadership was forced to accept black suffrage, to show courage and defy injustice. They had the right, duty, and support of their political patrons to be stewards for the welfare of their own kind. This sentiment must have contributed to the courage of the black jurors who determined that St. Paul's white Democratic criminal justice system had failed to make its case or had it wrong about Willis Harris. With courage and the full weight of the powerful Republican Party to secure what they had achieved, black men stood "equal before the law with their fellow men of other races, every opportunity thrown open to them, every barrier torn down, left free to work out the highest destiny of which they were capable." But to what extent Donnelly's words influenced the jurors when they deliberated Harris's verdict is unknown.[25]

These black jurors were proud men. They were steadfast Republicans, loyal to the party that had given them the right to vote, whose martyred standard-bearer had emancipated them from slavery. And they were a community creating a new identity that embraced and affirmed their race. These "insolent nagurs" had left behind subordinate ways to come to a land where they could be proud black men. With their arrival had come a new black presence in Minnesota.[26]

Unlike many of the earliest black settlers—who separated them-

selves from the new arrivals, content to live in modest acculturation
with white society or at least within an outdated sense of their own
culture and race—the new arrivals were political men, *race* men.
Men like Israel Crosby, James Hilyard, and Jacob Pritchard, many
of whom were the first "pilgrims," launched black advancement or-
ganizations such as the Pioneer Lodge of the Masonic Order in
1866. One year earlier, R. T. Grey, Maurice Jernigan, and Ed
James established the Golden Key Club, "a literary association for
the young men of St. Paul." All three lobbied Republican leaders in
an effort to bring the black suffrage question to a popular vote, organized the convention to celebrate the ultimate success of that effort, and founded the first statewide civil rights group, the Sons of
Freedom.[27]

In 1868 the sight of blacks organizing for the third suffrage referendum prompted St. Paul's Democratic newspapers to print stories of "negro outrage." In one issue the *Daily Pioneer* ran a story
of a black man having raped a white girl and another about Tennessee blacks denying white union troopers their right to vote.
Meanwhile, the *Pioneer Press* scared its readers with accounts of
race riots and alleged disenfranchisement of Irishmen in the South,
as well as of antiwhite abuses by "negro governments" in Haiti and
Liberia.[28]

Yet in August 1868—months before they knew whether the Republican establishment, after two failed attempts, could deliver the
votes to make them citizens at last—this new black community
within a hostile white community celebrated Great Britain's emancipation of the slaves of the West Indies in 1831, an event observed
by free blacks and abolitionists in other Northern cities through
the antebellum period. They clearly showed their resolve to be
seen, heard, and respected as black people.[29]

At the root of this activity were men who shared a common out-
look and profession—most of these early leaders were barbers from
the urban centers of Minnesota. Historian David Taylor reported
that between 1860 and 1870, while "opportunities for acquisition
of wealth and property were abundant[,] it was usually beyond the
reach of persons relegated to the margins of society."[30]

Limited in their ability to obtain necessary resources, blacks were also limited in their ability to amass surplus capital for investment. Nonetheless, some blacks were able to acquire substantial real estate holdings and personal assets. Black men supported themselves by barbering, cooking, and serving as porters and laborers, with barbering the first successful business enterprise within the black community. It required a skill easily obtained and a small capital outlay, its fees and tips bringing in an income that with frugality made possible the accumulation of surplus capital. Thus, by the end of the decade, black males became business proprietors and property owners.[31]

Barbers like Maurice Jernigan, who were proprietors of shops or in partnerships catering exclusively to white clientele, were the most successful of this class. With this success came respectability. The *Daily Press* described in extravagant detail "Professor R. J. Stockton's Superb Establishment—The Marble Palace," with its "exquisite marble ornaments, consisting of three marble pedestals surmounted by rich and costly mirrors, and a solid marble wash stand of octagon shape, with its pedestal of beautiful Tennessee marble capped by a globe of stained glass." With so much to lose, Democratic leaders might logically assume Stockton and Jernigan were amenable to generous and loyal customers whose patronage made their success possible.[32]

Again, the emergence of Maurice Jernigan as a leader of the black community and his recognition by powerful whites as "an esteemed colored gentleman of this city" during the late 1860s illustrate how a black barber proprietor could ascend to significance. Yet little is known about him.[33]

As early as 1863, when Robert Hickman settled in St. Paul with his Pilgrims, Jernigan had established a parlor in the Merchant Hotel, which he was able to maintain even after he had temporarily moved to Stillwater in 1864. In 1866 R. T. Grey joined him in partnership at the Merchant Hotel. The next year, he expanded his operation to the International Hotel, where he created a partnership with R. J. Stockton. By 1869 he had become so successful that he opened a new parlor on a different site he prominently advertised—"The Artistic Hair Cutter . . . where one can always get a nice clean shave or an artistic haircut"—in the *St. Paul Daily Press,* itself an indication of the degree to which he had become a well-connected businessman.[34]

Such success reflects the strength of the contacts he established with influential Republican officials, who no doubt had made it possible for him and his fellow organizers of the Convention of the Colored Citizens to hire the professional, all-white Seibert Band; rent as sites for celebration two sumptuous halls—the Ingersoll and the Odeon—in downtown St. Paul; and secure free passage on stage and railroad lines for all who wanted to attend the convention.

Barbering in quarters frequented by powerful Minnesotans did more than provide a crucial connection with the white world; it also gave powerful whites a view of industrious blacks who seemed to be fulfilling middle-class aspirations. When Jernigan and R. T. Grey established the Golden Key Club, they intended to portray themselves as men capable of demonstrating cultivation and refinement. In 1865 when the two men led a twelve-man delegation of their literary society to acknowledge the efforts of key legislators who had supported the first black suffrage initiative, they presented a gold-headed cane to Charles Griswold of Winona County, who authored the bill that passed the House. The choice of the cane as a gift—an emblem of gentlemanly refinement—showed the two barbers as possessing "the political leadership and sagacity of Minnesota's black community."[35]

These were the new black men of Minnesota; they wanted white Minnesota to think of them whenever black people were considered, certainly not of the black suspects who weekly appeared in police court or the harmless, impoverished black septuagenarian who told stories about strange places called Kaposia and Pig's Eye.

This was the image of the new black men that other black men were to follow. In their newly acquired high profile as race leaders and the embodiment of the promise of racial betterment, they knew that they were being judged by Minnesota in general. But of the multitude of "judges" watching their every step, they knew which ones mattered and which did not. The St. Paul Democrats, who in selecting them for jury service and later in calling for a school choice for black parents and their children, offered choices too little, too late, and too transparent. The important choices had already been made. The judgment of the Republican leadership was what mattered.

In the end, with every success of the black man, the Republicans felt vindicated in their party's identity as the steward of black freedom and advancement, vindicated in their belief that all could achieve the Yankee Protestant work ethic and middle-class values, vindicated in their vision of a liberal civilization in which all men in a real political sense were created equal.

Yet their clear vision did not allow them to see the paradox of their own making. As they memorialized in the state seal their concept of a civilized man as a self-reliant farmer behind his plow, they also expected the black man they had emancipated to be politically grateful, residentially urban, and, with some exceptions, economically dependent.

Republicans had placed their civic faith in the power of education and suffrage as antidotes for the racial stigma that whites placed upon blacks—but mixed bloods, "civilized" Indians, and the Irish Catholics of St. Paul, all enfranchised for a longer period, lived under the stigma of race and religion. The bad acts of a few reflected poorly on the whole. Though these men could vote, they were not equal to the Yankee Protestant elite—Republican or Democrat.

Still, the black man was no longer a slave. He could vote. He could expect his government to provide his children with equal access to public education. He could expect the protection that came not only with citizenship but also from a deeper and uniquely intimate connection between himself and the party of Lincoln.

Living at the head of the navigable waters of the Mississippi River, still in the corner of America where frontier and civilization met on the edge of social convention, the black man just might be able to define himself in his own terms. In this sense he lived the Minnesota experience, in which a slave could become a free man of property, where political equality might be extended solely on the basis of principle.

Notes

Notes to Chapter 1

1. William W. Folwell, *A History of Minnesota* (St. Paul: Minnesota Historical Society Press [hereafter MHS Press], 1956), 1:159–60; Marcus L. Hansen, *Old Fort Snelling, 1819–1858* (Iowa City: State Historical Society of Iowa, 1918), 181–85.

2. Lawrence Taliaferro, "Autobiography of Maj. Lawrence Taliaferro," *Minnesota Historical Society Collections* 6 (1894): 214–19; Lea VanderVelde and Sandhya Subramanian, "Mrs. Dred Scott," *Yale Law Journal* 106 (Jan. 1997): 1047, 1056.

3. Edward D. Neill, "Occurrences in and around Fort Snelling from 1819 to 1840," *Minnesota Historical Society Collections* 2 (1889): 115.

4. Ibid., 115.

5. Alfred Brunson, *A Western Pioneer* (Cincinnati: Hitchcock and Walden, 1879), 2:83–84. Taliaferro, "Autobiography," 235; William H. Forbes, "Traditions of the Sioux Indians," *Minnesota Historical Society Collections* 6 (1894): 413; Earl Spangler, *The Negro in Minnesota* (Minneapolis: T. S. Dennison, 1961), 18.

6. VanderVelde and Subramanian, "Mrs. Dred Scott," 1080.

7. U.S., 1 Stat. 51 (1787); Melvin I. Urofsky and Paul Finkelman, *A March of Liberty: A Constitutional History of the United States* (New York: Oxford University Press, 2002), 1:87.

8. U.S., 1 Stat. 51 (1787); Urofsky and Finkelman, *A March of Liberty*, 1:87; Eugene H. Berwanger, *The Frontier against Slavery: Western Anti-Negro Prejudice and the Slavery Extension Controversy* (Urbana: University of Illinois Press, 1971), 7–8.

9. Urofsky and Finkelman, *March of Liberty*, 341–42.

10. Robert R. Dykstra, *Bright Radical Star: Black Freedom and White Supremacy on the Hawkeye Frontier* (Cambridge: Harvard University Press, 1993), 3–4.

11. Ibid., 5–6, 44, 61.

12. VanderVelde and Subramanian, "Mrs. Dred Scott," 1050.

13. Richard Kluger, *Simple Justice: The History of Brown v Board of Education and Black America's Struggle for Equality* (New York: Knopf, 1976), 39.

14. Urofsky and Finkelman, *March of Liberty*, 378; Alan Brinkley, *The Unfinished Nation: A Concise History of the American People,* 3d ed. (Boston: McGraw-Hill, 2000), 228, 252.

15. For a listing of slaves in Crawford County, Wisconsin Territory, see Reuben Gold Thwaites, ed., *First Census of Wisconsin Territory, 1836* (Madison: Wisconsin Historical Society, 1895), 254.

16. Don Fehrenbacher, *Slavery, Law, and Politics: The Dred Scott Case in Historical Perspective* (New York: Oxford University Press, 1981), 124; VanderVelde and Subramanian, "Mrs. Dred Scott," 1042, 1044, 1070; Hiram F. Stevens, *History of the Bench and Bar of Minnesota* (Minneapolis, 1904), 1:30.

17. VanderVelde and Subramanian, "Mrs. Dred Scott," 1047–50.

18. Booker T. Washington, *Up from Slavery* (New York: Oxford University Press,

1995), 21; Kluger, *Simple Justice,* 69; Theodore C. Blegen, *Minnesota: A History of the State* (Minneapolis: University of Minnesota Press, 1975), 126.

19. Folwell, *History of Minnesota,* 1:141–42.

20. Taliaferro, "Autobiography," 234–35; VanderVelde and Subramanian, "Mrs. Dred Scott," 1041.

21. Albert Raboteau, *Slave Religion* (New York: Oxford University Press, 1978), 183.

22. Taliaferro, "Autobiography," 235; Gary Clayton Anderson and Alan R. Woolworth, *Through Dakota Eyes: Narrative Accounts of the Minnesota Indian War of 1862* (St. Paul: MHS Press, 1988), 85; Stevens, *History of the Bench and Bar,* 30; Brunson, *Western Pioneer,* 2:83–84.

23. Lawrence Taliaferro, Journals, 29 May 1826, Lawrence Taliaferro Papers, 1813–1868, Minnesota Historical Society, St. Paul (hereafter MHS); VanderVelde and Subramanian, "Mrs. Dred Scott," 1048.

24. Taliaferro, Journals, 28 March 1831.

25. Ibid.

26. VanderVelde and Subramanian, "Mrs. Dred Scott," 1052–53.

27. Ibid., 1053; Helen M. White and Bruce White, *Fort Snelling in 1838: An Ethnographic and Historical Study* (St. Paul: Turnstone Historical Research, 1998), 56, 60. For a general discussion of antiblack sentiment among the Irish, see, for example, Noel Ignatiev, *How the Irish Became White* (New York: Routledge, 1995); and David R. Roediger, *The Wages of Whiteness: Race and the Making of the American Working Class* (New York: Verso, 1991).

28. Fehrenbacher, *Slavery, Law, and Politics,* 126; Hansen, *Old Fort Snelling,* 65–66; VanderVelde and Subramanian, "Mrs. Dred Scott," 1070. See also White and White, *Fort Snelling in 1838,* 86.

29. *First Census of Wisconsin Territory, 1836,* 254; VanderVelde and Subramanian, "Mrs. Dred Scott," 1071, 1122.

30. VanderVelde and Subramanian, "Mrs. Dred Scott," 1049, 1055.

31. Neill, "Occurrences in and around Fort Snelling," 115; Folwell, *History of Minnesota,* 1:216–17.

32. *Rachel v Walker,* 4 Mo. 350 (1836).

33. Ibid., 350–51.

34. VanderVelde and Subramanian, "Mrs. Dred Scott," 1072. See also Paul Finkelman, *An Imperfect Union: Slavery, Federalism, and Comity* (Chapel Hill: University of North Carolina Press, 1981), 221–28.

35. *Rachel v Walker,* 351–52.

36. Ibid., 354.

37. Ibid.

38. Urofsky and Finkelman, *A March of Liberty,* 1:320–21.

39. *Rachel v Walker,* 352–54.

40. VanderVelde and Subramanian, "Mrs. Dred Scott," 1083n216; Urofsky and Finkelman, *March of Liberty,* 390–91.

41. Taliaferro, Journals, 26 Nov. 1835; VanderVelde and Subramanian, "Mrs. Dred Scott," 1056–57.

42. Fehrenbacher, *Slavery, Law, and Politics,* 124.

43. Ibid., 124–25.

44. Brunson, *Western Pioneer,* 2:75–76.

45. Ibid.

Notes to Chapter 2

1. Brunson, *Western Pioneer,* 2:75. When Brunson purchased and freed Jim Thompson is not clear. His autobiography is contradictory, stating that he purchased

Thompson both in 1836 and fourteen years before the 1851 Methodist conference where he and a critic resolved a dispute (ibid., 2:63–65).

2. Ibid., 2:78.

3. Ibid.

4. Ibid., 2:78; Malcolm Cjesney Shurtleff, "The Introduction of Methodism to Minnesota" (master's thesis, University of Minnesota, 1922), 4.

5. Brunson, *Western Pioneer,* 2:83–84; Folwell, *History of Minnesota,* 1:205–6.

6. Brunson, *Western Pioneer,* 2:63.

7. Ibid.

8. Ibid., 2:64–65; Livia Appel, "Slavery in Minnesota," *Minnesota History Bulletin* 5 (Feb. 1923): 41–42.

9. Brunson, *Western Pioneer,* 2:64–65; Appel, "Slavery in Minnesota," 41–42; Spangler, *Negro in Minnesota,* 19–20.

10. Ella C. Brunson, "Alfred Brunson, Pioneer of Wisconsin Methodism," *Wisconsin Magazine of History* 2 (Dec. 1918): 140.

11. Stephen R. Riggs, "Protestant Missions in the Northwest," *Minnesota Historical Society Collections* 6 (1894): 136; Appel, "Slavery in Minnesota," 41; Ella Brunson, "Alfred Brunson," 140.

12. Folwell, *History of Minnesota,* 1:205. See also Chauncey Hobart, *History of Methodism in Minnesota* (Red Wing, MN: Red Wing Publishing, 1887), 15.

13. Folwell, *History of Minnesota,* 1:185; Charles Eastman, *Minnesota Archaeologist* 12, no. 1 (Jan. 1946): 7–11.

14. Eastman, *Minnesota Archaeologist,* 7–11.

15. Return I. Holcombe, *Minnesota in Three Centuries* (St. Paul: Publishing Society of Minnesota, 1908), 2:262–63; Hobart, *Methodism in Minnesota,* 15, 19.

16. Brunson, *Western Pioneer,* 2:95, 97, 100–101.

17. Brunson did not retire from public life; he was elected representative of St. Croix County in the Wisconsin territorial legislature in 1840 and appointed Ojibwe agent at La Pointe, 1842–43 (Brunson, *Western Pioneer,* 2:137, 140, 144, 206–7); Folwell, *History of Minnesota,* 1:204n68, for leaving post. Folwell, *History of Minnesota,* 1:206; Brunson, *Western Pioneer,* 2:95, for attendance. Taliaferro, Journals, 10 Aug. 1838; Folwell, *History of Minnesota,* 1:206n72, for Little Crow.

18. Brunson, *Western Pioneer,* 2:127–35. See also Folwell, *History of Minnesota,* 1:206.

19. Some historians have written that Thompson moved across the river to St. Paul in 1838, but this seems unlikely considering that there is no record of such a move and that Mary Thompson was pregnant with Sarah, born later that October. Thompson likely would not have moved from the mission where he could get care for his wife to a place that was barely a settlement.

20. Folwell, *History of Minnesota,* 1:206. See also a report by B. T. Kavanaugh to Corresponding Secretary of the Missionary Society of the Methodist Episcopal Church, 26 Aug. 1840, Methodist Episcopal Church Archives, Minnesota Annual Conference, United Methodist Church Archives, 122 W. Franklin, Suite 400, Minneapolis, MN 55404 (hereafter U.M. Arch.); Pope to Taliaferro, 24 Aug. 1838, U.M. Arch.

21. Pope to Henry Sibley, 22 May 1839, U.M. Arch.

22. Folwell, *History of Minnesota,* 1:205; Riggs, "Protestant Missions," 136; Spangler, *Negro in Minnesota,* 20.

23. Holcombe, *Minnesota in Three Centuries,* 2:262.

24. Gideon Pond, quoted in Holcombe, *Minnesota in Three Centuries,* 2:84.

25. Ibid.

26. Conversation with Thelma B. Boeder, archivist of the U.M. Arch., 19 Feb. 2003, notes in author's possession.

27. Ibid.; *The Doctrines and Discipline of the Methodist Episcopal Church* (New York: T. Mason and G. Lane, 1840), 53.

28. *Doctrines and Discipline of the Methodist Episcopal Church*, 80; Thelma Boeder to author, 14 Feb. 2003.

29. Kavanaugh to Brunson, quoted in Shurtleff, "Methodism to Minnesota," 20; Pond Family Papers, 1833–1970, MHS. See also Folwell, *History of Minnesota*, 1:206n72.

30. Folwell, *History of Minnesota*, 1:165.

31. Ibid., 1:166.

32. Ibid.

33. Ibid., 1:167; Taliaferro, Journals, 23 May 1839.

34. White and White, *Fort Snelling in 1838*, 53–54.

35. Folwell, *History of Minnesota*, 1:205; Holcombe, *Minnesota in Three Centuries*, 2:262.

36. Holcombe, *Minnesota in Three Centuries*, 2:84.

37. Ibid. Brown attended the Stillwater Convention, which drew up the first petition to Congress to establish the Territory of Minnesota. In 1849 he served on the Territorial Council and later in the U.S. House of Representatives. He owned the *Minnesota Pioneer*, one of the territory's first newspapers, and the *Henderson Democrat* and helped to develop the towns of Hastings, Henderson, and Browns Valley.

38. Folwell, *History of Minnesota*, 1:221.

39. Ibid., 1:220.

40. Ibid., 1:223.

41. Ibid., 1:223; Holcombe, *Minnesota in Three Centuries*, 2:85.

42. Holcombe, *Minnesota in Three Centuries*, 2:85; *St. Paul Sunday Pioneer Press*, 28 Aug. 1949, 7.

43. Hobart, *Methodism in Minnesota*, 19; Shurtleff, "Methodism to Minnesota," 10n37.

44. Depositions of Jacques Lefevre and François Chevalier taken by Henry Hastings Sibley, 26, 27 Jan. 1841, Henry H. Sibley Papers, 1815–1930, MHS.

45. Ibid.

46. Ibid.

47. Ibid.

48. The warrant is in the Sibley Papers; Henry H. Sibley, "Reminiscences of the Early Days of Minnesota," *Minnesota Historical Society Collections* 3 (1880): 266.

49. Sibley, "Reminiscences," 266.

50. Conversation with Professor Annette Atkins, 15 Feb. 2003, St. John's University, Collegeville, MN, notes in author's possession.

51. Joan Pepin Tschida, comp., *Marriages of the Churches of St. Peter (Mendota, MN) and St. Paul (St. Paul, MN), 1840–1854* (Minnesota, 2002), 2:30, copy in MHS collections; conversation with Professor Annette Atkins, 15 Feb. 2003.

52. Brown purchased 320 acres of land from François Chevalier on July 10, 1840. The land is "near the mouth of the River St. Croix, bounded on the south by the Mississippi River," near present-day Prescott, Wisconsin. One signature of a witness reads, "J. B. Deniger (his X mark)," Book "A" of Deeds, Washington County Courthouse, Stillwater, 4; Sumner Bright to Thelma Boeder, 31 Dec. 1989, copy in author's possession.

53. Sibley, "Reminiscences," 265–66.

54. Ibid., 265.

55. Ibid., 266.

56. Ibid.

57. Dykstra, *Bright Radical Star*, 26, citing *Laws of the Territory of Iowa (1839)*, 180–81, 188, 330, 404, and *Laws (1840)*, 33. See also Leon F. Litwack, *North of Slavery:*

The Negro in the Free States, 1790–1860 (Chicago: University of Chicago Press, 1961), 93.

58. Dykstra, *Bright Radical Star*, 26, citing *Laws of the Territory of Iowa (1839)*, 180–81, 188, 330, 404, and *Laws (1840)*, 33.

59. Eugene Berwanger, *The Frontier against Slavery: Western Anti-Negro Prejudice and the Slavery Extension Controversy* (Urbana: University of Illinois Press, 1971), 32–33.

60. Ibid., 32–33.

61. Lawrence M. Friedman, *A History of American Law* (New York: Touchstone/ Simon and Schuster, 1985), 160.

62. James Thompson, Affidavits No. 68–71, Sioux Affidavits, No. 150, Sarah Thompson, and No. 151, George Thompson, Roll of Mixed-Blood Claimants, 1856, Records Relating to Mixed Blood Claimants under the Treaty of Prairie du Chien, 1855–1856 (Record Group 75, Bureau of Indian Affairs, National Archives), microfilm copy in MHS.

63. Alan R. Woolworth (research fellow at MHS) to Sally Morehouse, 10 Oct. 1994, copy in author's possession.

64. *St. Paul Daily Press*, 3 June 1871, 4; *Minneapolis Daily Tribune*, 2 June 1885, 8.

65. Folwell, *History of Minnesota*, 1:223–24.

66. Thomas M. Newson, *Pen Pictures of St. Paul, Minnesota, and Biographical Sketches of Old Settler* (St. Paul: privately published, 1886), 1:10.

67. Ibid., 1:11.

68. Ibid.

69. J. Fletcher Williams, *History of the City of St. Paul to 1875* (St. Paul: MHS Press, 1983), 165; Patricia C. Harpole and Mary D. Cannon, eds., *Minnesota Territorial Census, 1850* (St. Paul: MHS Press, 1972), 44.

Notes to Chapter 3

1. Williams, *History of the City of Saint Paul*, 165, 170–71. Thompson, Brunson, Cavalier, Wilkinson, Larpenteur, Forbes, Ramsey, and Bass were listed in sequence by the census takers in order of visitation. Presumably, the families lived in the same neighborhood; *Minnesota Territorial Census, 1850*, 43–44.

2. Blegen, *Minnesota: A History of the State*, 161–63; Folwell, *History of Minnesota*, 1:234–38.

3. Blegen, *Minnesota: A History of the State*, 161–63; Folwell, *History of Minnesota*, 1:234–38.

4. Blegen, *Minnesota: A History of the State*, 161–63; William Anderson, *A History of the Constitution of Minnesota* (Minneapolis: University of Minnesota, 1921), 24; Folwell, *History of Minnesota*, 1:234–38.

5. Blegen, *Minnesota: A History of the State*, 162.

6. Ibid., 163.

7. Anderson, *History of the Constitution of Minnesota*, 9. See also Finkelman, *March of Liberty*, 1:86–88.

8. Anderson, *History of the Constitution of Minnesota*, 9; Northwest Ordinance, sec. 9.

9. Northwest Ordinance, secs. 3–8, as modified by the act of 7 Aug. 1789. For a discussion on the interrelationship between the Northwest Ordinance and the Missouri Compromise, see Anderson, *History of the Constitution of Minnesota*, 11.

10. *Congressional Globe*, 29th Cong., 2d sess. (1846–47), 53, 71, 441–45, 540, 572; *Congressional Globe*, 30th Cong., 1st sess. (1847–48), 136, 656, 772, 1052; *Congressional Globe*, 30th Cong., 2d sess. (1848–49), 693, 699; *Stats. at Large of USA* (1853), 9:403–9. Anderson, *History of the Constitution of Minnesota*, 207.

11. *St. Paul Pioneer*, 28 June 1849. See also Litwack, *North of Slavery*, 30–112; Berwanger, *Frontier against Slavery*, 7–59.

12. Williams, *History of the City of Saint Paul,* 229.
13. Ibid., 149; see also Anderson, *History of the Constitution of Minnesota,* 9.
14. T. S. Williamson to Slade, the former governor of Vermont, 1846, Thomas S. Williamson Papers, 1839-1939, MHS. See also Williams, *History of the City of Saint Paul,* 162.
15. E. S. Seymour, *Sketches of Minnesota, the New England of the West* (New York: Harper, 1850), 92-94.
16. Ibid.
17. In Newson, *Pen Pictures of St. Paul,* 1:12, the following portrait of Thompson appears: "In personal appearance, Mr. Thompson resembled Morton Wilkinson. He had a large, aquiline nose; a high forehead; small, round eyes; a well-set mouth; with a peculiar movement incident to the late senator. . . . His complexion was quite light, indicating Anglo-Saxon blood; and his white makeup clearly showed that he was away above the ordinary when a Southern slave, and fully equal both to the white or the Indian when a free man." In contrast, a caricature of Jim Thompson, singing "Old Beulah Land" while merrily hammering a shingle, appears in Nancy Fitzgerald, "Ex-Slave Helped Found Historical St. Paul Church," *St. Paul Sunday Pioneer Press,* 28 Aug. 1949, 7, copy in author's possession. Seymour, *Sketches of Minnesota,* 92-94.
18. Seymour, *Sketches of Minnesota,* 92-94.
19. *Minnesota Chronicle* (St. Paul), 28 June 1849; Seymour, *Sketches of Minnesota,* 92-94.
20. *Minnesota Pioneer* (St. Paul), 2 June, 15 Nov. 1849; see also *Minnesota Chronicle,* 21 June 1849. *Galena Advertiser,* 1849, is cited in Williams, *History of the City of St. Paul,* 213. For a profile of Minnesota's territorial newspapers, see George S. Hage, *Newspapers on the Minnesota Frontier, 1849-60* (St. Paul: MHS Press, 1967), 138.
21. Williams, *History of the City of Saint Paul,* 234-35; Christopher C. Andrews, *History of St. Paul, Minnesota* (Syracuse, NY: Mason and Company, 1890), 58.
22. *St. Paul Pioneer,* 25 Apr. 1850.
23. Harpole and Nagle, eds., *Minnesota Census of 1850;* Williams, *History of the City of Saint Paul,* 228, 266; David Vassar Taylor, "The Blacks," in *They Chose Minnesota: A Survey of the State's Ethnic Groups,* ed. June D. Holmquist (St. Paul: MHS Press, 1981), 73.
24. Andrews, *History of the Constitution of Minnesota,* 61.
25. *Minnesota Pioneer,* 3 Sept. 1849; Andrews, *History of the Constitution of Minnesota,* 61; Williams, *History of the City of Saint Paul,* 235-36. For the bill, see Minnesota, *House Journal,* 1849, 60-62.
26. Pond Family Papers, Manuscript Collection, MHS. For an account of Pond's early years in Minnesota, see "Annals of Minnesota," Works Progress Administration Papers, Pond Brothers—Samuel W. and Gideon H.
27. See Pond's speech to the Old Settlers' Association, 1874, Pond Family Papers.
28. Minnesota, *House Journal,* 1849, 62.
29. Ibid., 123, 146, 149.
30. *Acts Passed by the First Legislative Assembly of the Territory of Minnesota* (St. Paul, 1850), 53-54. The bill prohibiting blacks from being referees is found in *Revised Statutes of the Territory of Minnesota* (St. Paul: James M. Goodhue, Territorial Printer, 1851), 358. The bill prohibiting blacks from holding office in villages is also found in *Revised Statutes,* 183. Minnesota, *House Journal,* 1854, 255; see also Gary Libman, "Minnesota and the Struggle for Black Suffrage, 1849-1870: A Study in Party Motivation" (Ph.D. diss., University of Minnesota, 1972), 11-13.
31. *Minnesota Chronicle and Register,* 25 Aug., 29 Sept. 1849.

Notes to Chapter 4

1. *Seventh Census of the United States, 1850,* "Minnesota Territory" (1851), ix; *Ninth Census of the United States, 1870,* vol. 1, "Population" (1872), 40; Deborah Swanson, ed., "Joseph Farr Remembers the Underground Railroad in St. Paul," *Minnesota History* 57 (Fall 2000): 124; *Minnesota Territorial Census, 1850,* 45.

2. *Minnesota Territorial Census, 1850;* Taylor, "Blacks," 74.

3. James Goodhue to an unnamed correspondent in the East, J. M. Goodhue Papers, MHS; see also Williams, *History of the City of Saint Paul,* 232–33; Edmund Neill to Milton Badger, 19 July 1849, American Home Missionary Society papers (hereafter AHMS papers), MHS.

4. *Register* (St. Paul), 4 Aug. 1849.

5. *Minnesota Territorial Census, 1850.*

6. *St. Paul Pioneer,* 30 Sept. 1852.

7. *Revised Statutes of the Territory of Minnesota,* 45.

8. Minnesota Territory, *Journal of the Council* (1849), 12. For a discussion of antiblack sentiment, see Berwanger, *Frontier against Slavery;* Dykstra, *Bright Radical Star;* Litwack, *North of Slavery;* Minnesota Territory, *Journal of the House* (St. Paul: Brown and Olmstead, 1854), 206, 254–59.

9. For an example of such men, see Rhoda Gilman, *Henry Hastings Sibley* (St. Paul: MHS Press, 2004).

10. Minnesota Territory, *Journal of the House and Council* (1849), 12.

11. Williams, *History of the City of Saint Paul,* 60, 305.

12. Ibid., 307–08; Sarah P. Rubinstein, "The French Canadians and French," in *They Chose Minnesota,* ed. June Drenning Holmquist (St. Paul: MHS Press, 1981), 35; *Minnesota Democrat* (St. Paul), 19 July 1851.

13. "A Petition for a Memorial by the Mixed Bloods of Pembina, 17 Aug. 1849," in Minnesota Territory, *Journal of the House and Council* (1849), 197–98.

14. Gov. Ramsey to the Council and House of Representatives, 17 Aug. 1849, in Ibid., 50–51.

15. Ibid.

16. Ibid.

17. Neill to Badger, 14 Sept. 1849, AHMS papers, MHS.

18. Augustin Ravoux, *Reminiscences: Memoirs and Lectures of Monsignor A. Ravoux, V.G.* (St. Paul: Brown, Treacy and Company, 1890), 52, 84–85.

19. Albert Barnes, *Home Mission: A Sermon in Behalf of the American Home Missionary Society Preached in the Cities of New York and Philadelphia* (New York, 1849), 13–14. See also this sermon for a discussion on the "Americanization of the West" movement among missionaries during the preterritorial period of Minnesota. The sermon was first preached before the Society for Promoting Collegiate and Theological Education in the West, in 1846. See also Barnes's sermon in Donald B. Marti, "The Puritan Tradition in the 'New England of the West,'" *Minnesota History* 40 (Spring 1966): 2–4. For an excellent synthesis of the movement in Minnesota, see J. K. Benson, "New England of the West: The Emergence of the American Mind in Early St. Paul, Minnesota, 1849–1855" (master's thesis, University of Minnesota, 1970).

20. Barnes, *Home Mission,* 13–14.

21. Ray A. Billington, "Anti-Catholic Propaganda and the Home Missionary Movement, 1800–1860," *Missionary Valley Historical Review* 22 (1935): 361–62, 377.

22. *Minnesota Chronicle,* 2 Aug. 1849. The only French Minnesotan elected to either body was Alexis Bailly of Mendota, and with William Forbes he constituted the legislature's only Catholics. For results of the election, see *Minnesota Chronicle,* 2 Aug. 1849; Minnesota Territory, *Journal of the House and Council* (1849), 4; Minnesota Territory, *Second Annual Report of the Superintendent of Common Schools of the Territory of Minnesota* (St. Paul, 1853), 4.

23. Minnesota Territory, *Second Annual Report of the Superintendent of Common Schools* (St. Paul, 1853), 4.

24. Ibid.; Benson, "New England of the West," 36–38.

25. Ravoux, *Reminiscences,* 63; James M. Reardon, *The Catholic Church in the Diocese of St. Paul: From Earliest Origin to Centennial Achievement* (St. Paul: North Central, 1952), 72–78; A. McNulty, "The Chapel of St. Paul," *Acta et Dicta* 1, no. 1 (1907): 68.

26. Harriet Bishop, *Floral Home: My First Years of Minnesota* (New York, 1857), 99; Ravoux, *Reminiscences,* 52.

27. Alexander Ramsey, *Diaries,* entries on 10 June, 5, 26 Aug., 5, 26 Sept. 1849; 18 Mar., 21, 28 July, 10 Aug., 3 Nov., 8 Dec. 1850; 8 June, 9 Nov., 21, 29 Dec. 1851. For references to Ramsey's desire to establish a Whig presence in Minnesota, see Ramsey, *Diaries,* 19 June 1849; Wilson P. Shortridge, *The Transition of a Typical Frontier: With Illustration from the Life of Henry Hastings Sibley, Fur Trader, First Delegate in Congress from Minnesota Territory and First Governor of the State of Minnesota* (Menasha, WI, 1919), 61–63.

28. Though there was no black church during the early 1850s, evidence suggests that the majority of blacks was Protestant (Taylor, "Blacks," 76).

29. U.S. Bureau of the Census, *The Seventh Census, Report of the Census for December 1, 1852* (Washington, DC, 1853), 16–19; U.S. Bureau of the Census, *The Eighth Census, Population of the United States in 1860* (Washington, DC, 1864), 262.

30. *U.S. Census of 1850 for the Minnesota Territory: Occupational Structure, by Nativity, of Population of St. Paul, 1850,* MHS. For an excellent study of immigration, economic opportunity, and social stratification in St. Paul, see Benson, "New England of the West," 42–78. For the laws that incorporated these businesses, see Minnesota Territory, *Collated Statutes of the Territory of the Minnesota and Decisions of the Supreme Court,* MHS.

31. Ramsey, *Diaries,* 25 July 1852; *St. Paul Pioneer,* 8 Jan. 1852; letter to the Executive Committee of the American Home Missionary Society, 15 July 1853, AHMS papers, MHS; *Annals of the Minnesota Historical Society* (1853), 4:39.

32. U.S. Bureau of the Census, *The Seventh Census: Report of the Superintendent of the Census for December 1, 1852* (Washington, DC, 1853), 16–19, and *Eighth Census: Population of the United States in 1860* (Washington, DC, 1864), 262; U.S. censuses of 1850, 1857, and 1860 for Minnesota, MHS.

33. Benson, "New England of the West," 56, 71–72; see also "Letters of Daniel J. Fisher, A Seminarian in St. Paul," *Acta et Dicta* 1, no. 1 (1907): 45, 48.

34. *St. Paul Pioneer,* 29 July 1852; "Letters of Daniel J. Fisher," 45.

35. Folwell, *History of Minnesota,* 1:379; *Minnesota Democrat,* 5 Apr., 30 June 1854; Ravoux, *Reminiscences,* 63; Reardon, *Catholic Church in St. Paul,* 99–101; Anatole Oster, "Personal Reminiscences of Bishop Cretin," *Acta et Dicta* 1, no. 1 (1907): 76.

36. *Minnesota Democrat,* 7 Oct. 1851.

37. Ibid., 7 Dec. 1853.

38. Ibid., 1 Feb. 1854; *Weekly Minnesotian,* 18 Feb. 1854. Throughout the 1840s and 1850s anti-Catholic sentiment intensified in northern cities over such issues as public financing for Catholic schools and trusteeship disputes over church property. In an effort to settle matters, the Vatican sent Papal Nuncio Bedini to tour American cities. Bedini was ill-suited for the task, however, after having established himself in 1849 as a ruthless reactionary who suppressed revolutionary uprisings in papal states. As historian Tyler Anbinder noted: "Bedini had never dealt with Catholic issues in a predominately Protestant country, and he lacked the tact necessary to strengthen American Catholicism without alarming sensitive Protestants." The incident in Cincinnati, perpetrated not by Protestants but by German- and Italian-born immigrants, reflected the depth of hostility felt by Catholics who knew Bedini's reputation and still harbored resentment

over the role that the Catholic Church had played in suppressing their short-lived republics (Tyler Anbinder, *Nativism and Slavery: The Northern Know-Nothings and the Politics of the 1850s* [New York: Oxford University Press, 1992], 27–28).

39.   Shortbridge, *The Transition of a Typical Frontier*, 63–65; Folwell, *History of Minnesota*, 1:379; *Minnesota Democrat*, 30 June 1854.

40.   "Letters of Daniel J. Fisher," 45.

41.   St. Paul formally became designated a "city," which sounded more elevated than "town." *Weekly Minnesotian*, 3 Mar. 1854; *St. Paul Pioneer*, 20 Jan. 1853; Williams, *History of the City of Saint Paul*, 336, 348–55 (for an account of the Yu-ha-zee case, see pp. 331, 335); *Daily Minnesotian*, 30 Dec. 1854, 2; see also John D. Bessler, *Legacy of Violence: Lynch Mobs and Executions in Minnesota* (Minneapolis: University of Minnesota Press, 2004), 3–4.

42.   Spangler, *The Negro in Minnesota*, 26; "Biographies of Black Pioneers," *Gopher Historian* (Winter 1968–69): 17.

43.   Swanson, "Joseph Farr Remembers the Underground Railroad in St. Paul," 126.

44.   Ibid.

45.   Ibid..

46.   Fugitive Slave Act of September 15, 1850, ch. 60, 9 Stat. 462; Litwack, *North of Slavery*, 248–50.

47.   For examples of how the Fugitive Slave Act ensnared free Northern-born blacks who had established themselves within Northern communities, see Paul Finkelman, *Slavery in the Courtroom* (Washington, DC: Library of Congress, 1985), 59–60, 80–136. See also Herbert Aptheker, ed., *A Documentary History of the Negro People in the United States* (New York: Citadel Press, 1968), 1:299, 323, 334; Litwack, *North of Slavery*, 250; Swanson, "Joseph Farr Remembers the Underground Railroad in St. Paul," 126.

48.   *St. Paul Times*, 23 Sept. 1854, 2 (this weekly summarized the events of several days).

49.   Ibid.

50.   Ibid.

51.   Ibid.

52.   Section 5 of the St. Paul charter denied blacks the right to vote, for it entitled only those persons who were eligible "to vote in territorial or county election" (*Weekly Minnesotian*, 11 Mar. 1854); Taylor, "Blacks," 74.

53.   *Minnesota Pioneer*, 30 Sept. 1852; Taylor, "Blacks," 74.

54.   Minnesota Territory, *Journal of House and Council* (1854), 258–59. For the 1807 Ohio "black law," see Chase, ed., *Ohio Statutes I*, 555–56, cited in Berwanger, *Frontier against Slavery*, 23; Finkelman, *An Imperfect Union*, 156.

55.   Minnesota Territory, *Journal of House and Council*, 258–59; Finkelman, *An Imperfect Union*, 156.

56.   For a full discussion, see Paul Finkelman, "Prelude to the Fourteenth Amendment," *Rutgers Law Journal* (1986).

57.   Robert Watson, *Notes on the Early Settlement of Cottage Grove and Vicinity* (Northfield, MN, 1924), 18.

58.   More contemporary historians have determined that Rolette was in fact French Canadian, having virtually no Indian blood, and that his identity as a mixed blood was really an invention meant to cultivate the colorful aspect of his personality. For more information about research on Rolette, see Bruce M. White, "The Power of Whiteness or, The Life and Times of Joe Rolette, Jr.," in *Making Minnesota History, 1849–1858*, ed. Anne Kaplan and Marilyn Ziebarth (St. Paul: MHS Press, 1999), 27, 29, 37.

59.   William D. Green, "Race and Segregation in St. Paul Schools, 1849–1869," *Minnesota History* (Winter 1997): 138–49.

60.   Ibid., 144.

61. Green, "Race and Segregation," 141–42; *Territorial Census of Minnesota, 1857,* 183.
62. Swanson, "Joseph Farr Remembers the Underground Railroad," 129n18.

Notes to Chapter 5

1. Finkelman, *March of Liberty,* 1:366–68.
2. Berwanger, *Frontier against Slavery,* 8.
3. Ibid., 18.
4. Ibid., 11.
5. The treaties of Traverse des Sioux and Mendota in 1851 opened southern Minnesota to white settlement.
6. Aileen S. Kraditor, *Means and Ends in American Abolitionism: Garrison and His Critics on Strategy and Tactics, 1834–1850* (New York: Vintage, 1969), 144, 145, 146.
7. *Weekly Minnesotian* (St. Paul), 8 Apr. 1854.
8. *Daily Minnesotian* (St. Paul), 26 June 1854; *Weekly Minnesotian,* 8 July 1854.
9. Charles Gordon Ames, *Charles Gordon Ames: A Spiritual Autobiography* (Boston: Houghton Mifflin, 1913), 64–65; Carlton C. Qualey, "John Wesley North and the Minnesota Frontier," *Minnesota History* 35 (Sept. 1956): 101–16.
10. Qualey, "John Wesley North," 102, 103.
11. Lucile M. Kane, "Governing a Frontier City: Old St. Anthony, 1855–72," *Minnesota History* 35 (Sept. 1956): 117.
12. Qualey, "John Wesley North," 104.
13. Kane, "Governing a Frontier City," 118.
14. *St. Anthony Express,* 14 Feb. 1852.
15. Ibid., 29 Nov. 1851, 24 Jan. 1852.
16. Qualey, "John Wesley North," 105.
17. William D. Green, "Eliza Winston and the Politics of Freedom in Minnesota, 1854–1860," *Minnesota History* 57 (Fall 2000): 116.
18. Lucile M. Kane, *The Falls of St. Anthony: The Waterfall That Built Minneapolis,* rev. ed. (St. Paul: MHS Press, 1987), 24.
19. *Minnesota Republican* (St. Anthony), 29 Mar. 1855; Anderson, *History of the Constitution of Minnesota,* 38.
20. *Minnesota Republican,* 5 Apr. 1855.
21. Ibid.
22. *St. Anthony Express,* 12 Apr. 1855.
23. *St. Paul Daily Times,* 14 July 1854.
24. For an account of the Republicans' debate over whether Marshall or Ramsey should be the standard-bearer for the congressional delegate seat, see Folwell, *History of Minnesota,* 1:375–76. The platform can be found in *Minnesota Republican,* 5 July 1855; *Daily Minnesotian,* 27, 28 July 1855; Eugene Smalley, *A History of the Republican Party* (St. Paul: Pioneer Press Company, 1896), 150–53.
25. Anderson, *History of the Constitution of Minnesota,* 38.
26. Gustav Rolf Svendsen, *Hennepin County History: An Illustrated History* (Minneapolis: Hennepin County Historical Society, 1976), 48.
27. Emily O. Goodridge Grey, "The Black Community in Territorial St. Anthony: A Memoir," *Minnesota History* 49 (Summer 1984): 45, 48.
28. Ibid., 48.
29. Ibid., 48, 50.
30. Ibid., 51–52. In 1860 three free black men and one free black woman lived in St. Anthony, and three free black men and five free black women lived in Minneapolis, of a total population of 3,254 and 2,535, respectively (*Eighth Census, Population of the United States in 1860* [Washington, DC, 1864], 254, 257).

31. Grey, "Black Community in Territorial St. Anthony," 49–50.
32. Ibid., 51–52.
33. For an account of the controversy faced by clergymen who preached antislavery sentiments from the pulpit, see Charles W. Nichols, "Henry M. Nichols and Frontier Minnesota," *Minnesota History* 19 (Sept. 1938): 254–55.
34. Grey, "Black Community in Territorial St. Anthony," 53.

Notes to Chapter 6

1. Anderson, *History of the Constitution of Minnesota*, 73–75; *St. Paul Pioneer and Democrat*, 1 July 1857.
2. Anderson, *History of the Constitution of Minnesota*, 73–75; *St. Paul Pioneer and Democrat*, 1 July 1857.
3. *Daily Minnesotian*, 6 Apr. 1857; Anderson, *History of the Constitution of Minnesota*, 72.
4. Anderson, *History of the Constitution of Minnesota*, 75, 78.
5. Ibid., 78.
6. Ibid., 78–79.
7. Ibid., 79.
8. Ibid.
9. Ibid., 79–80.
10. Ibid., 80–81.
11. Ibid., 85–86; Minnesota Constitutional Convention, *Debates and Proceedings of the Constitutional Convention for the Territory of Minnesota* (Republican) (1857), 337–85.
12. For an excellent discussion of black suffrage, see Gary Libman, "Minnesota and the Struggle for Black Suffrage," 28–41; William D. Green, "Minnesota's Long Road to Black Suffrage, 1849–1868," *Minnesota History* 56 (Summer 1998): 68–84.
13. Anderson, *History of the Constitution of Minnesota*, 99.
14. Ibid.
15. Ibid., 92–93, 99; Folwell, *History of Minnesota*, 1:417.
16. Minnesota Constitutional Convention, *Debates* (Republican), 337–38.
17. Ibid., 350.
18. Ibid., 341.
19. Anderson, *History of the Constitution of Minnesota*, 99–101; Minnesota Constitutional Convention, *Debates* (Republican), 337, 361–62, 365–66, 572, 575–82.
20. Libman, "Minnesota and the Struggle for Black Suffrage," 29.
21. Minnesota Constitutional Convention, *Debates* (Republican), 371.
22. Minnesota Constitutional Convention, *Debates and Proceedings of the Minnesota Constitutional Convention* (Democratic) (1857), 427; Green, "Black Suffrage," 74; Libman, "Minnesota and the Struggle for Black Suffrage," 30.
23. Anderson, *History of the Constitution of Minnesota*, 230.
24. *Minnesota Republican* (St. Anthony and Minneapolis), 13 Aug. 1857.
25. *Dred Scott v Sandford*, 60 U.S. (19 Howard) 393 (1857). For discussions of the decision, see Fehrenbacher, *Slavery, Law, and Politics*, 183–213; Finkelman, *An Imperfect Union*, 274–84; Litwack, *North of Slavery*, 49–50, 59, 62.
26. *Minnesota Republican*, 30 Apr. 1857.
27. Minnesota Constitution, art. 1, sec. 2 (the pre-1974 version). In one notable instance, former adjutant general Sylvanus Lowry of St. Cloud, a resident of Minnesota and Tennessee, kept slaves at his Minnesota home. In 1858 fiery abolitionist Jane Grey Swisshelm launched an attack against him in her newspaper, resulting in him leading a group of men who, one night, threw her printing press into the Mississippi River

(Blegen, *Minnesota: A History of the State,* 237; William D. Green, "Eliza Winston," 106, 111).

28. In 1860 New York's highest court ruled in *Lemmon v The People* (1860) that a slave brought into the state for one day became free. The Civil War prevented any appeal of the case. See Finkelman, *March of Liberty,* 349. For a more thorough examination of Lemmon, see Finkelman, *An Imperfect Union,* 296–312.

29. *Minnesota Republican,* 30 Apr. 1857.

30. *Lake Area* (Minneapolis), Jan. 1988, 24.

31. *Minnesota Republican,* 15 Jan. 1857.

32. *Minneapolis Sunday Tribune,* 18 Nov. 1934, 54–55.

33. *Stillwater Democrat,* 19 May 1860.

34. Mortimer Robinson and Family Papers (1859–1874), 10, 17 Jan. 1860, microfilm, MHS; Litwack, *North of Slavery,* 250.

35. Robinson Papers, 7 Feb. 1860.

36. Robinson Papers, 7 Feb., 6 Mar. 1860.

37. Minnesota, *Journal of the House,* 1860, 677–78.

38. *State Atlas* (Minneapolis), 10 Mar. 1860, MHS.

39. *State Atlas,* 10 Mar. 1860; *Eighth Census of the United States* (1864), 254; Regarding Coggswell's views on slavery in Minnesota and black suffrage, see *Falls Evening News* (St. Anthony and Minneapolis), 8 Mar. 1860, 2.

40. Minnesota, *Journal of the Senate* (1859–60), 599–601; *Falls Evening News,* 6 Mar. 1860.

41. *Falls Evening News,* 20 Mar. 1860; *Minnesota State News,* 24 Mar. 1860.

42. *Minneapolis Plain Dealer,* 25 Aug. 1860; see also *Falls Evening News,* 22 Sept. 1860; *Pioneer and Democrat,* 23 Aug. 1860.

43. Louis Filler, *The Crusade against Slavery, 1830–1860* (New York: Harper and Row, 1960), 28; *Falls Evening News,* 23 Aug. 1860.

44. *Falls Evening News,* 25 Aug. 1860.

45. *Minnesotian,* 19, 21 July 1860; *Pioneer and Democrat,* 19 July 1860.

46. *Minnesotian,* 21 July 1860.

47. Ibid.

48. *Minnesotian,* 23 July 1860.

49. *Minnesotian,* 21, 23, 25 July 1860.

50. *Minnesotian,* 1 Aug. 1860.

51. Green, "Eliza Winston," 107–22.

52. Finkelman, *An Imperfect Union,* 285.

53. Ibid., 117.

54. Ibid., 112–13.

55. Ibid., 114.

56. St. Anthony had indeed changed. Franklin Steele and other St. Anthony businessmen whose fortunes were tied to waterpower on the eastern side of the falls had difficulty getting financing from their New York investors. Jobs were growing scarce, and population increases slowed as Minneapolis, led by W. D. Washburn, outspent St. Anthony in economic growth. The boom on the eastern side of the river had begun to wane (Kane, *Falls of St. Anthony,* 56–57; see also Folwell, *History of Minnesota,* 1:428–34). Robinson Papers, 12 Oct., 16 Dec. 1860.

57. *State Atlas,* 24 Oct. 1860; *Minneapolis Plain Dealer,* 20 Oct. 1860; Robinson Papers, 12 Oct., 16 Dec. 1860.

58. Leon Litwack, "The Emancipation of the Negro Abolitionist," in *Blacks in the Abolitionist Movement,* ed. John H. Brace Jr., August Meier, and Elliott Rutnick (Belmont, CA: Wadsworth, 1971), 67–68; W. H. Pease and Jane H. Pease, "Antislavery Am-

bivalence, Immediacy, Expediency, Race," in *Blacks in the Abolitionist Movement,* 95, 97.
59. Pease and Pease, "Antislavery Ambivalence," 95, 97. See also Mamie E. Locke, "From Three-Fifths to Zero," in *"We Specialize in the Wholly Impossible": A Reader in Black Women's History,* ed. Darlene Clark Hine, Wilma King, and Linda Reed (Brooklyn, NY: Carlton, 1995), 225, 227.
60. Robinson Papers, 10 Jan., 20 Feb., 13 Mar. 1860; Litwack, "Emancipation of the Negro Abolitionist," 96. None of the names Grey mentioned in her memoir appeared in any records, newspaper accounts, letters, or minutes of the abolitionists of the St. Anthony-Minneapolis area.
61. Robinson Papers, 12 Oct. 1860; *State Atlas,* 21, 28 Nov., 5, 12 Dec. 1860.
62. Robinson Papers, 7 Jan. 1861.
63. Ibid.; *State Atlas,* 13 Feb. 1861 (emphasis added).
64. Minnesota, *Journal of House and Senate* (1861), 421-22; *State Atlas,* 6 Mar. 1861; Folwell, *History of Minnesota,* 1:54-55.

Notes to Chapter 7

1. Article 7, section 1, of Minnesota's 1860 constitution states: "Every male person of the age of twenty-one years or upwards, belonging to either of the following classes, who shall have resided in the United States one year, and in this State for four months next preceding any election, shall be entitled to vote at such election, in the Election District of which he shall at the time have been for ten days a resident, for all officers that now are, or hereafter may be, elective by the people. First. White citizens of the United States. Second. White persons of foreign birth, who shall have declared their intention to become citizens, conformably to the laws of the United States upon the subject of naturalization. Third. Persons of mixed white and Indian blood, who have adopted the customs and habits of civilization. Fourth. Persons of Indian blood residing in this State, who have adopted the language, customs, and habits of civilization, after an examination before any District Court of the State, in such manner as may be provided by law, and shall have been pronounced by said Court capable of enjoying the rights of citizenship within the State." *Falls Evening News,* 24 Mar. 1860; *State Atlas,* 24 Mar. 1860.
2. Anderson, *History of the Constitution of Minnesota,* 123.
3. White, "Power of Whiteness," 194.
4. Ibid., 191.
5. Williamson and Riggs to Reverend Rufus Anderson, 20 June 1857, Correspondence, American Board of Commissioners for Foreign Missions (ABCFM), transcript, microfilm in MHS.
6. U.S. Commissioner of Indian Affairs, *Report, 1856* (Washington, DC, 1857), 65.
7. Riggs to Selah B. Treat, 31 July 1856, ABCFM. The sixth article asked "separate division of what enured them from the sale of land." What the article meant is uncertain. Harriet C. Bell, "The Hazelwood Republic," typescript, 1937, copy in MHS.
8. Bell, "Hazelwood Republic," 5.
9. *St. Paul Financial, Real Estate, and Railroad Advertiser,* 13 Dec. 1856, 2.
10. U.S. Commissioner of Indian Affairs, *Report, 1860,* 56; Riggs to Treat, 20 Nov. 1857, ABCFM.
11. Riggs to Treat, 13 Aug. 1857, ABCFM.
12. Ibid.
13. Folwell, *History of Minnesota,* 1:325.
14. Riggs to Treat, 13 Aug. 1857, ABCFM.
15. Ibid.
16. Ibid.

17. Charles E. Flandrau, *The History of Minnesota and Tales of the Frontier* (St. Paul: E. W. Porter, 1900), 393.

18. Ibid.

19. Ibid.

20. Ibid.

21. Ibid.

22. *St. Paul Financial, Real Estate, and Railroad Real Estate, and Railroad Advertiser,* 6 June 1857. See also Anderson, *History of the Constitution of Minnesota,* 73–74. For Flandrau's speech, see Minnesota Constitutional Convention, *Debates* (Democratic), 431–32 (emphasis added). *St. Paul Pioneer and Democrat,* 1 July 1857.

23. Anderson and Woolworth, *Through Dakota Eyes,* 194–97.

24. Ibid.

25. Riggs to J. M. Gordon, treasurer, 5 May 1858, ABCFM.

26. Ibid.

27. Folwell, *History of Minnesota,* 1:221–22.

28. Riggs to Treat, 30 Nov. 1857.

29. Ibid.

30. Minnesota Constitutional Convention, *Debates* (Democratic), 430.

31. Ibid., 432.

32. Anderson, *History of the Constitution of Minnesota,* 123–24.

33. For reports on local conditions, see Commissioner of Indian Affairs, *Reports, 1856–1862.*

34. Riggs to Treat, 9 Dec. 1859, ABCFM.

35. Ibid.

36. Ramsey to Treat, 30 Jan. 1860, ABCFM.

37. *St. Paul Daily Press,* 28 June 1861.

38. Ibid.

39. Folwell, *History of Minnesota,* 2:222–23; *Henderson Democrat,* 16 June 1858. For accounts of the Dakota War, see Anderson and Woolworth, *Through Dakota Eyes;* Kenneth Carley, *Dakota War of 1862;* Carol Chomsky, "The United States–Dakota War Trials: A Study in Military Injustice," *Stanford Law Review* 45 (Nov. 1990): 13–99.

40. Flandrau, *History of Minnesota,* 395.

41. Anderson, *History of the Constitution of Minnesota,* 45.

42. Ibid.

43. *Report to the Commissioner of Indian Affairs,* 1863, 286; Folwell, *History of Minnesota,* 2:234.

44. Walt Bachman, "Joseph Godfrey: Black Dakota," in *Race, Native Roots and African American Relations,* ed. Terry Straus (Chicago: Albatross Press, 2005), 377–78.

45. Folwell, *History of Minnesota,* 2:234; *St. Paul Press,* 21 Sept. 1862; *St. Paul Pioneer,* 16 Sept. 1862.

46. Folwell, *History of Minnesota,* 2:380; Minnesota Board of Commissioners, *Minnesota in the Civil and Indian Wars, 1861–1865* (St. Paul, 1890–93), 1:418; conversation with Hampton Smith, MHS archivist, 22 July 2003.

47. Anderson and Woolworth, *Through Dakota Eyes,* 15, 25–26; Carley, *Dakota War of 1862,* 17. Galbraith's account of recruiting the Rangers appears in *Report to the Commissioner of Indian Affairs,* 1863, 275.

48. Chomsky, "United States–Dakota War Trials," 92–93.

49. *St. Paul Daily Press,* 5 Feb. 1863.

50. Blegen, *Minnesota: A History of a State,* 280; *St. Paul Daily Press,* 28 Jan. 1863.

51. "The Indian War—A Few Suggestions," *St. Paul Daily Press,* 30 Aug. 1862.

52. *St. Cloud Democrat,* 11, 18 Sept. 1862.

53. Sylvia S. Hoffert, "Gender and Vigilantism on the Minnesota Frontier: Jane

Grey Swisshelm and the U.S.-Dakota Conflict of 1862," *Western Historical Quarterly* (Autumn 1998): 354, 357. For a discussion on the relationship of the abolition movement and Indians during the nineteenth century, see Linda K. Kerter, "The Abolitionist Perception of the Indian," *Journal of American History* 62 (Sept. 1975): 271–95.

54. Folwell, *History of Minnesota,* 2:263.

55. United States, *Statutes at Large,* 12:819; Folwell, *History of Minnesota,* 2:263; *Henderson Democrat,* 16 June 1858.

56. *Report to the Commissioner of Indian Affairs,* 1863, 91.

57. Ibid.

58. Anderson and Woolworth, *Through Dakota Eyes,* 100, 119–20, 194–95, 205–6.

59. Folwell, *History of Minnesota,* 2:259.

60. Ibid., 2:258.

61. Ibid., 2:259.

62. *St. Paul Daily Press,* 5 May 1863.

63. Ibid.

64. Ibid., 16 May 1863.

65. Ibid.

66. Folwell, *History of Minnesota,* 2:259.

67. *St. Paul Daily Press,* 2 June 1863.

Notes to Chapter 8

1. Paul M. Angle, ed., *The Lincoln Reader* (New Brunswick, NJ: Rutgers University Press, 1947), 403; see also John G. Nicolay and John Hay, *Abraham Lincoln: A History* (New York: Century Company, 1914), 6:153.

2. Frank Klement, "The Abolition Movement in Minnesota," *Minnesota History* 32 (Mar. 1951): 22; Ignatiev, *How the Irish Became White,* 87–88, for quote; Iver Bernstein, *The New York City Draft Riots: Their Significance for American Society and Politics in the Age of the Civil War* (New York: Oxford University Press, 1990), 143–44, for Lincoln.

3. *Weekly Pioneer and Democrat,* 12 July 1861.

4. Benjamin Quarles, *The Negro in the Civil War* (New York: Da Capo Press, 1989), 29–31, for federal law. Folwell, *History of Minnesota,* 2:380; *Minnesota in the Civil and Indian Wars,* 1:418; Kenneth Carley, *Minnesota in the Civil War: An Illustrated History* (St. Paul: MHS Press, 2000), 163, for Renville Rangers. Klement, "Abolition Movement," 29; William S. McFeely, *Frederick Douglass* (New York: W. W. Norton, 1991), 214–15, for Lincoln's proclamation.

5. *St. Cloud Democrat,* 2 Oct. 1862; Folwell, *History of Minnesota,* 2:341.

6. United States, *Statutes at Large,* 12:1268; J. G. Randall and David Donald, *The Civil War and Reconstruction* (Boston: D. C. Heath and Company, 1961), 197.

7. Writers Project, Slave Narratives, "Robert Hickman," Box 230 (Works Project Administration: Hickman); "Biographies of Black Pioneers," *Gopher Historian* (Winter 1968–69): 7, 17; David Vassar Taylor, "Pilgrim's Progress: Black St. Paul and the Making of an Urban Ghetto, 1870–1930" (Ph.D. diss., University of Minnesota, 1977), 24–26; Dykstra, *Bright Shining Star,* 196.

8. Vicksburg, Mississippi, the last fortified Confederate outpost on the river, fell to the Union army on July 4, 1863.

9. Writers Project, Slave Narratives, "Robert Hickman"; "Biographies of Black Pioneers," 7, 17; Taylor, "Pilgrim's Progress," 24–26; Dykstra, *Bright Shining Star,* 196.

10. The term "contraband" was used to label slaves who had sought refuge with the Union army. For a full discussion of the term, see Urofsky and Finkelman, *A March of Liberty,* 430–31; Patricia L. Faust, ed., *Historical Times Illustrated Encyclopedia of the Civil War* (New York: Harper and Row, 1986), 161–62.

11. Writers Project, Slave Narratives, "Robert Hickman"; "Biographies of Black Pioneers," 7, 17; Taylor, "Pilgrim's Progress," 24–26; Dykstra, *Bright Shining Star*, 196.

12. *St. Paul Press*, 6 May 1863.

13. For an example of black victims of a mob attack being arrested "in order to avoid further violence," see Litwack, *North of Slavery*, 100. For an example of official containment of riots, see Ignatiev, *How the Irish Became White*, 131–35.

14. *St. Paul Daily Press*, 16 May 1863.

15. Ibid.; 16 May 1863; Taylor, "Pilgrim's Progress," 8, 9.

16. Minnesota Territory, *House Journal, 1854*, 258–59.

17. Minnesota, *House Journal, 1860*, 242.

18. *St. Paul Daily Press*, 10 Feb. 1863; *St. Paul Daily Press*, 9 May 1863; Folwell, *History of Minnesota*, 2:344.

19. *St. Paul Daily Press*, 9 May 1863; Folwell, *History of Minnesota*, 2:344.

20. *St. Paul Daily Press*, 12 May 1863.

21. Ibid., 16 May 1863, 1.

22. Ibid.

23. Ibid.

24. *Mankato Semi-Weekly Record*, 14 June 1862; Spangler, *Negro in Minnesota*, 50; Blegen, *Minnesota: A History*, 136; Williams, *History of the City of Saint Paul*, 173–74. For a general discussion of Sibley's career, see Gilman, *Henry Hastings Sibley*. The financial vitality of the city was best reflected in the establishment of its banking system. In December 1863 the First National Bank, "one of the earliest established in the country," became the first of seven additional banks that were established over the next few years (Williams, *History of the City of Saint Paul*, 410–12).

25. Twice Union generals issued orders to free slaves residing in their respective departments—John C. Frémont in command of the Department of the West, headquartered in St. Louis, and David Hunter, who in 1862 decreed that all slaves living in Georgia, Florida, and South Carolina be freed. Twice Lincoln reversed the order, but it was Lincoln's response to Frémont's order that best characterizes the president's rationale in the Missouri case. On August 30, 1861, General Frémont instituted "martial law throughout the state of Missouri and proclaimed that the property of all rebels would be confiscated and their slaves 'declared free men.'" Klement continued, "President Lincoln, trying to keep the border states in the Union and soliciting the support of Northern conservatives, soon reversed Frémont's order and later removed him from command" (Klement, "Abolition Movement," 23, 26).

26. Bernstein, *New York City Draft Riots*, 7–9.

27. Anbinder, *Nativism and Slavery*, 271; Bernstein, *New York City Draft Riots*, 43; Williams, *History of the City of Saint Paul*, 412. For an example of Democratic condemnation of the conscription law, see *St. Paul Weekly Pioneer and Democrat*, 27 Mar. 1863.

28. Observing this transformation, Frederick Douglass wrote, "The Irish, who at home (in Ireland), readily sympathize with the oppressed everywhere, are instantly taught when they step onto our soil to hate and despise the Negro. They are taught to believe that he eats the bread that belongs to them. The cruel lie is told to them, that we deprive them of labor and receive the money which would otherwise make its way into their pockets. Sir, the Irish-American will one day find out his mistake" (Frederick Douglass, *Life and Times of Frederick Douglass Written by Himself* [New York: Collier Books, 1962], 298). See also Regan, "The Irish," 130; Sterling D. Spero and Abram Harris, *The Black Worker: The Negro and the Labor Movement* (New York: Atheneum, 1968), 13; Litwack, *North of Slavery*, 74–75; Kenneth Neill, *An Illustrated History of the Irish People* (Dublin: Gill and Macmillan, 1985), 197–98. For an account of Douglass's tour of Ireland, see William S. McFeely, *Frederick Douglass* (New York: W. W. Norton, 1991), 119–30; Ignatiev, *How the Irish Became White*, 31.

29. *St. Paul Daily Press,* 16 May 1863.
30. Ibid.
31. Taylor, "Blacks," 76–77; *St. Paul Daily Press,* 17 May 1863.
32. Taylor, "Blacks," 75; Taylor, "Pilgrim's Progress," 28.
33. Williams, *History of the City of St. Paul to 1875,* 409.
34. *St. Paul Daily Press,* 3 Feb., 27 Mar. 1863.
35. Swanson, "Underground Railroad," 128–29n7; Anderson and Woolworth, *Through Dakota Eyes,* 241.
36. Kerter, "The Abolitionist Perception of the Indian," 294, citing *Boston Standard,* 29 May 1869.

Notes to Chapter 9

1. This chapter is based in part on my article "Minnesota's Long Road to Black Suffrage, 1849–1868," *Minnesota History* 56 (Summer 1998): 68–83.
2. Minnesota, *House Journal, 1866,* 295–97; Minnesota, *Senate Journal, 1866,* 242; see also Folwell, *History of Minnesota,* 3:3.
3. Libman, "Minnesota and the Struggle for Black Suffrage," 49, citing James McPherson, *The Struggle for Equality: Abolitionists in the Civil War and Reconstruction* (Princeton: Princeton University Press, 1964), 270, 276–77.
4. Ibid.
5. Minnesota, *House Journal, 1865,* 65, 66, 101, 109, 122, 139; *St. Paul Daily Press,* 21, 28, 31 Jan. 1865; *St. Paul Pioneer,* 28, 31 Jan., 2, 7 Feb. 1865.
6. *St. Paul Daily Press,* 21, 28, 31 Jan. 1865; *St. Paul Pioneer,* 28, 31 Jan., 2, 7 Feb. 1865.
7. *St. Paul Daily Press,* 20 Jan. 1865. For information on the Golden Key Club, see *St. Paul Daily Press,* 8 Jan. 1865.
8. *St. Paul Pioneer,* 7 Feb. 1865.
9. Ibid.; Minnesota, *House Journal, 1865,* 142.
10. Minnesota, *House Journal, 1865,* 154, 165.
11. *Preston Republican,* 17 Feb. 1865; *Mantorville Express,* 3 Nov. 1865; *St. Paul Daily Press,* 21 Sept. 1865, for expediency; *St. Paul Daily Press,* 1 Mar. 1865, for cane; *Chatfield Democrat,* 18 Mar. 1865, for quote.
12. *Mankato Union,* 17 Mar. 1865; *Wilton News,* reprinted in *Chatfield Democrat,* 2 Sept. 1865; *Hastings Conserver,* reprinted in *Winona Democrat,* 26 Aug. 1865, for suffrage; *Mankato Weekly Record,* 4 Feb. 1865, for quote.
13. *Chatfield Democrat,* 19 Aug. 1865 (paragraphing added).
14. See, for example, *Shakopee Weekly Argus,* 12 Sept. 1865; *St. Paul Pioneer,* 7 Nov. 1865. Such expressions of the fear of miscegenation reflected the degree to which racism had spread into Minnesota. Interracial marriage among blacks, whites, and Indians was common long before the American flag flew above Minnesota soil. Yet in 1865 such expressions were rhetorically effective in helping to defeat the proposition. Still, Minnesota's marriage law never resembled those of most other states banning interracial marriage. Instead, it banned marriages on the basis of consanguinity and "insane, epileptic, imbecile" and "deaf, dumb, blind" conditions (*State Laws Limiting Marriage Selection* [Cold Spring Harbor, MN, 1913], 54). See also *Chatfield Democrat,* 18 Feb., 5, 26 Aug., 9 Sept. 1865; *St. Paul Pioneer,* 5 Nov. 1865.
15. *Chatfield Democrat,* 20 May 1865.
16. *St. Paul Pioneer,* 12, 22 Oct. 1865.
17. Ibid., 1, 10 Oct. 1865.
18. Ibid., 14, 22 Oct. 1865; *Shakopee Weekly Argus,* 2 Sept. 1865, for white laborers. *St. Paul Pioneer,* 14, 22 Oct. 1865; *Shakopee Weekly Argus,* 2 Sept. 1865, for influence. Whether all veterans were antisuffrage is questionable. Letters written by soldiers of

the First Minnesota Regiment indicate that veterans more likely shared the full range of sentiments reflected by the people of Minnesota. See Richard Moe, *The Last Full Measure: The Life and Death of the First Minnesota Volunteers* (1993; St. Paul: MHS Press, 2001), 34, 80–81, 113–14; Libman, "Minnesota and the Struggle for Black Suffrage," 76–86, for Republicans.

19. Minnesota, Secretary of State, "Census of the State of Minnesota," *Annual Report, 1865,* 119.

20. *St. Paul Daily Press,* 10 Jan. 1866, for Hewson; *Annual Message of Governor Miller and Inaugural Address of Governor Marshall to the Legislature of Minnesota* (St. Paul: Press Printing, 1866), 21, 22, 35.

21. Minnesota, *House Journal, 1866,* 150, for vote; *Stillwater Messenger,* 13 Feb. 1866, for quote and following.

22. Libman, "Minnesota and the Struggle for Black Suffrage," 123–24. See also John Cox and Lawanda Cox, *Politics, Principles and Prejudice, 1865–1866* (New York: Atheneum, 1969), for a discussion on Johnson and his Conservative Party.

23. McPherson, *Struggle for Equality,* 367; William Gillette, *The Right to Vote: Politics and the Passage of the Fifteenth Amendment* (Baltimore: Johns Hopkins University Press, 1965), 28–31; Bruce M. White et al., *Minnesota Votes: Election Returns by County for Presidents, Senators, Congressmen, and Governors, 1857–1977* (St. Paul: MHS, 1977), 68; *St. Paul Daily Press,* 18, 20 Nov., 20 Dec. 1866.

24. Minnesota, *House Journal, 1867,* 114–15; Minnesota, *Senate Journal, 1867,* 154; *St. Paul Daily Press,* 5, 7, 9 Feb. 1867; *St. Paul Pioneer,* 10 Feb. 1867, for suffrage bill. *St. Paul Pioneer,* 15, 17 Oct., 5, 13 Nov. 1867; *Chatfield Democrat,* 26 Oct. 1867; *Mankato Weekly Record,* 19 Oct. 1867, for remainder.

25. *Records of the State Legislature, 1867,* House Bills, H.F. No. 1., Archives Division, MHS; *St. Paul Pioneer Press,* 16 Oct. 1867; *St. Paul Daily Press,* 20 Oct. 1867, for amendment; *St. Paul Daily Pioneer,* 3, 14 Nov. 1868, for last quote.

26. Libman, "Minnesota and the Struggle for Black Suffrage," 137, 138, for voting. For an interesting breakdown of voting patterns and causes for the defeat, see Ibid., 135–46. *Faribault Central Republican,* 20 Nov. 1867, for backsliders quote. See also *Goodhue County Republican* (Red Wing), 7 Feb. 1867. *St. Paul Daily Press,* 31 Jan., 5 Feb. 1868, for remainder. See also Alan Harmon letter to the *Minneapolis Tribune,* 22 Nov. 1867. For a comment on the timidity of certain county committees in placing the amendment on the Republican ballot, see also *Mower County Register* (Austin), 21 Nov. 1867; *St. Paul Pioneer,* 6 Nov. 1867; *Rochester Post,* 23 Nov. 1867.

27. *St. Paul Daily Press,* 11 Jan. 1868.

28. Ibid.; see also Gordon's speech, in Hanford L. Gordon Papers, 1868–1920, MHS.

29. *St. Paul Daily Press,* 23 Oct. 1868; *St. Paul Dispatch,* 23 Oct. 1868, for first quote. The warning about the effect of Wilkinson's statement was printed in the *Mower County Register,* 22 Oct. 1868. *Stillwater Republican,* 13 Oct. 1868; *Minneapolis Tribune,* 16 Oct. 1868; *St. Paul Daily Press,* 23 Oct. 1868, for amendment quote. Of the 43,722 who voted for Gen. Ulysses S. Grant for president, 39,493 voted for the amendment. *Legislative Manual 1868,* 89–93. For a thorough interpretation of the returns, see Libman, "Minnesota and the Struggle for Black Suffrage," 169–84.

30. Minnesota, *Senate Journal, 1870,* 9, 21; Minnesota, *House Journal, 1870,* 29; *St. Paul Pioneer,* 11 Jan. 1870.

31. *Proceedings of the Convention of Colored Citizens of the State of Minnesota* (St. Paul: Press Printing, 1869), 3–5 (hereafter *Proceedings*).

32. Ibid.

33. Ibid.

34. Ibid., 3–5, for votes; *St. Paul Daily Press,* 29 Dec. 1868.

35. *Proceedings*, 5.
36. Ibid., 5, 6.
37. Ibid., 6.
38. *St. Paul Daily Press*, 29 Dec. 1868; *Proceedings*, 7; *St. Paul Daily Press*, 13 Nov. 1868.
39. *Proceedings*, 7.
40. Ibid.
41. Ibid.
42. *St. Paul Daily Press*, 8 Jan. 1869; *St. Paul City Directory*, 1869; *U.S. Census, 1870*, microfilm, roll 10, 1035.
43. *Proceedings*, 8.
44. Ibid.
45. Ibid.
46. Ibid., 29–31; Spangler, *Negro in Minnesota*, 59. The men chosen as vice presidents were A. Miles of Winona, William Liggins of Minneapolis, James Griffen of Wright County, Maurice Jernigan of St. Paul, and Andy Sanderline of Faribault. Thomas Jackson of St. Paul remained secretary, and Addison Drake, also of St. Paul, was assistant secretary. Bank appointed Jackson Overalls of Hastings to serve as chair of the resolutions committee (ibid., 7–9).
47. Ibid., 9, 10; see also *St. Paul Press*, 8 Jan. 1869, for transcript of the day's session.
48. *Proceedings*, 10–11.
49. Ibid. (emphasis added).
50. Ibid.
51. Ibid.
52. Ibid.
53. Ibid., 14, 16.
54. Ibid., 16.
55. Ibid.
56. Ibid.
57. Ibid.
58. Ibid.
59. *St. Paul Daily Press*, 8 Jan. 1869.
60. *Proceedings*, 18.
61. Ibid. (emphasis added).
62. Ibid.
63. Ibid., 20–26 (emphasis added).
64. Ibid. (emphasis added).
65. Ibid.
66. Ibid.
67. *St. Paul Daily Press*, 8 Jan. 1869.
68. Ibid.
69. Ibid.
70. Ibid., 13 Nov. 1868.
71. Ibid., 8 Jan. 1869.
72. *St. Paul Pioneer*, 3 Jan. 1869; *St. Paul Weekly Pioneer*, 8 Jan. 1869.
73. *St. Paul Pioneer*, 3 Jan. 1869; *St. Paul Weekly Pioneer*, 8 Jan. 1869.
74. *St. Paul Pioneer*, 3 Jan. 1869; *St. Paul Weekly Pioneer*, 8 Jan. 1869.
75. *Minneapolis Tribune*, 5 Jan. 1869.
76. *St. Paul Daily Press*, 8 Jan. 1869. The campaigns for black suffrage in Iowa and Wisconsin took different routes. In Republican-dominated Iowa, the referendum of 1857 was defeated 49,511 to 8,489, reflecting that while state Republicans were against the extension of slavery, they also were adamantly opposed to black political equality

(Berwanger, *The Frontier against Slavery,* 41). Not until 1868, during Grant's presidential campaign, did the suffrage campaign in Iowa gain traction. In comparison to Minnesota, where state party leaders provided critical leadership for the campaign, in Iowa Grant is credited as the key to victory. In the final hour of his campaign, Grant (despite his policy of remaining silent on the matter) reportedly said that he "hoped the people of Iowa, where soldiers achieved such immortal renown in the field, could be the first state to carry [black] suffrage through unfalteringly." In November, Grant took 62 percent of the ballot, and 90 percent of his supporters voted for the amendment (Dysktra, *Bright Radical Star, 227*). In Wisconsin, which historian Berwanger termed "the most liberal state in the Old Northwest," the state constitution in 1848 made black suffrage available by popular vote. In the general election of 1849, 31,759 people voted, but only 5,265 voted for suffrage, and only 4,075 opposed it. Because officials determined that the amendment must be ratified only with the support of a majority of those voting in the general election, the proposition was defeated. A second referendum, in 1857, was overwhelmingly defeated. In *Gillespie v Palmer, et al.,* 20 Wisc. 572 (1866), the state supreme court decided that the constitution required for ratification only a majority of the votes cast on the issue. Therefore, the black men of Wisconsin had legally possessed the right to vote for seventeen years (Berwanger, *The Frontier against Slavery,* 42n31).

77. *Proceedings,* 16, for quote.

Notes to Chapter 10

1. *St. Paul Daily Press,* 5 Oct. 1864. This chapter is based in part on my article "Race and Segregation in St. Paul Schools, 1849–1868," *Minnesota History* 55 (Winter 1997): 138–49.

2. *St. Paul Daily Press,* 5 Oct. 1864.

3. Ibid., 4 Oct. 1864.

4. Ibid., 15 Aug. 1865.

5. *St. Paul Daily Pioneer,* 10 Oct. 1865; Spangler, *Negro in Minnesota,* 34.

6. *St. Paul Daily Pioneer,* 10, 15 Oct. 1865, 6 Sept. 1867; *St. Paul Daily Press,* 8 May 1865, 30 Nov. 1867, 30 Jan. 1868.

7. *A Century of Service: St. Paul Public Schools* (St. Paul, 1956), 3.

8. Folwell, *History of Minnesota,* 3:13.

9. Ibid.

10. Ibid.

11. Donnelly served Minnesota in both state and federal politics. Relentlessly opposing the railroad, lumber, and wheat-milling monopolies, he put issues above party affiliation, becoming Democrat, Republican, Greenbacker, Granger, Farmers' Alliance supporter, Populist, and Fusionist. He was also a journalist, editor, and successful novelist. For a study of his life, see Martin Ridge, *Ignatius Donnelly: The Portrait of a Politician* (Chicago: University of Chicago Press, 1962; St. Paul: MHS Press, 1991).

12. Author's assumption of Donnelly's rationale.

13. *St. Paul Daily Pioneer,* 10 Nov. 1865.

14. Minnesota Constitution, art. 13, sec. 1 (emphasis added).

15. *St. Paul Daily Press,* 28 Feb. 1869.

16. *Minnesota Laws, 1869,* 99.

17. *St. Paul Press,* 20 Jan., 22 Feb. 1865; *Owatonna Gazette,* reprinted in *Chatfield Democrat,* 12 Aug. 1865.

18. *Mankato Union,* 17, 24 Mar. 1865.

19. *St. Paul Weekly Press,* 1 Mar. 1869; *Minnesota Laws, 1869,* 7.

20. *St. Paul Daily Press,* 14 Mar. 1869.

21. Spangler, *Negro in Minnesota,* 35; *St. Paul Daily Pioneer,* 13 Apr. 1869.

22. *St. Paul Daily Pioneer,* 13 Apr. 1869.

23. St. Paul Board of Education, "Minutes," 19 Apr. 1869, MHS. The calls by white citizens for separate schools persisted for several years. As late as 1909, a committee of white parents appeared before the board of education to protest the admission of black students to Mattocks School ("Minutes," 1 Sept. 1909). See also Frank W. Cummings, "Segregated Education in St. Paul, Minnesota" (master's thesis, Macalester College, 1961), 36.

Notes to Chapter 11

1. *St. Paul Weekly Pioneer,* 26 Mar. 1869; *St. Paul Press,* 24 Mar. 1869; *Minneapolis Tribune,* 25 Mar. 1869.

2. *St. Paul Weekly Pioneer,* 26 Mar. 1869; *St. Paul Press,* 24 Mar. 1869; *Minneapolis Tribune,* 25 Mar. 1869.

3. Williams, *History of Saint Paul,* 391. How Heard came to defend Harris is unclear. He may have been appointed in the manner of a public defender, or at least as likely, the Democrats in control of the city (remember the ward bosses sitting in the back row at the Convention of Colored Citizens) arranged for Harris's defense to demonstrate their party's benevolence toward blacks.

4. *St. Paul Weekly Pioneer,* 26 Mar. 1869.

5. For biographical sketch of Robertson, see Williams, *History of Saint Paul,* 283; Charles Flandrau, *Encyclopedia of Biographies of Minnesota: History of Minnesota* (Chicago: Century Publishing and Engraving Company, 1900), 1:431–32; Newson, *Pen Pictures of St. Paul,* 1:217–18. An example of his influence was reflected in his retaining two judges to represent him in a series of civil actions concerning land claims. *St. Paul Daily Press,* 14 Apr. 1869. His wealth and sophistication were reflected not only in his land holdings but also in the quality of his personal library, which included a newspaper published in 1721 by James Franklin, older brother of Benjamin. *St. Paul Daily Press,* 16 May 1869.

6. *Minneapolis Tribune,* 26 Mar. 1869.

7. Ibid.

8. *St. Paul Weekly Pioneer,* 26 Mar. 1869.

9. At which point the rest of the white jurors were selected is not clear, but the newspapers listed them all: James Pendergast, N. B. Brisbin, Willis Stanton, Daniel Flavin, I. S. Elliot, Joseph Lewis, and I. S. Larpenteur. *St. Paul Weekly Press,* 25 Mar. 1869; *St. Paul Weekly Pioneer,* 26 Mar. 1869.

10. *St. Paul City Directories,* 1863–1869; *U.S. Census, 1870.*

11. *St. Paul Weekly Pioneer,* 26 Mar. 1869, for discharge; *St. Paul Daily Press,* 24 Mar. 1869; *St. Paul Weekly Pioneer,* 26 Mar. 1869.

12. The growing discontent of farmers was transforming the Grange into a political organization that would serve as a springboard for the creation of a third party called the Anti-Monopoly Party. Col. Daniel Robertson worked closely with Grange founder Oliver Kelley, both later joined by Ignatius Donnelly. In 1869 the chapter organized by Robertson in St. Paul became the heart of the statewide movement.

13. Coalition building also came to bear when in 1884 Grover Cleveland became the first postwar Democrat elected president of the United States, in part due to the defection of Northern black voters discouraged by Republican lethargy regarding race relations and black civil rights. Rayford Logan, *The Betrayal of the Negro, 1877–1901* (New York: Collier Books, 1965), 57–58.

14. *St. Paul Pioneer,* 8 Jan. 1869.

15. *St. Paul Weekly Pioneer,* 8 Jan. 1869.

16. D. A. Robertson to Victor Robertson, 31 Jan. 1885, Daniel A. Robertson and Family Papers, 1814–1933, MHS.

17. Joel Best, "Keeping the Peace in St. Paul: Crime, Violence, and Police Work, 1860–1874," *Minnesota History* 47 (Summer 1981): 246.

18. Ibid., 245–46, citing *U.S. Census, 1870, Population,* 41.

19. Ibid., 246. See also *St. Paul Pioneer,* 7 June 1870. The Irish were 10 percent of the population and 34 percent of those arrested in 1870.

20. *Proceedings,* 24.

21. *St. Paul Daily Press,* 15, 26 May 1869.

22. *Proceedings,* 21.

23. Ibid.

24. Ibid., 26 (emphasis added).

25. Ibid., 21.

26. *St. Paul Daily Press,* 16 May 1863, for quote.

27. *St. Paul Pioneer Press,* 8 Jan. 1865, for Masonic and Golden Key. In September 1866, two months before Pilgrim Baptist Church's incorporation, Moses Dixon, Joseph Parr, Israel Crosby, James Hilyard, and Jacob Pritchard organized the lodge under the aegis of Prince Hall Grand Lodge (Taylor, "Pilgrim's Progress," 29).

28. *St. Paul Daily Pioneer,* 17 Nov. 1868; *St. Paul Pioneer Press,* 31 Oct., 14 Nov. 1868.

29. *St. Paul Daily Press,* 4 Aug. 1868; Taylor, "Pilgrim's Progress," 33.

30. Taylor, "Pilgrim's Progress," 73–76.

31. Ibid.

32. *St. Paul Daily Press,* n.d. The *Daily Press* further reported, "Since this establishment has been thrown open to the public it has been visited by thousands not only from our citizens, but also from different portions of this and other States. There is but one sentiment expressed in regard to it, that of unqualified admiration. As the visitor first enters the main palace, he involuntarily stops and when his eyes have roamed over the large apartment taking in at a glance its magnificent and costly appointments, and the great taste displayed in the arrangement of the rich ornaments of the room, he can not fail to give vent to his sentiments in terms of unbound admiration and delight, and he will for a time forget that he is in a far western State, and wonder whether this gorgeous palace of beauty is indeed a reality, or only a creation of imagination. A closer inspection, however, will dispel his doubts and his delight and wonder will be increased as he makes a tour of the Palace and examines all its conveniences and adornments in detail."

33. *St. Paul Daily Press,* 22 June 1866.

34. *St. Paul City Directories,* 1863–1869; *St. Paul Press,* 20 Mar. 1869, 4.

35. For a sense of the festivities, see *St. Paul Press,* 8 Jan. 1865; see also Libman, "Minnesota and the Struggle for Black Suffrage," 60.

Index

abolitionists and abolitionism: in 1850s, 71–82; harassment of Southern tourists, 91–92, 98–99; legislative proposals and resolutions, 93, 99, 100; meetings and rallies, 74, 77, 78, 79; at state constitutional convention, 83–100. *See also* Hennepin County Antislavery Society

Adams, John Quincy, politician, 71

Adams Division school, 166

agriculture. *See* farmers and farming

Alabama, secession, 100

alien suffrage rights, 113

American Anti-Slavery Society, 139

American Fur Company, 23, 111

American Home Missionary Society, 56

Ames, Charles Gordon (Rev.), abolitionist, 75, 78, 91, 92

Anbinder, Tyler, historian, quoted, 135, 194n38

Anderson, William, quoted, 40, 84–85, 87, 116–17

Andrews, Christopher C. (Gen), 144, 148, 152–53, 157

Anoka, support for black suffrage, 142

Anti-Monopoly Party, 207n12

Atchison, John (steamboat captain), 26

Aunt Mornin (slave), 6

Babbitt, W. D., abolitionist: abolition activities, 78, 92, 99, 100; assistance to Eliza Winston, 97, 98; St. Anthony resident, 77

Bacon, Francis, philosopher, 167

Bailly, Alexis, slaveholder, 11, 23–24, 193n22

Banks, Robert, civic leader, 152–53, 157, 162

Barnes, Albert (Rev.), 56, 193n19

Becker, George L., convention delegate, 112–13

Bedini, Gaetano, papal nuncio, 62, 194n38

Beecher, Henry Ward, abolitionist, 127–28

Bell, Harriet, quoted, 106

Berry, Eugene, riverboat worker, 64

Berwanger, Eugene, historian, quoted, 32, 72, 205n76

Best, Joel, sociologist, 179, 180

Big Thunder, Ojibwe leader, 18

Bigelow, S., abolitionist, 92

Bishop, Harriet, teacher, 58

blacks: abolition of slavery linked to civil rights, 78; assistance to fugitive slaves, 64; business and civic leaders, 181–85; civilizable characteristics, 159, 160–61, 163; contraband labor, 131–32, 134, 136, 138; courting by Democratic Party, 177–78, 207n13; crimes and convictions, 179–80; emancipation celebration, 182; "good conduct" codes, 68–69; interracial sexual relationships prohibited, 138; Irish laborers compared to, 133–35; jury service, 173–76, 179, 180–81; life of emancipated slaves in Minnesota Territory, 17–36; migration ban and registration proposed, 131–32; military service prohibited, 119, 128; mob containment practices in Northern cities, 130–31; neighborhood relationships in St. Anthony, 81–82, 100; occupations, 51, 65, 133, 134, 137, 157–58, 182–83, 184; population statistics, 50, 143, 179; property ownership rights and protections, 49, 79; racial segregation during 1850s, 49–70; relationship with white laborers, 65–67, 131; rural versus urban opportunities, 157–58; second-class citizenship, 37–48; similarities with

WILLIAM D. GREEN is professor of history at Augsburg
College in Minneapolis. He is author of *Degrees of Freedom:
The Origins of Civil Rights in Minnesota, 1865–1912* (Minnesota,
2015).